AF255656

"The concrete realization and manifestation of the kingdom or rule of God *on earth*, is indeed the central theme of Scripture. Sean Finnegan demonstrates that most clearly, covering all the issues in an exceptionally engaging but sharply analytical style. Indeed, this message has the potential to revive the gospel message in a way that can transform the world."

—JAMES D. TABOR, retired professor of Christian origins,
University of North Carolina at Charlotte

"In this intensely personal, yet thoroughly researched book, Sean Finnegan invites us to join him on a journey of exploration to discover the authentic biblical vision of the kingdom of God—and why it matters. Interweaving his own story with biblical exposition and historical investigation, Finnegan challenges the reader to embrace God's marvelous plan to transform this broken world into the new heavens and the new earth."

—J. RICHARD MIDDLETON, professor of biblical worldview and exegesis,
Northeastern Seminary at Roberts Wesleyan University

"I greatly appreciate and recommend Sean Finnegan's book *Kingdom Journey*. With a fantastic review of kingdom theology in church history, from the church fathers to the Middle Ages, to Weiss and Schweitzer, to Ladd and Wright, the author tells of his journey concerning the kingdom. With a practical emphasis on family life, church leadership, mission work, and diligent study, Finnegan is an excellent guide through his life story, through his education, and through Scripture, to lead us into a clearer picture of the practical, real, kingdom of God that Jesus and the prophets focused on."

—JOE MARTIN, retired president, Atlanta Bible College

"A captivating quest for the unsung message of the historical Jesus—a gospel of earthly restoration rather than heavenly escape—and a clarion call for the rediscovery of its meaning for the Christian faith and life. Sean Finnegan's exploration of not only what was lost, but how it was lost and how to retrieve it, marks a step forward in the 'earthly turn' of Christian eschatology."

—KEGAN CHANDLER, Researcher, Department for the Study of Religions,
University of Cape Town

Kingdom Journey

Kingdom Journey

A Call to Recover the Central Theme of Scripture

SEAN P. FINNEGAN

WIPF & STOCK · Eugene, Oregon

KINGDOM JOURNEY
A Call to Recover the Central Theme of Scripture

Wipf & Stock
An Imprint of Wipf and Stock Publishers
199 W. 8th Ave., Suite 3
Eugene, OR 97401

www.wipfandstock.com

PAPERBACK ISBN: 978-1-6667-8595-1
HARDCOVER ISBN: 978-1-6667-8596-8
EBOOK ISBN: 978-1-6667-8597-5

12/20/23

To my wife, Ruth, without whose steady love and support I would have shipwrecked long ago. You are my lighthouse, who not only warns me of danger but also shows me the way home.

Contents

Preface

THE EUROPEAN COMMON CUCKOO lays her egg in the nest of another species. The cuckoo egg hatches earlier than the other eggs and grows faster than the other chicks. Often the baby cuckoo will even push other eggs and other chicks out of the nest to monopolize the resources of the host mother. Tragically, the mother tires herself out caring for this invader while her own brood are marginalized. What an injustice!

This, I fear, is what has happened to the Bible's teaching about the kingdom of God. A new idea came in from a foreign source and began to grow in the nest of early Christianity. Over time the idea that Christ's followers go to heaven at death grew stronger and kicked out the old kingdom-on-Earth doctrine. Rather than dreaming of a world made new, Christians fantasized about a bodiless existence in a heavenly ether, eternally gazing on God's effulgence.

What I find particularly horrifying about this issue is that many leaders in the church of today continue to protect, nourish, and support this foreign heaven idea. It's reinforced in our worship songs, Sunday sermons, and funeral services. Books purporting to provide reliable accounts of near-death experiences sell like hotcakes while the old biblical passages describing God's dreams for the future remain ignored and covered in dust.

For millennia, the Hebrew people believed in a physical kingdom that God would establish on the last day. They understood the kingdom to be a time when God extends his reign to Earth, transforming our world into a flourishing paradise where injustice, sickness, and death will be gone forever. Never again will we hear about drunk drivers killing innocent families or single mothers getting aggressive cancer. Wars will go extinct along with government corruption and propaganda. No more will counterfeit ideas and fake news hold sway among honest-hearted people. Rather, truth—God's truth—will win the day when "the earth shall be full of the knowledge of the LORD as the waters cover the sea" (Isa 11:9).

The kingdom of God has been unknown to all but a few Christians for nearly seventeen centuries now. But today, in our time, God is doing something. A growing movement is spreading around the globe, calling Christians back to their Bibles to discover God's grand plan for our world. Rather than floating on clouds, smoking cigars, or playing harps, many are coming to see that God's goal is to renew this world when Christ comes back.

In fact, among scholars, this truth has been common knowledge since the turn of the twentieth century. Every Hebrew prophet spoke of it, and Jesus focused his preaching on the kingdom. Yet still, pastors, podcasters, and influencers routinely favor a disembodied escape from our planet in the place of Jesus's clear teaching that "the meek will inherit the earth" (Matt 5:5).

What happened? How was the biblical hope buried? Why did Christianity reject the kingdom? This is the story I've spent countless hours investigating. I'm here to explain what happened and call for a kingdom revolution. It's time to get back to the Bible and restore this ancient truth to its proper place.

In this book, I'll share my own quest of discovery. From youth camp to Bible college to seminary and beyond, I'll explain how I learned what the kingdom is and what happened to it. This journey changed my life forever, and after a decade of research, I'm confident to tell what I found to others.

Christians need to know this truth. I'm not talking about an esoteric doctrine that is fun to ponder but doesn't affect real life. The kingdom is huge. It's central to Jesus's gospel proclamation and it has major lifestyle implications for believers today. Jesus put it this way: "Seek first the kingdom of God and his righteousness" (Matt 6:33). How dare we demote it to secondary curiosity!

Simply put, the biblical teaching of the kingdom changes everything. It affects how we treat people, how we think about creation, and how we deal with anxiety and depression. This message needs to get out there. Not only will it open the eyes of many Christians, but it will also equip us with a compelling message that will connect with the lost.

During my twenty years as a pastor, I've watched this message transform the lives of many Christians. Having a clear vision of tomorrow is key to navigating life today. I've watched people who were bored with church, bored with the Bible, and most of all, bored with the thought of going to heaven come alive when they learned about the kingdom. Suddenly their faith felt relevant to the real world. Suddenly they found motivation to pursue righteousness. Suddenly they had a message they were proud to tell others.

As many see this truth, they see the Bible come to life. The Old Testament prophets become relevant to theology. Jesus's teaching and miracles start to fit together in new and powerful ways. Beyond making the Bible clearer and more relevant, this understanding provides both moral direction as well as moral imagination and motivation.

I pray that this book would not only educate readers, but also inspire them to become kingdom ambassadors, eager to share this good news with others. Together we can contribute to the reformation already underway in Christianity today.

Acknowledgments

I AM GRATEFUL TO the generous people who supported me to pursue graduate studies full-time. My time in Boston enabled me to do the research that made this book possible.

Professor James Walters gave me permission and guidance on writing my master's thesis on why mainstream Christianity lost the kingdom. This thesis served as the basis for this book.

Over many breakfast dates, my beloved wife, Ruth Finnegan, kindly read through every word of the first draft of the manuscript and offered many suggestions for improvement.

Daniel Fitzsimmons read through a portion of the manuscript and gave helpful advice.

Anna Brown not only fixed innumerable grammatical peccadillos, she also helped immensely in editing the content to avoid ambiguities, idiosyncrasies, and monotonous style. I am indebted to her.

Lastly, I want to thank my dad for having the courage to investigate this topic and change his beliefs while I was a fairly clueless teenager. Because of him, I came to believe in restorationism—the process by which one seeks to recover authentic Christianity by testing beliefs against Scripture.

The stories in this book reflect my recollection of events. Some names, locations, and identifying characteristics have been changed to protect the privacy of those depicted. Dialogue has been recreated from memory.

Abbreviations

ANF   *Ante-Nicene Fathers*

BDAG   *A Greek-English Lexicon of the New Testament and Other Early Christian Literature*, by Walter Bauer, F. W. Danker, William F. Arndt, and F. Wilbur Gingrich

NPNF[1]   *Nicene and Post-Nicene Fathers, Series I*

NPNF[2]   *Nicene and Post-Nicene Fathers, Series II*

NT   New Testament

OT   Old Testament

Introduction

Could we be wrong about heaven and hell? These two destinations are so enmeshed in our culture today that it's hard to even question them. Where else would we go? Heaven is in our songs, our funerals, our sermons, our cartoons, our tracts, and our books. Heaven is where Christians go when they die. Hell is where everyone else goes—at least bad people. Everyone knows that.

But here's the problem. The Scriptures seem wholly focused on another idea. Sure, they mention heaven as the realm where God and the angels live. But they don't say people go there when they die. Instead, prophets like Isaiah and Daniel talk about a final judgment followed by an Edenic age when God makes everything wrong with the world right. The people of God will live on a renewed Earth without fear, sickness, or death in an eternal era: the kingdom of God.

Jesus took for granted that his hearers already knew what the kingdom of God was based on their knowledge of the Hebrew Bible. He did not redefine the kingdom as the church or claim some new understanding that would replace or spiritualize the old notion.

My goal with this book is nothing short of igniting a revolution in the church's understanding of the kingdom of God. By and large, scholars already know the truth, but most everyday Christians have a muddled understanding of the topic. My desire is that the Bible's cardinal doctrine would once again become central in the church. I want to see a reformation whereby Bible readers connect with Scripture in a fresh and relevant way.

To accomplish this goal, I've opted for a "Bible plus history" approach. This book breaks into two main parts. The first part covers what the Bible says about the kingdom of God; not only is it the destiny of the righteous, it is also the gospel we preach. What's more, a clear kingdom vision of the future is key to living out our Christianity today, as ethicists have long noted. As a Bible-believer myself, this part of the book is primary. Because theology books tend to be dry, I've included personal anecdotes to invite the reader into my own journey of discovery.[1]

Of course, there are a smattering of texts here and there that informed Bible students might think of as problematic for believing in a future kingdom on Earth. I did not want to divert the reader's attention to explain these misunderstood texts in the main body of the book. However, I recognize the importance of understanding all the texts, not just the ones that *prima facia* support my thesis. Consequently, I decided to include a collection of appendices, in which I offer explanations to dozens of key texts that occasionally get pressed into service to argue for heaven at death, that the church is the kingdom, or that the kingdom is in heaven.

The second part of the main book narrates my investigation to answer the question: what happened to the kingdom? Although many Bible-believing Christians don't delve into church history in depth, I felt that it would be critical to pair the biblical case for the kingdom with a thorough examination of what happened to the idea and why. Attending graduate classes at Boston University, Boston College, and Harvard University afforded me huge opportunities to access world-class teachers, theology libraries, and digital resources to understand why Christianity came to reject the kingdom in favor of a heavenly hope. After much research, I discovered three main reasons: early Christians thought the old kingdom idea was too Jewish, too crude, and too hedonic. Though these reasons would utterly fail to appeal to us today, they were decisive in the third, fourth, and fifth centuries of the church.

After describing how the church lost the kingdom, I explore how three independent movements rediscovered this doctrine in the sixteenth, nineteenth, and twentieth centuries. I was astounded to learn that the kingdom idea is known in the academy, among Adventist churches, and in some Anabaptist circles. It appears to me that God has been working with people in recent centuries to get this truth out. I believe we are now approaching a tipping point when many will come to see the kingdom for what it is.

In the last chapter, I draw together the practical implications of recovering a kingdom theology. Firstly, I point out that since the kingdom mattered to Jesus, it should matter to us. In fact, to claim to know Jesus and not know the primary focus of his heart, words, and actions is problematic. Additionally, the kingdom of God is our north star, guiding our

---

1. I am indebted to Nehemiah Gordon for the idea to begin each chapter with a personal story. When he gave me his book, *Shattering the Conspiracy of Silence*, I had no intention of reading it. However, on the plane ride home, I took a gander at the first chapter. His engaging style so gripped me that I found myself helpless to resist reading the whole book.

way through the darkness. Having a clear vision of what God plans to do in our world in the future helps us understand how we should live today. Lastly, recovering the kingdom can provide the church with much needed prosocial power to combat the tribalism of our age, both inside and outside the church. I conclude by calling readers to become kingdom ambassadors who challenge, persuade, and popularize this lost central truth.

My prayer is that this book will light a fire in your heart as you come to understand your Bible and Jesus better. May you earnestly seek to share this good news with others—both fellow Christians and the lost who are in desperate need of hope, wholeness, and salvation.

1

Earth Renewed

The preacher droned on about the kingdom of God while I sat in the stiff grey chair in the sweltering heat, on the verge of breaking into a sweat. I was at a week-long Christian retreat for teens at a YMCA facility on Lake George, New York. I sat in the ancient stone meeting hall surrounded by dozens of my peers from all walks of life. Since I was a pastor's kid, I had been going to these camps every year since I was old enough. Usually, the sermons merely served as the backdrop against which the real action and drama—sailing, basketball, the ever-present opposite sex—played out during the week. But today was different.

"So, as you can see from these verses," intoned the minister, "no one is going to heaven. Heaven is the storehouse—the place where our treasures are laid up. It is like a bank. When you retire, do you move into the bank?"

I had to admit he had a point there. But what in the world was he saying? No one is going to heaven? Perhaps I was daydreaming or too distracted by the cute girl sitting next to me, but did he just say that we aren't going to heaven? Regardless of my intermittent focus up to this moment, I resolved to zero in on what he was saying.

"The Bible teaches about the kingdom of God. The meek will inherit the Earth. In the end, God will restore everything back to the way it was in the beginning—in the garden of Eden."

What? This pastor was clearly saying something provocative, yet his monotone voice and the general disinterest among the rest of the people in the room conspired together to make me even more incredulous. "How can this guy get up there and in one hour demolish the hope for billions of

Christians," I thought to myself, "and no one has a problem with that?" I continued concentrating, trying to find the flaw in his case.

After the teaching, we sang. We ate. We mingled. No one said anything about what had just happened, as if everyone had just glazed over during the sermon—everyone, that is, except my roommate, Victor.

"Hey, what did you think of that?" said Victor.

"He just abolished heaven? I thought we were going to heaven. Can he just do that?" I replied.

"Well, he just did."

"I think he's wrong. He must be wrong. My whole life, I've been on my way to heaven, and now I'm just supposed to change my beliefs? I mean, just think of all the songs we sing about going to heaven!"

"Let's prove him wrong," Victor said with a sparkle in his eye. "When we get back to our room tonight, we'll find that verse that says we are going to heaven."

I can't remember what the evening activity was that night—basketball, manhunt, or a talent show—but what I'll never forget was that Victor and I, for the first time ever, cracked open our Bibles after hours and pored over the text. Even though we had both grown up in solid Christian families that revered the Bible as God's inspired, authoritative book, neither of us had read it much on our own. Sure, we had read parts of it here and there, but the thick Shakespearean English contained in our King James Versions barred us from really digging into it.

We used the subject index at the back of our Bibles and flipped around to any place where we thought we might find something to disprove this ludicrous anti-heaven idea. Nothing. After some frustration, Victor said, "Hey, what was the name of that workshop we were in?"

"How to Study the Bible," I replied.

"Well, I guess he succeeded." Victor continued, "I wonder if the other ministers here know what he just taught us. Do you think they are in on it?"

They were. As time went on, our local group of house churches began reconsidering our beliefs. Christian groups tend to see their role as preserving the traditions of the founders, so when we began seeing several doctrines differently, it was both unnerving and exciting. In those days, our preachers, notably my father, began encouraging our church to adopt a "Berean attitude" towards truth. According to the book of Acts, the Bereans were noble-minded because "they received the word with all eagerness, examining the scriptures daily to see if these things were so" (Acts 17:11). The people of that ancient Greco-Roman city neither accepted nor rejected Paul's new teaching about Jesus; rather, they tested it against the Scriptures to see if it was true. My dad could hardly preach a single sermon without saying, "Don't believe it because I said it. Check this out for yourself and see if it's true."

During this transitionary time, I began looking at the broad storyline of the Bible, and I saw that the beginning and end tie together marvelously. The Bible opens with "In the beginning God created the heavens and the earth." The statement is as plain as it is powerful—God made our world. Next, God speaks as water separates, land appears, vegetation sprouts, animals multiply, and humans take shape. Five times over, the magnificently crafted creation account resounds with the refrain, "it was good." Then, on the sixth day, God surveys all his work and concludes "it was very good." Reading Genesis today, I am compelled to affirm the primal goodness of the universe. From the shining stars to the flowing seas, all is the product of a brilliant creator who lovingly and powerfully spoke it into existence.

The more I reflect upon creation, the more I appreciate how spectacular it truly is. For example, plants come from seeds. What is a seed? Is it alive or dead? On the one hand, seeds appear to be dead because they can sit for years in a package and never change a bit; on the other hand, they begin growing into massive trees as soon as they are activated.

How do we unlock the incredible life-generating power of a seed? Do we crush it to pieces and form a paste, hang it on an existing plant, or affix it to the skin of an animal? No: we unleash the mysterious life force of a seed by sticking it in dirt. Dirt. We put a semi-dead husk in dirt and sprinkle some water on it—which makes mud—and that somehow transforms an inanimate pod into a growing baby plant. The plant feeds on dirt, water, sunlight, and carbon dioxide, four of the most plenteous and non-endangered resources on the planet. It grows taller, produces leaves, emits oxygen, and brings forth many more seeds. This utterly common process is actually spectacular.

What's more, God's ingenious seed idea is incredibly resilient. Plants spring up everywhere, from the spaces between sidewalk slabs to the tiny cracks in asphalt parking lots. If someone doesn't patch and repair the road regularly, weeds will quietly and steadily spread the asphalt apart, bit by bit, until they take over completely. This is just one aspect of God's creation, but it teaches us something about the inherent goodness of God's handiwork. When God says, "Let the earth sprout vegetation, plants yielding seed," the result is a diverse panoply of robust and stunning organisms that continue their life cycle eon after eon (Gen 1:11). From massive redwoods to little clovers to colorful roses, creation is replete with grandeur.

At the end of God's creative activity appears the climax of God's creative process: the human body. Although the Creator makes plants and animals with a mere word, Genesis uses different terms to describe God's act of making humanity. He forms us from the dust and breathes into our nostrils the breath of life (Gen 2:7). These words convey intimacy, as if God bent over and blew our first breath directly into our nostrils. The scene bespeaks the care with which God fashioned humanity.

As medicine and technology have improved, we have increasingly come to understand just how masterfully crafted and magnificently complicated we are. Containing approximately twenty-two square feet of skin, 206 bones, twenty-five feet of intestines, forty-five miles of nerves, and 100,000 miles of blood vessels, the human body is nothing short of an engineering marvel.

Further, the human body is a masterpiece capable of extraordinary versatility. Humans live all over the globe—from icy regions where the snow never melts to the tropical islands where snow never falls. Our skin provides us with temperature regulation, sensory input, and a waterproof barrier against the external world. Our fingers are capable of both finely tuned maneuvers like playing the trumpet as well as feats of strength like swinging a hammer. Our wrists enjoy 160 degrees of motion, enabling our hands to accomplish complex tasks like throwing Frisbees and riding motorcycles. Our shoulder's ball-and-socket joint enables 360 degrees of motion, allowing us to lift an object from the ground over our heads in one fluid motion. Our hearts are exceptional pumps, capable of displacing two thousand gallons of blood each day without rest. Our stomachs produce hydrochloric acid so powerful that it could literally digest solid metal. Our bipedal design enables marathon runners to traverse great distances and ballerinas to achieve impeccable balance. Our ears pick up sounds from the quiet gurgling of a creek in the distance to the raucous jamming of an indoor rock concert.

We are capable of whispering, speaking, yelling, and singing. Having two eyes ensures depth perception and makes available nearly 180 degrees of horizontal vision. Our brains process the sensory input of our skin, the sounds our ears pick up, the visual picture our eyes take in, and the tastes and smells our mouths and noses detect, and somehow make sense of it all.

The human brain is capable of advanced cognitive functions like language and love, comprehension and compassion, invention and imagination. We humans have accomplished architectural feats from the Burj Khalifa, a skyscraper in Dubai more than a half mile high, to the Danyang-Kunshan Grand Bridge in China, spanning more than a hundred miles. We have mastered terrestrial travel via bicycles, automobiles, and trains. We traverse the high seas with cruise ships, transport barges, and aircraft carriers. We fly through the air in balloons, helicopters, and jets. We float through space on rockets, shuttles, and space stations.

Humans have charted nearly a billion stars, over a million species of animals, and almost half a million plants. We paint canvasses, play sports, listen to music, invent machines, make love, explore creation, decipher codes, build relationships, and think abstractly. Humans have written everything from gripping adventure novels to precise legal tomes, totaling approximately 130 million books. In addition, we have composed tens of millions of pieces of music and produced more than two million movies. We have penetrated the vast distances of empty space with powerful telescopes and peered deep into the world of cells and DNA with electron microscopes. Whatever someone may think of our origin, we must all admit that humans are remarkable creatures, nearly unlimited in our potential.

I spend so much time contemplating the grandeur of God's creation because it's important to understand that God did a masterful job making everything. Our world is not "plan B," held together by duct tape like a broken bumper on an old pickup truck. This world—from seeds to *Homo sapiens*—is our brilliant designer's original idea.

So it makes sense that God would rather rescue it than evacuate it. In fact, how we understand the beginning influences how we think about the end. For example, the ancient gnostics believed physical creation came into existence when *Yaldabaoth*, a naughty angelic being, rebelled against the supreme God. The true believers, they said, were indwelt with a spark of the divine that originated from a heavenly realm beyond this physical universe. According to the gnostics, the purpose of life was to gain secret knowledge (*gnosis*) so we could ascend beyond this physical universe at death. Eventually God would destroy all matter, leaving only the spiritual realm.

The Bible, however, offers a significantly different storyline. Instead of beginning in heaven, humans originate from the dust of the Earth. Rather than falling *before* creation, we commit our first sins *after* creation. Thus, creation is inherently good, not evil.

Although in the gnostic scenario, creation itself is the consequence of rebellion, in the biblical narrative, creation is God's original plan. God did not create the universe "a waste place," insists Isaiah, "but formed it to be inhabited" (Isa 45:18). God does not plan to evacuate the planet but to fill it with people—his people. Whereas the gnostics wanted to escape from our physical world, the Bible looks forward to a future when God heals our world, restoring it back to the paradise Adam and Eve enjoyed before the fall.

This is why the first two chapters of the Bible look so similar to the last two. In both, we read about humans living in paradise on Earth, complete with the tree of life and the presence of God. Between these two bookends, we read the story of how humanity got off track and how God works within his creation to restore it back to its original glory. The Bible ends where it begins.

Further, the Hebrew seers also envisioned a day when God would heal the world—our world, this world. If we believe that we'll live in heaven, the many prophecies about God's renewal of the Earth seem irrelevant. However, if we believe that we'll be on Earth, the prophecies about what happens here are of prime importance.

For example, Isaiah speaks of "the last days" when all nations would come to God's mountain to learn his ways (Isa 2:2–3). From Jerusalem, the word of the Lord will radiate forth to everyone. God will judge the nations and put an end to violence (Isa 2:4). In fact, the world will melt down its weapons of warfare and make them into tools for agriculture. God will put a human ruler in charge of this global renovation—one who will trust God's Spirit when making decisions rather than what his eyes see and ears hear (Isa 11:2–3). He will judge the poor justly without perverting justice for the sake of a bribe (Isa 11:4).

What would our world look like if true justice prevailed and a qualified arbiter handled international disputes such that even the study of war proved as irrelevant as learning how to operate an abacus?

But the kingdom vision doesn't stop there. In the age to come, the handicapped and outcasts will enjoy the closest proximity to God, dwelling on Mount Zion itself (Mic 4:6–7). In fact, anyone with a physical malady will enjoy permanent healing and restoration. The blind will see, the deaf will hear, the lame will leap, and the mute will shout for joy (Isa 35:5–6). Those suffering from disease, depression, or chronic pain will finally find relief.

What's more, not only people, but even the animals will change. Isaiah puts this so beautifully that I will quote him in full:

> The wolf shall dwell with the lamb,
> and the leopard shall lie down with the young goat,
> and the calf and the lion and the fattened calf together;
> and a little child shall lead them.
> The cow and the bear shall graze;
> their young shall lie down together;
> and the lion shall eat straw like the ox.
> The nursing child shall play over the hole of the cobra,
> and the weaned child shall put his hand on the adder's den. (Isa 11:6–8)

It's difficult to imagine a world where animals don't run away from us or kill each other, yet that is precisely the kind of world Isaiah holds out before us.

God's healing does not stop at establishing global peace for humans and animals, but it extends to the land itself. One of the problems with our world is uninhabitable land. For example, though the Sahara Desert—the largest hot desert—is larger than the continental United States and growing every year, it's only the third largest desert in the world. Geologists classify Antarctica and the Arctic lands as the two biggest deserts. If all three of these regions became habitable, it would be like getting a new continent bigger than South America, North America, or even Africa!

Of course, if God is going to fix our world, it makes sense that he would address this issue as well. He will cause the parched deserts to run with water so that the scorched ground will give way to bushes, flowers, and mighty trees (Isa 35:1–2). Where desolation once reigned, springs of water will bubble up causing grasses and reeds to flourish (Isa 35:7).

After he has repaired our world, God himself will take up residence with us, making Jerusalem his habitation, illuminating that city with his presence (Isa 60:19). Finally, God and humanity will enjoy a relationship, unfettered by dysfunction, guilt, or rebellion. All of God's people will be righteous (Isa 60:21).

It is hard to imagine a world where humankind seeks God's will all the time. But rather than everyone looking out for their own interests, they will genuinely care about others, even those who are different than they are. Rather than many religions and philosophies yanking people in different directions, at that time "the LORD will be king over all the earth. On that day the LORD will be one and his name one" (Zech 14:9).

God's original intent was for mankind to rule the Earth (Gen 1:26), and we learn from the prophet Daniel, "The God of heaven will set up a kingdom that shall never be destroyed" (Dan 2:44). This "kingdom of God" or "kingdom of heaven"—two phrases that are entirely interchangeable— will not be a temporary fix. It will last forever. Three times, God emphasizes this fact in this vision of Daniel:

> I saw in the night visions,
> And behold, with the clouds of heaven
> One like a Son of Man was coming,
> And He came up to the Ancient of Days
> And was presented before Him.
> And to Him was given dominion,
> Glory and a kingdom,
> That all the peoples, nations and men of every language
> Might serve Him.
> His dominion is an everlasting dominion
> Which will not pass away;

And His kingdom is one
Which will not be destroyed. (Dan 7:13–14)

This prophecy is so important for understanding God's plans for our world. He is going to give the Son of Man "dominion, glory, and a kingdom." This kingdom will hold sway over all "peoples, nations, and languages." This dominion is "an everlasting dominion, which will not pass away . . . nor be destroyed."

And finally, God has plans to obliterate the overwhelming pall of death cast over all nations once and for all (Isa 25:7–8). Many of those who sleep in the dust of the ground will awake to enjoy eternal life (Dan 12:2).

God's plan is to take over planet Earth. His kingdom will reign over America, China, and Russia, encompassing English, Mandarin, and Russian speakers. It is not just going to last a thousand years, but it will endure forever. Nothing and no one will ever destroy it. Furthermore, God will give all the kingdoms under the whole heaven to his people (Dan 7:27). One could even say it is the inheritance of God's children. As the creator, he longs to restore the world to its former glory, including putting quality rulers in power to care for and steward his world. When he does that, he will call upon us, his people, to inherit that kingdom.

As I considered how many Scriptures talk about the restoration God will bring to pass on this world in the last day, I remember feeling confused. Why do so many of us believe in going to heaven instead? Why is it that in virtually all funerals, the officiant says, "he's gone to a better place," or "she's with the Lord now"? Why do so many songs like "When We All Get to Heaven" and "I'll Fly Away" reinforce the heaven idea? Why do the radio preachers and bestselling Christian books likewise endorse a heavenly hope?

Was I missing something? I had learned so much at my church in New York, but I wanted to dig even deeper. At the time I had no idea how deep the rabbit hole would go. I naively conceived of the kingdom as just an interesting doctrine to study. As time went on, I would discover how central it is to understanding God's heart, Jesus's identity and ministry, and even Christian morality.

Discovering the kingdom was not like finding out an ancestor from the Middle Ages was royalty; it was more like finding out I had a child I knew nothing about. It's not just an idea; it's a revolution of the mind with serious practical, this-worldly ramifications. My journey would take me not only to the American south, but also to Africa and New England as I learned about the kingdom and investigated how this idea had been lost to Christianity. I had only just begun to glimpse the tip of a mighty iceberg, the majority of which remained invisible beneath the surface.

I applied to the Atlanta Bible College in Georgia. My by-then wife, Ruth, and I packed our bags and loaded up our car. We were headed south, ready for adventure.

2

Gospel Message

I HAD JUST BEGUN working at a steakhouse in Georgia when I made my blunder: I greeted a table of locals with the words "Hey guys. I'm Sean. I'll be taking care of you today."

The group of young adults looked as if I had just insulted them. One of them drawled, "Excuse me, there are ladies at the table." Naturally, in New York, ladies are "guys," too, but here, in the Deep South, I had transgressed the protocol for greeting. I knew then that adjusting to the culture of the South was going to take some effort.

After apologizing for my cultural faux pas, I asked, "Can I get you something to drink?"

"Sure," one said, "I'm fittin' to get me some sweet tea." I knew enough to get the woman her iced tea, but I was already puzzled by this strange term: "fittin.'"

Before long, I would come to learn that "fittin'" is short for "fixing," which really means "preparing" or "getting ready." In the South, it seemed like people were always "fixing" to do something. Someone would say, "I'm fixing to go to the store." What was with all the fixing? Why not just say, "I'm going to the store"? I never did quite figure it out.

These linguistic idiosyncrasies were not the only quirk that caught my attention. Attending classes at the Atlanta Bible College likewise took some adjusting. Growing up, church had been a tightly regulated affair. People did not just erupt in exclamation during the sermon, nor did people talk or sing during someone else's prayer. We practiced a strict protocol taken from 1 Corinthians chapter 14, "everything done decently in order," which we interpreted to mean one person speaking at a time. But matters were quite different in the Bible Belt.

I remember my first class like it was yesterday. I was in Old Testament Survey, sitting next to my wife, Ruth, and never before had I felt like such a minority. Our teacher, though not a native Georgian, was nevertheless a southerner through and through. He was from Pumpkin Center, Louisiana, a tiny place that sounded larger than life from the jaw-dropping tales he told about his childhood. Unusually, he went by "Dr. Joe" rather than "Dr. Martin," an informality that formed, for me, another on a growing list of cultural abnormalities. Dr. Joe would begin each class speaking in a normal, audible tone about assignments and then ramp up his intensity as he got into the lecture for the day. As he reached points he wanted to emphasize, he would shout and smack the lectern. Though this was a bit jarring, at least I was somewhat familiar with the style of preaching. What I wasn't ready for were the sudden outbursts from everyone around me.

"Amen brother!" shouted the lady in the corner.

"Glory," replied another.

"Halleluuuuuuujah," crooned a third.

My wife and I were taken aback. We looked at each other, not sure if we should laugh or join in. As the lecture wore on, the call and response occasionally intensified into nearly 100 percent participation, and we began to find ourselves joining in. I even muttered a "that's right" and my sweet, northern wife likewise let fly a "Thank you Jesus."

We giggled the whole way home, impressed by the fervor, but tickled by how out-of-place it seemed to us.

As the weeks wore on, I began to record the students' unique exclamatory phrases. Everyone had their favorite: have mercy, glory, yes Lord, mm hmm, uh oh, powerful, that's right, tell it brother, come on with it, hello, and my personal favorite, 'hank ya Jeeeeesus.

The following semester, a professor said something to the effect of, "If Satan is in chains now then apparently he's on a long leash," to which a classmate blurted out, "Let the dog roam!"

But that was the only time I heard that one.

Beyond learning to liberate my inner voice and discovering that fried chicken was its own food group, I also learned a good deal of theology during my sojourn in the South. In particular, I learned that the kingdom of God is not just something that would one day come on Earth, but it was also gospel.

I remember the first time I met Sir Anthony Buzzard, sitting next to him at lunch. Nearly the first words he addressed to me were, "What do you make of Luke four forty-three?"

I fumbled around a bit, trying to conjure the verse from memory, and eventually mumbled, "I'm not sure I remember what it says."

"I must preach the kingdom of God to the other cities also, for I was sent for this purpose," he eagerly quoted with his top-shelf British accent, grinning at me over wire-framed glasses. "This is Jesus's purpose statement," he continued. "Jesus came for the purpose of preaching this kingdom message as gospel from town to town. That's what God commissioned him to do. Isn't that magnificent? The whole truth is wrapped up in one simple verse."

I'll admit, even while I politely nodded agreement, I didn't quite grasp what he was so blooming excited about. Little did I anticipate that during my second semester, I would have the opportunity to study the New Testament with the Oxford-educated professor. He was always on about "the gospel." I hadn't thought about what the word "gospel" meant before. Of course, I knew of gospel music and the Gospels in the Bible, but neither of these were what Buzzard had in mind.

"Gospel" derives from the Greek word *evangelion*,[1] which means "good message" or "good news." It is the evangelistic word spoken to bring about conversion. The gospel is not just a general word about God or the Bible; it is the message we need to believe in order to receive eternal life. According to Paul, Christ "abolished death and brought life and immortality to light through the gospel" (2 Tim 1:10). Thus, getting the gospel right is the single most significant task a Bible student can ever face.

"If you get the message that people must believe in to be saved wrong, then you've lost everything," explained Buzzard. "If I were the devil, this is precisely what I would go after. Let people sing their Christian songs; let them pray; let them have church; but muddle their understanding of the gospel."

I hadn't thought much about the message I needed to believe to be saved. The only verse I knew on that subject was Rom 10:9, which talks about confessing Jesus as Lord and believing God raised him from the dead. But Buzzard started showing text after text about what Jesus himself preached.

I decided to write a paper about the gospel message and began looking up dozens of websites and collecting evangelical tracts. What I found was almost eerie. No matter what ministry I took them from or what their other theological commitments might be, these invitations to accept Christ all followed the same basic pattern. For example, consider the Sinner's Prayer:

1. Although the Erasmian pronunciation of Greek is more common in universities, I learned the modern Greek pronunciation; transliterations will follow that way of pronouncing the language.

Dear God,
I know I'm a sinner, and I ask for your forgiveness.
I believe Jesus Christ is Your Son.
I believe that He died for my sin and that you raised Him to life.
I want to trust Him as my Savior and follow Him as Lord, from
this day forward.
Guide my life and help me to do your will.
I pray this in the name of Jesus. Amen.[2]

In this salvation statement, like most others, I found three primary elements: first, the confession of guilt; next, the belief that Jesus died for "my" sins; and last, a declaration of belief. I saw this pattern repeatedly in popular evangelistic techniques, i.e., the Roman Road, the Four Spiritual Laws, and the Way of the Master. In fact, no matter where I looked, I never found anything whatsoever about the kingdom of God.

Buzzard claimed that the kingdom referred to a time when God makes everything wrong with the world right. This massive concept of restoration is one of the major themes of all Scripture. The Bible begins with paradise lost and ends with paradise restored. All the prophets proclaimed how God is going to judge the wicked and establish lasting peace and righteousness for all. The psalmists sang about it, the sages wrote about it, the apostles preached it to crowds. God will send his Messiah to rule again on the throne of David over all nations. This is going to happen, and it's going to change everything.

It is good news. But is it gospel? Is it *the* good news?

Either Buzzard was some maverick whose pet theory amounted to little more than his private interpretation, or he had identified the most significant omission in all of evangelical and mainstream Christianity. Could he be right? What if he *was* right?

The thing about Buzzard was that he was always pointing to Scripture. It is very difficult to disprove someone who constantly lists evidence for his or her position. For example, he would point out that it wasn't until the sixteenth chapter of Matthew that Jesus even *began* to tell his disciples that he would die. And when he did, they not only didn't believe him, but Peter actually took Jesus aside and rebuked him! Yet for the fifteen chapters before this, Jesus had preached tirelessly, sent out the twelve to preach, and even commissioned another seventy to do the same.

What were Jesus and his followers preaching this whole time? We don't have to guess—Matthew tells us,

2. Billy Graham Evangelistic Association, "Begin Your Journey to Peace."

> And he went throughout all Galilee, teaching in their synagogues and proclaiming the gospel of the kingdom and healing every disease and every affliction among the people. (Matt 4:23)

> And Jesus went throughout all the cities and villages, teaching in their synagogues and proclaiming the gospel of the kingdom and healing every disease and every affliction. (Matt 9:35)

> These twelve Jesus sent out, instructing them, "Go . . . to the lost sheep of the house of Israel. And proclaim as you go, saying, 'The kingdom of heaven is at hand.'" (Matt 10:5–7)

Jesus preached the kingdom from town to town and he sent out the twelve with the same message. I had to admit that Buzzard had a point. It seemed hard to deny that Jesus and his original disciples all preached the same kingdom message, which did not have anything to do with him dying for our sins.

If this is true, then why don't any of the evangelistic tracts talk about the kingdom at all? Did Jesus take the kingdom out of the message after his crucifixion? Once again, we don't have to guess about this, because Luke tells us that Jesus spent forty days with his closest followers after his resurrection, "speaking about the kingdom of God" (Acts 1:3). Now, to be sure, the apostles started preaching about the cross and resurrection as well, but they did not get rid of the kingdom message. Instead, they added to it. For example, when Philip went to Samaria, he "preached good news about the kingdom of God and the name of Jesus Christ" (Acts 8:12). Paul, likewise, preached the kingdom throughout his missionary journeys (Acts 19:8). Towards the end of his life, Paul still, even while under house arrest, welcomed whoever would come, "proclaiming the kingdom of God and teaching about the Lord Jesus Christ" (Acts 28:31).

I had to admit that it sure didn't seem like the kingdom aspect of preaching had fizzled out after Christ ascended. It was still there as prominent as ever. I also had to admit that Buzzard was quite convincing. I decided to try out this "kingdom as gospel" idea in evangelism and see what happened.

Finding a non-Christian back home is as easy as getting bit by a mosquito on a summer evening. However, in Georgia, no matter whom I talked to, everyone self-identified as a Christian, and nearly everyone went to church regularly. I thought this would be the perfect environment to test out what I had been learning in class. Surely, all of these locals would already know about the cross of Christ and his resurrection, but would they know about the kingdom? Was I the only one who was clueless or was my ignorance commonplace?

I went out with a friend and a survey. I carried around a clipboard and a pen and went up to strangers at Clayton State University, next door to the Atlanta Bible College. We asked four main questions:

1. What are the first and last books of the Bible?

2. What was the main message of Jesus?

3. How do you get eternal life?

4. What is the kingdom of God?

We designed the first question as a diagnostic. Most people knew the answers were Genesis and Revelation. However, the next question, about the main message of Jesus, confirmed my suspicions. No one ever mentioned the kingdom gospel.

Throughout the Gospels, Jesus constantly speaks about the kingdom. Most of his parables are about the kingdom. His title is Christ, which means God's anointed one to rule the kingdom. And yet *no one seemed to know about it.*

The third question asked about the gospel message again, but from a different angle. To our minds, asking about eternal life revealed what information our interviewees thought was necessary for salvation. And once again, no one mentioned the kingdom. People said, "believe in Jesus," or, "do good deeds," or, "confess Jesus as Lord," or, "accept Christ's death for my sins," but not a single soul, out of the dozens we asked, ever said *anything* about the kingdom.

On the last question, which directly asked how our interviewees understood the kingdom, people had no idea what to say. It was like I was asking them how many angels can dance on the head of pin. After a puzzled look, some people made up answers. They said "heaven," others, "the church," still others, "Jesus reigning in my heart," but most just couldn't come up with anything, staring at me blankly. Almost no one said, "the age when Christ comes back to rule the world."

Now these were good Christian folks who had sat in church their whole lives, listening to countless sermons. We had spoken with the old and the young, foreigners and Americans, students and staff, and they were all just like I had been—clueless about Jesus's message.

Could it be that universally respected preachers and innumerable others were preaching a gutted gospel? At best, their message was partial, at worst, impotent. I felt like I was at a fork in the road, not knowing which way to turn, but knowing that they could not both be right. On the one hand, I had a load of biblical texts clearly stating that Jesus and his disciples preached relentlessly about the kingdom, and on the other, I had the testimony of honest-hearted Christians all around me.

The simplest explanation was that Buzzard was wrong and everyone else was right. But he made his case on the basis of the Bible. Listening to my professor, either the Bible was wrong or Christians were wrong. Honestly, I didn't like either possibility, but in the end, I would have to choose.

This choice, to reject common Christian teaching or the Bible, was the same decision Martin Luther had to make when he initiated the Protestant Reformation. He had to choose between popular Christian doctrines, like the medieval belief about indulgences, and what the Scriptures said. His conclusion was as follows:

> Unless I am convinced by scripture and plain reason—I do not accept the authority of the popes and councils, for they have contradicted each other—my conscience is captive to the Word of God. I cannot and I will not recant anything for to go against conscience is neither right nor safe. God help me. Amen.[3]

Luther would not accept the "authority of the popes and councils." In other words, he did not accept what the church of his time was saying when it contradicted plain reason and the Bible. Luther risked his life in this defining moment, and yet the stand that this lone monk took changed the world forever.

Maybe the world is ripe for another reformation.

Even if I couldn't swallow all the implications of what Buzzard was saying, I also couldn't find any compelling arguments to disprove his kingdom-gospel hypothesis. In fact, the more time I spent with Buzzard, both inside and outside the classroom, the more I came to realize that he was a man driven to get this message out whatever the cost. He had written books, put together a website, published a monthly newsletter, taught classes, ran conferences, and recorded a radio show—all to get Christians to preach a gospel centered on the kingdom. Not only this, but he also spent much of his free time corresponding with truth-seekers from all over the world.

He was completely consistent with the truth he discovered. He was not standing idly by, muttering, "it's all in God's hands" or some other adage. He was on the front lines of a movement, eagerly heralding the kingdom message any way he could. His passion was contagious, and I found myself

---

3. Luther, *Luther's Works*, 32:112–13.

swept up in it, eagerly looking for opportunities to share with others what I had discovered.

After my first year at Bible college, Ruth and I went on a missionary trip to Africa. Halfway around the world, spending time with some of the poorest people on Earth, I began to understand the profound alienation I had from the world of Jesus and the people of his time. It was there that I would learn some of the richest truths about Jesus and his kingdom message.

3

Hope of the World

WE SAT IN A cold bungalow, staring down at my wife's feet. From her toes to her ankles, they were so swollen they looked like oversized, puffy marshmallows. My poor wife Ruth couldn't even fit them in her sneakers. We didn't know how long they were going to stay that way but figured the puffy appendages would return to normal soon enough. She took a picture of them and we went out for hamburgers.

As part of a five-person missionary team, we had flown sixteen hours over the Atlantic Ocean from Atlanta to Johannesburg, where we were staying overnight before catching another flight to our destination, a narrow country in southeastern Africa called Malawi. Anticipation filled my heart, knowing I was about to see and experience an exciting adventure. I was on my first missionary trip, summer break after my first year of Bible college.

The next day, we arrived to our concrete apartment in the partially industrialized city of Blantyre. Though the lodging resembled what we would call "the projects" here in the United States, over there it was more like an upscale flat—fit for a doctor or lawyer. Electricity was spotty, coming and going, and the water depended on gravity to make its way down to us from a large cistern on the roof. To get enough water pressure to wash adequately, we squatted in the bathtub and used a little hose of cold water.

As a middle-class suburbanite from upstate New York, I was out of my element. The apartment had an old TV that barely picked up one channel through the static: programming in Chichewa, the local language. Concrete walls armed with defensive shards of jagged glass surrounded our building. Police were scarce and unreliable, so having an intimidating wall was the first line of defense from thieves. Many people with means also hired private security to protect their homes.

I've never felt so much like an outsider than when I was in Africa. Everything was different: the people, the food, even the stars. I couldn't speak the language or navigate my way anywhere. I completely depended on our leaders who, in turn, were relying on the driver and our indigenous pastor-translators to help us along the way. Of course, the mission team leaders had been on this trip a dozen times before. But for me, all of this was brand new.

We visited a town in the neighboring country of Mozambique; there a baby cried and cried when he saw my wife. Her pale skin terrified him—he was seeing his first white person. Even though she tried to console him, something was terribly unnerving about these ghostly foreigners. As we pulled up to each village, people would surround us with singing and dancing, escorting us the final few hundred yards to our destination. We were *zungus,* white folks, an unusual sight in these remote places, and the local villagers came from near and far just to see us and hear what we had to say.

We went to over a dozen churches during our time in Africa. Each day we would wake up early in the morning and pile into the van. Our driver would take us over bumpy roads—sometimes asphalt, sometimes gravel, sometimes dirt—until we got to our destination. One time we even had to get out of the van to push it through the deep sand left by a wadi. By the time we reached the village, we felt like paint cans, thoroughly mixed by the constant bouncing up and down. When we exited the vehicle, the local pastors and church folks greeted us exuberantly with handshakes and smiles. Then we would all squeeze into the small, thatched church for a long service. Oftentimes the churches did not have walls at all, though sometimes they had brick walls and tin roofs. Furniture was expensive, so everyone usually sat on the ground. However, in order to honor their guests, sometimes the churches placed outdoor plastic chairs in the front for us to sit in. I remember how awkward that was, sitting apart from the people.

At each church, the congregation would begin by singing songs, harmonizing, clapping, and dancing effortlessly. I remember how impressed I was by the little children, who could sing and dance in perfect rhythm, while I awkwardly struggled even to sing and clap at the same time. Next, one or more of us would preach through a translator. Each service lasted between two and three hours. Sometimes we would leave right away and go to another church to lead another service; other times we would head home to repeat the cycle the next day. It was exhausting. I remember being so tired one night that we went to bed at 7:30 p.m.

I was careful to monitor my bodily functions while in Africa. One time I was out in a tiny village in the middle of nowhere and had to use the bathroom. The village did not have bathrooms like we have here; instead, the locals had constructed a small, open-roofed, three-sided hut, about the size of a closet, over a hole. Made of sticks and tall grass, the *chimbuzi*, as they called it, was where everyone went to relieve themselves. I told Ruth where I was going and nonchalantly snuck behind the church to the *chimbuzi*.

"Strange," I thought to myself when I looked inside. "This one doesn't have a hole in the ground." I thought no more of it, and relieving myself in the rickety structure, made my way back into the church. I was met by my wife—laughing in embarrassed dismay. She said, "Sean, that was their changing room! The *chimbuzi* is over there!"

Thankfully, no one made an issue out of it.

Poverty was everywhere. Most of the villages I visited had no internet, no electricity, and no plumbing whatsoever. People lived in thatch huts or, sometimes, in homemade brick houses. Only the wealthiest had tin roofs. No one had glass windows. Women cooked food outside, in large pots over small fires. The primary food was *nsima*, a tasteless porridge resembling cream of wheat. Meat was a luxury Malawians could seldom afford. People ate with their hands after washing in a common bowl of water passed around the room.

At one meeting, I remember seeing an elderly man sitting in the front wearing just one flip-flop. He was so poor that he didn't even own two, but he had evidently decided one was better than none at all. Many women wore the traditional *chitenje*, a large, rectangular piece of fabric that worked as a skirt, head wrap, or baby sling, depending on the need of the moment. Some of the men wore suits, but others sported an array of American hand-me-downs advertising products that they would never be able to buy. Once, I even saw a grown man proudly dressed in a Boy Scout uniform, complete with badges and pins, probably unaware of what they signified.

I was way out of my element. What could I, a white, suburban yuppie, possibly have to say to these people whose lives differed so drastically from my own? My idea of hardship was when the barista at Starbucks put too much cream in my coffee, or when the doctor's office made me wait a few extra minutes when I went in for a physical. But these people were worrying about getting enough food to survive or about staying dry during the rainy season.

The grinding poverty left me shocked and overwhelmed. Then I read this verse:

> Listen, my beloved brothers, has not God chosen those who are
> poor in the world to be rich in faith and heirs of the kingdom,
> which he has promised to those who love him? (Jas 2:5)

Just before these words, James had been reproving Christians for paying attention to those wearing gold rings and fine clothes, assigning them the good seats while making the poor stand in the corner or sit on the floor. To James, Christianity, especially the kingdom message, was for "those who are poor in the world" but "rich in faith." I began to catch sight of how the kingdom message I wanted to preach could meet these people in a relevant and life-changing way.

As I read the Gospels, I discovered how similar the village context in Malawi was to Jesus's own situation in Galilee. These were precisely the kind of people who would turn out in droves to hear Jesus teaching on the mount, on the plain, or from the sea. As we preached the kingdom of God from village to village, I remember how, suddenly, Jesus's teaching that the last will be first felt relevant. For example, see his Sermon on the Plain:

> Blessed are you who are poor, for yours is the kingdom of God.
> Blessed are you who are hungry now, for you shall be satisfied.
> Blessed are you who weep now, for you shall laugh . . .
> But woe to you who are rich, for you have received your consolation.
> Woe to you who are full now, for you shall be hungry.
> Woe to you who laugh now, for you shall mourn and weep.
> (Luke 6:20–25)

In rural Africa, a text which had always seemed difficult in my own American context suddenly came alive. *Here* were the poor, the hungry, and the weeping.

At that time, the life expectancy of a local African person was forty-eight years. Nearly 70 percent of area hospital beds held patients fighting HIV and AIDS. To such people, Jesus's statements that the first will be last and the last will be first were good news, indeed. Jesus pronounces the poor blessed and promises them an inheritance far beyond what they could ever afford—the kingdom of God. In that day, these people will enjoy satisfaction and laughing without all of the instability and hardship that they faced each day.

Now, to be clear, I'm not saying that riches are inherently evil or that poverty is virtuous. Right from the first generation of the movement, we find wealthy Christians. To be sure, riches often block someone from putting their trust in God, but that is not always the case. Nevertheless, the wealthy in Jesus's time were often those who participated in the system of economic injustice.

In this poor country, explaining such nuances was unnecessary. These dear brothers and sisters eagerly soaked in the Bible's simple message of hope, grasping the meaning without theological hairsplitting.

In addition to what the Bible promises the poor, I came to appreciate the tactile language God uses in the prophets when he describes his plan for the world. Isaiah describes Jerusalem's future in this way:

> Then you [Jerusalem] shall see and be radiant;
> your heart shall thrill and exult,
> because the abundance of the sea shall be turned to you,
> 　the wealth of the nations shall come to you.
> A multitude of camels shall cover you,
> the young camels of Midian and Ephah;
> all those from Sheba shall come.
> They shall bring gold and frankincense,
> and shall bring good news, the praises of the Lord.
> . . . .
> Foreigners shall build up your walls,
> . . . .
> Your gates shall be open continually;
> day and night they shall not be shut,
> that people may bring to you the wealth of the nations,
> with their kings led in procession.
> . . . .
> Whereas you have been forsaken and hated,
> with no one passing through,
> I will make you majestic forever,
> a joy from age to age.
> . . . .
> Instead of bronze I will bring gold,
> and instead of iron I will bring silver;
> instead of wood, bronze,
> instead of stones, iron.
> I will make your overseers peace
> and your taskmasters righteousness.
> Violence shall no more be heard in your land,
> devastation or destruction within your borders;
> you shall call your walls Salvation,
> and your gates Praise.
> The sun shall be no more
> your light by day,
> nor for brightness shall the moon
> give you light;
> but the Lord will be your everlasting light,
> and your God will be your glory.
> . . . .
> Your people shall all be righteous;

> they shall possess the land forever,
> the branch of my planting, the work of my hands,
> that I might be glorified. (Isa 60:5–21)

I love how this vision of the kingdom is so *concrete*. Isaiah talks about walls, gates, gold, and bronze. He portrays a city overflowing with abundance, including camels and frankincense. At long last, people will live in a world without systemic injustice and crushing poverty. The time will come, Isaiah says, when people will inherit and enjoy wealth and prosperity in addition to the arrival of God's healing and glory.

Although most Western Christians could barely read the words of this passage before immediately allegorizing or spiritualizing them to make them fit with the typical theology about heaven, this was precisely the kind of text that the Malawians could sink their teeth into. Here, God promises to address their real needs.

In addition, we read in verse 18 that "violence shall no more be heard" in the land. This resonated in the Malawian culture around me, where police and security forces sometimes took matters into their own hands, using excessive force with impunity. In such a society, some might find it tempting to envy or even join the wrongdoers. But to this notion, the Scripture says the following:

> For the evildoers shall be cut off,
> But those who wait for the LORD shall inherit the land.
> In just a little while, the wicked will be no more;
> though you look carefully at his place, he will not be there.
> But the meek shall inherit the land
> And delight themselves in abundant peace.
> . . . .
> for those blessed by the LORD shall inherit the land,
> but those cursed by him shall be cut off.
> . . . .
> For the LORD loves justice;
> he will not forsake his saints.
> They are preserved forever,
> But the children of the wicked shall be cut off.
> The righteous shall inherit the land and dwell upon it forever.
> . . . .
> Wait for the LORD and keep his way,
> and he will exalt you to inherit the land;
> you will look on when the wicked are cut off. (Ps 37:9–34)

Though evildoers often take control of governments large and small, God's promise is that he will judge the wicked and give the land to the righteous. This is a fact which Jesus himself preached in his famous Sermon on the Mount, when he said, "Blessed are the meek, for they shall inherit the earth" (Matt 5:5). We need not fret when we see the wicked prospering as if God is blessing them. They are under a curse and will not enjoy the land forever. The righteous, however, "shall inherit the land and dwell upon it forever."

Dietrich Bonhoeffer, the famous theologian-spy who lived under one of the most oppressive and unjust regimes in human history, Nazi Germany, wrote these words about this issue:

> They [the meek] show by every word and gesture that they do not belong to this earth. Leave heaven to them, says the world in its pity, that is where they belong. But Jesus says: "They shall inherit the earth." To these, the powerless and the disenfranchised, the very earth belongs. Those who now possess it by violence and injustice shall lose it, and those who here have utterly renounced it, who were meek to the point of the cross, shall rule the new earth. . . . God does not forsake the earth: he made it, he sent his Son to it, and on it he built his Church.[1]

Such words seemed especially relevant to the Malawians, as I came to see that they were such a peace-loving and humble people. Once again, the Scripture fit so well with their situation.

We Westerners, on the other hand, live in such an artificial society. We encounter airbrushed pictures of unusually proportioned women on huge billboards lining our roads, in magazines at the checkout line, and in online ads on millions of websites. We use a wide variety of toiletry and cosmetic products to artificially shape our hair, mask our natural odors, and beautify our faces. Oftentimes our clothes are impractical, but stylish. Most of us have no idea what it's like to walk ten miles. On the contrary, many of us live far away from our jobs so that we can find more affordable housing, commuting to work an average of twenty-five minutes each way.[2]

We live in cities, where we never see plants, apart from how urban planners neatly arrange them, or animals, apart from how zoos present them. The modern supermarket has so separated us from our food that most of us have never killed an animal or even seen the butchering process. A couple of years ago, I put on a pig roast in my backyard in honor of my friend's upcoming marriage. I'm not at all a squeamish person, but watching someone break the pig's vertebrae one by one with a knife—so it would

---

1. Bonhoeffer, *Cost of Discipleship*, 110.

2. Copeland, "Americans' Commutes Aren't Getting Longer," para. 2.

cook faster—made me queasy. In our time, less than 2 percent of Americans farm, producing enough food for everyone in the country (as well as plenty for export).[3] Advances in food transportation, mostly due to the refrigerated container, enable even low-income Westerners to enjoy a stable supply of produce all year round, shipped to us from warmer climates.

As a result of all of these technological and processing transformations, the Bible's portrayals of paradise can fail to capture our hearts the way it does in agrarian societies. For this reason, it's worthwhile to try and read these texts like the Malawians did. Here is an example from Amos:

> "Behold, the days are coming," declares the Lord,
> "when the plowman shall overtake the reaper
> and the treader of grapes him who sows the seed;
> the mountains shall drip sweet wine,
> and all the hills shall flow with it.
> I will restore the fortunes of my people Israel,
> and they shall rebuild the ruined cities and inhabit them;
> they shall plant vineyards and drink their wine,
> and they shall make gardens and eat their fruit.
> I will plant them on their land,
> and they shall never again be uprooted
> out of the land that I have given them,"
> says the Lord your God. (Amos 9:13–15)

How could a plowman overtake a reaper? To put the question another way, why are people still harvesting when it is time to plow and plant?

The picture is one of prolific abundance. Normally, harvest is a relatively brief but intense time for farmers, filled with hard work. Growers have to gather their produce and sell it or process it so that they can store it through the winter. But in this prophecy, reaping continues all the way until the season for sowing.

Likewise, with grapes, the treaders are busy only during the harvesting time; but in this passage they are still making juice when it's time to sow seed. These Scriptures made perfect sense to the saints in Malawi and Mozambique as they licked their lips, imagining such bounty.

Now what if, instead of Isaiah's portrait of agricultural abundance, I had come to these tiny villages with the promise that one day they would "prepare heavenly dishes" or "polish rainbows"?[4] Would that have resonated with these people?

3. American Farm Bureau Foundation for Agriculture, "Fast Facts," para. 11.

4. Graham, *Hope for the Troubled Heart*, 214.

To most, floating around as a disembodied soul, staring at God's glory as if locked into a tractor beam, doesn't appeal. Randy Alcorn relates the following conversation he had with a pastor friend:

> A pastor once confessed to me, "Whenever I think about Heaven, it makes me depressed. I'd rather just cease to exist when I die."
> "Why?" I asked.
> "I can't stand the thought of that endless tedium. To float around in the clouds with nothing to do but strum a harp. . . . It's all so terribly boring."[5]

Unlike the ancient Greek philosophers, who disparaged the human body and ridiculed resurrection, the God of the Bible envisions a future for his people with dirt under their fingernails, farming a land that yields bounteously. He invented soil, plants, and the human body, so it makes sense that he wouldn't want to scrap them, but redeem them.

Even if I could not solve the problems causing the poverty these dear people faced, I could at least tell them about a hope that made sense to them. As I taught them what God promised in the age to come, they taught me how spectacularly relevant the Bible is when taken at face value.

The message is so simple: God plans to heal our world. He is going to topple the systems of oppression that impede peace and prosperity while simultaneously blessing the land and those who dwell in it. This is his dream, repeated throughout the Hebrew Bible and echoed by Jesus and his apostles, and over and over, I watched as God's dream captured the hearts and imaginations of the villagers in Malawi. They felt its pull and dreamed along with him of an age without suffering, sickness, and death.

We find one of the most magnificent depictions of what God dreams for our world in the last book of the Bible:

> And I heard a loud voice from the throne saying, "Behold, the dwelling place of God is with man. He will dwell with them, and they will be his people, and God himself will be with them as their God. He will wipe away every tear from their eyes, and death shall be no more, neither shall there be mourning, nor crying, nor pain anymore, for the former things have passed away." And he who was seated on the throne said, "Behold, I am making all things new." Also he said, "Write this down, for these words are trustworthy and true." And he said to me, "It is done! I am the Alpha and the Omega, the beginning and the end. To the thirsty I will give from the spring of the water of life without payment." (Rev 21:3–6)

5. Alcorn, *Heaven*, 5–6.

This prophecy shows God's heart for his creation. He intends to eliminate the sources of sorrow in our world. He does not demolish our planet; instead, he renews it, restoring it back to its primal glory. He makes all things new. Such hope can help us weather the most turbulent storms of our lives "as a sure and steadfast anchor of the soul" (Heb 6:19).

That month I spent in Africa helped me understand Jesus and his context so much better. Even so, I had a way to go before I fully grasped the implications of the kingdom of God for daily life. The next stage in my journey was a four-year period I spent pastoring my home church in upstate New York. It was then that I would begin to glimpse how the kingdom message provided the key to Christian ethics.

4

The Heart of Ethics

After I graduated from the Atlanta Bible College, I went back to New York to serve as an assistant pastor. While I was in Georgia, my church back home had become embroiled in a controversy with another church in our state. Their lead pastor, who I'll call Johnny Jones, had started teaching that all genuine Christians should commit to passive nonresistance, an extreme form of Christian pacifism. In fact, I remember attending one of his summer seminars when he said that if someone attacked his wife, he would do nothing. Nothing. Over time, I kept waiting for him to clarify or add an exception, but he left me with no doubt.

Although most of us in my home church were not too bothered by Jones's radical new position, he began insisting that agreement with him was necessary for fellowship. In other words, Jones would no longer attend our big summer gatherings or allow members of his church to go. Ironically, the "pacifist" was bullying everyone into accepting his beliefs—or else.

A split loomed on the horizon, forcing everyone to take sides. At the time, I felt the pressure more than most because many of my young adult friends were in Jones's church. Were they seriously going to stop talking to me ever again because I had a different belief? Yes: that's exactly what they were prepared to do. Regardless of our previous relationship, from their perspective, I was either with them or against them.

As a brand-new assistant pastor, this was a lot to carry on my shoulders.

Still, I couldn't make a doctrinal decision based on what friends I might lose. I felt compelled to investigate the topic and come to a settled view based on the biblical evidence, careful reasoning, and real-world application. I began reading books about pacifism from older authors like Leo

Tolstoy and Dietrich Bonhoeffer as well as newer ones like Gregory Boyd and Lee Camp. The more I read, the more I noticed how saturated these books were with references to the kingdom of God.

This really surprised me. While I had come to understand that the kingdom of God was both hope (what Christians look forward to) and gospel (the message we share with unbelievers), I did not yet understand how believing in the kingdom affects ethics (how we live now). I thought of it as only something yet to come—something tied to the return of Christ, when he establishes lasting justice and peace on Earth.

As I continued my research, I began to see how my belief about the future was the key to understanding how I should live now. For example, Jesus couldn't help but mention the kingdom eight times in the Sermon on the Mount—a teaching about how to live *in the present*. Even if my initial reason for delving into Christian ethics was to evaluate pacifism, I now started to catch sight of a much bigger picture. I was beginning to see how the future kingdom affected my present reality.

Around this time, I was also listening to a lot of N. T. Wright's lectures. I remember how he interpreted Jesus's ministry as the bringing forward of God's vision for the future into his own time and place. Here is how Wright puts it:

> The Bible doesn't speak, as so many Christians imagine, of a disembodied heaven, but rather of new heavens and new earth. And the point about God's future world is that it will be *more* real, more solid, more tangible and visible and tasteable than the present world. And that for a good reason: the present world is full of corruption and decay, of violence and sorrow and sin and death. But the whole point is that what God has decided to do about all this, precisely because he's the creator who loves the world he made, is to do away with all that corruption and sorrow and death and so leave the way clear for the world to be renewed from top to bottom, so that everything that's pure and lovely and beautiful and noble and wise will shine out all the more brightly. . . .
>
> And what Jesus did was to bring the plan forward so that instead of it happening at the end of history, it happened, decisively, in and through him, in the middle of history. . . . The resurrection is the sign, among many other things, that God's new creation has begun, that the future has come bursting into the present.[1]

---

1. Wright, "God's Future in Person," paras. 7, 8.

For Wright, Jesus's ministry provided a window into the future, as he demonstrated how the kingdom will look. Taking my cue from Wright, I imagined how Jesus's contemporaries would have interpreted his ministry.

Right from his inaugural sermon in his hometown of Nazareth, Jesus talked about the kingdom. He read from Isa 61, a chapter prophesying about the age to come, and then audaciously said, "Today this Scripture has been fulfilled in your hearing" (Luke 4:21). Then, he traveled from village to village preaching the kingdom, saying, "The time is fulfilled, and the kingdom of God is at hand; repent and believe in the gospel" (Mark 1:15). In addition to his gospel preaching, Jesus constantly talked about the kingdom in his other teachings. Jesus taught we should "seek first the kingdom of God and his righteousness," rather than worrying about clothing and food (Matt 6:33). Likewise, Jesus used parables to teach about the kingdom. He would say that the kingdom was like a mustard seed, or that it was like leaven, or that it was like a treasure hidden in a field, etc.

However, Jesus's kingdom ministry didn't culminate in mere words. Beyond teaching, he enacted the kingdom through miracles.

We can see this clearly in Luke chapter 7. In the narrative, after word spreads about Jesus raising the widow of Nain's son from the dead, John sends disciples to ask Jesus if he is the expected one (the Messiah). When these disciples arrive, Jesus is in the act of healing many from diseases, plagues, evil spirits, and blindness. He answers their question:

> Go and tell John what you have seen and heard: the blind receive their sight, the lame walk, lepers are cleansed, and the deaf hear, the dead are raised up, the poor have good news preached to them. And blessed is the one who is not offended by me. (Luke 7:22–23)

What is Jesus saying? This statement includes quotations from Isa 35 and 61—both chapters that prophecy about the kingdom. John wants to know whether or not Jesus was the Messiah—the one to usher in the kingdom age. Jesus responds by pointing to his kingdom miracles.

If someone wants to know what the kingdom will be like, all he or she needs to do is look at Jesus in action. Jesus's ministry gave people a taste of the coming kingdom, and in so doing, it authenticated his own messianic identity.

This is rather like asking someone in plain clothes if they are an orchestral conductor. A layman could not conduct even an experienced ensemble. But even without an orchestra, a competent conductor could still prove himself. He could explain music theory, rehearsal techniques, and the challenges of performance. He could play different parts on a piano and describe how they fit together. He might not yet be in the proper setting to show his identity in all its glory, but he can give a taste of who he is and what he does. Then it would be up to the questioner to decide whether or not to trust if he really is who he says he is.

This is what Jesus did for John's disciples—he pointed to his messianic work to validate his claim of being the genuine Messiah, the one who would establish God's kingdom.

Just as Jesus interpreted his miracles as proof of his messianic identity, he understood his exorcisms in light of the kingdom. He said, "But if it is by the Spirit of God that I cast out demons, then the kingdom of God has come upon you" (Matt 12:28). Each time Jesus liberated someone from the oppressive darkness of unclean spirits, it was like the kingdom dropped out of the sky for that moment, setting right what was wrong with someone. The future age was breaking into the present through Jesus's ministry. When the kingdom arrives, will people suffer from demonic possession? Of course not! So, when Jesus encountered unclean spirits, he cast them out, restoring people to wholeness.

Lastly, Jesus's titles brought kingdom flavor to his ministry. For example, he preferred to call himself "the Son of Man," which can mean merely a "human being," or it can refer to the one who receives the kingdom from the Ancient of Days in Daniel's famous vision (Dan 7:13–14).[2]

"Son of Man" is perfectly ambiguous; it forces people to make their own decisions about Jesus. He is a son of man to be sure, but he's also the Son of Man—the one who will rule over all peoples, nations, and languages, whose kingdom will last forever, not pass away, and never be destroyed. This distinctive kingdom flavor was behind why Jesus preferred this title so much.

From his miracles and exorcisms to his favorite way of referring to himself, Jesus led a kingdom-saturated ministry. Everything he did brought fresh signs of God's future into the present as a witness to what is to come. He restored defective eyes and legs; he restored sinners back to their communities; he restored demon-possessed people to sanity. Jesus's ministry was all about restoration, not only because of his compassionate heart but to show people what the kingdom will be like.

Wherever Jesus went there was a pocket of the kingdom. When villagers came near enough to Jesus, they got to a glimpse of the future. Lee Camp explains,

> And even though that coming aeon remains yet in the future,
> there is in Jesus' life and ministry something occurring which

2. See chapter 1.

> embodies that future coming reign. The word *proleptic* is a
> helpful adjective here: *proleptic* is that which represents or char-
> acterizes something in the future as having already occurred,
> or already having been accomplished in the present. Jesus' life
> and ministry—and subsequently the life and ministry of the
> church—thus proleptically realizes that coming age, in which
> the enemies of God will be entirely defeated. . . . We might pic-
> ture the overlapping of two aeons, of the new having broken into
> the old; the old still holds on to its pitiful existence, while the
> new is even now in our midst, its triumph assured. The escha-
> ton, the end, is even *now* in our midst, but *not yet* fully.[3]

Camp believes that Jesus is the man of the future, who brings the coming
age into our present age with his words and actions. I was beginning to see
a whole new dimension of the kingdom.

Now, I want to be careful here; I'm not saying that the kingdom has
already come or that the kingdom is the same as the church. If we define
the kingdom on the basis of the Hebrew prophets, then it refers to the time
when God sets everything wrong with the world right. For example, Daniel's vision of the Son of Man emphasizes how God's kingdom will include
every nation. So if there is even one nation rebelling against God, we can
safely conclude that God's kingdom has not yet arrived.

Even so, this future is available to live now, at least in part, that is,
proleptically. This is not to say that Christians should enact the kingdom *po-
litically* by taking over the world's governments and forcing everyone to live
as Christians in preparation for reigning with Christ. What it does mean is
that we can *prophetically* embody the age to come by practicing the lifestyle
of the age to come, even while living in this present evil age.

Jesus saturated his ministry with kingdom activity. In what practical
ways can we, his followers, likewise anticipate the kingdom's coming? One
way becomes clear when we read Paul's rebuke to the Corinthians for suing
each other:

> When one of you has a grievance against another, does he dare
> go to law before the unrighteous instead of the saints? Or do you
> not know that the saints will judge the world? And if the world is
> to be judged by you, are you incompetent to try trivial cases? Do
> you not know that we are to judge angels? How much more, then,
> matters pertaining to this life! So if you have such cases, why do
> you lay them before those who have no standing in the church?
> (1 Cor 6:1–4)

---

3. Camp, *Mere Discipleship*, 75–76.

Paul couldn't believe that Christians would take each other to court. Why couldn't they figure out their issues among themselves? Here they were, claiming they knew the Messiah, preaching about the kingdom, believing they were going to rule the world one day, and yet, they couldn't figure out how to deal with internal disputes! Asking an unbeliever to solve their disagreements undermined their central claim to be the kingdom people.

Paul rebuked the Corinthians because they weren't proleptically appropriating their beliefs about the future into the present. Their hope should have affected how they lived.

For us, the first question is, "How will it be in the kingdom?" The next is, "How can I embody kingdom living now in this situation?" In the age to come, will people lie to one another? Of course they won't, so it makes sense that the kingdom people would already put away lying. In the kingdom, will people make fun of one another and put each other down? Of course they won't. On this basis, we should treat each other with respect and build each other up now.

I'm not saying we can reflect the age to come in our current lives *perfectly*, but, to a large degree, we can. We may be broken mirrors, but people should still glimpse God's glorious future age when they look at our lives.

My good friend Victor Gluckin beautifully casts the vision with these words:

> When people come and interact with Christians, they should get a small taste of what it will be like in the kingdom. It should be different than when they interact with people living for this age. The gathering of the church is an embassy for the kingdom. When we are together, you sense the kingdom Spirit. When we leave, we are ambassadors for the king.[4]

The story doesn't end there though. It is not as though we must grit our teeth and force our way into living righteously. God has provided spiritual empowerment to live the future in the present.

I stumbled onto this truth while puzzling over the question the disciples asked just before Jesus ascended. Jesus had just told his disciples to stay in Jerusalem until they received the baptism of the Spirit when they asked, "Lord, will you at this time restore the kingdom to Israel?" (Acts 1:6). In their minds, the disciples associated "spirit" with "kingdom." Jesus promised that, in just a few days, they would receive the Spirit, and they thought that meant the kingdom was now coming. Why did the disciples think about the restoration of the kingdom when Jesus promised the coming of the Spirit?

4. Gluckin, "Kingdom Story," 2.

Christian commentators have sometimes criticized the disciples for holding to a nationalistic, this-worldly hope over against Jesus's message about a spiritual, instead of physical, kingdom. Here are several statements about this text from well-regarded Christian commentators:

> John Calvin: "There are as many errors in this question as words."[5]
> John Wesley: "They still seemed to dream of an outward, temporal kingdom, in which the Jews should have dominion over all nations."[6]
> Matthew Henry: "Our Lord knew that his ascension and the teaching of the holy spirit would end these expectations, and therefore only gave them a rebuke."[7]
> Peoples' New Testament Commentary: "They still held to their old ideas of a worldly restoration of the kingdom of Israel. Their only question was, Wilt thou restore it 'now?' After the Holy Spirit was given, this delusion was dismissed, and they understood that Christ's kingdom is not of this world."[8]

But were the disciples really so clueless? It's hard for me to believe that after Jesus spent years teaching them, they still got his central message wrong. No: Jesus never redefined or spiritualized the ancient kingdom prophecies, rather, he added to them, promising his disciples that they would sit on twelve thrones judging the twelve tribes of Israel (Luke 22:29–30). Jesus taught that "the meek [will] inherit the earth" (Matt 5:5), that "people will come from east and west . . . and recline at table in the kingdom" (Luke 13:29) and that "When the Son of Man comes. . . . Before him will be gathered all the nations, and he will separate people one from another" (Matt 25:31–32).

Furthermore, I see no evidence that Jesus was frustrated with the disciples' question about restoring the kingdom to Israel. In the text, Jesus does not rebuke them for believing in a national kingdom. Here is how the conversation goes:

> And while staying with them he ordered them not to depart from Jerusalem, but to wait for the promise of the Father, which, he said, "you heard from me; for John baptized with water, but you will be baptized with the Holy Spirit not many days from now." So when they had come together, they asked him, "Lord, will you at this time restore the kingdom to Israel?" He said to

5. Calvin, *Commentary on Acts*, 24.

6. Wesley, *Notes on the New Testament*, 248.

7. Henry, *Matthew Henry's Concise Commentary*, 1702.

8. Johnson, *People's New Testament*, 417.

them, "It is not for you to know times or seasons that the Father
has fixed by his own authority. But you will receive power when
the Holy Spirit has come upon you, and you will be my wit-
nesses in Jerusalem and in all Judea and Samaria, and to the end
of the earth." (Acts 1:4–8)

Jesus did not accuse the disciples of misunderstanding the kingdom, he
merely clarified the timing. God will restore the kingdom to Israel, but he
had not revealed to them when that will happen. Even so, the Spirit was
coming soon to enable them to testify about Jesus.

If the disciples weren't asking an off-the-wall question here, why in the
world did their minds jump to the kingdom when Jesus mentioned baptism
in the Spirit? As is so often the case, the answer lies in their Bible, our Old
Testament, where the outpouring of the Spirit is frequently linked with the
coming kingdom. Here is an example from Isaiah:

> For the palace is forsaken,
> the populous city deserted;
> the hill and the watchtower
> will become dens forever,
> a joy of wild donkeys,
> a pasture of flocks;
> until the Spirit is poured upon us from on high,
> and the wilderness becomes a fruitful field,
> and the fruitful field is deemed a forest.
> Then justice will dwell in the wilderness,
> and righteousness abide in the fruitful field.
> And the effect of righteousness will be peace,
> and the result of righteousness, quietness and trust forever.
> My people will abide in a peaceful habitation,
> in secure dwellings, and in quiet resting places. (Isa 32:14–18)

This text—and others like it[9]—clearly link the outpouring of the Spirit to
the age to come, when all that is wrong with the world will be made right.
Likewise, John the Baptist prophesied about the baptism of the Spirit in the
context of another aspect of the kingdom, the final judgment:

> John answered them all, saying, "I baptize you with water, but
> he who is mightier than I is coming, the strap of whose sandals I
> am not worthy to untie. He will baptize you with the Holy Spirit
> and fire. His winnowing fork is in his hand, to clear his thresh-
> ing floor and to gather the wheat into his barn, but the chaff he
> will burn with unquenchable fire." (Luke 3:16–17)

9. See Isa 44:1–5; Ezek 11:17–20; 36:24–28, 33–35; 37:12–14; 39:25–29; Joel 2:28—3:2.

According to John the Baptist, the baptism of the Holy Spirit and the baptism of fire will occur at the same time. When the Messiah comes, he will pour out God's Spirit on the righteous (the wheat) and burn up the wicked (the chaff).

Like Isaiah, John the Baptist was not aware of any interim period between the coming of the Spirit and the coming of the kingdom. The outpouring of the Spirit properly belongs to the future kingdom age. This is why when the Spirit came on Pentecost, Peter immediately jumped to the prophecy in Joel about the last days (Acts 2:16–21).

The Spirit is a piece of the kingdom we can experience now. It is a down payment of what is to come.[10] It is "the guarantee of our inheritance until we acquire possession of it" (Eph 1:14). When someone pays the down payment on a house, the bank can be sure he or she will pay the rest in the future. So it is with God. The kingdom is coming, but in the meantime, he gives the church a taste of the kingdom, some way to drink of the kingdom, refreshing and strengthening us to bring forth signs of God's future into our present world.

Because of what the Messiah has accomplished, we have experienced enlightenment, drunk from the heavenly gift, shared in the Holy Spirit, and tasted the goodness of God's message as well as the powers of the age to come (Heb 6:4–5). God's Spirit enables us to conduct our lives according to the culture of the age to come, even while we live in this tired old world, full of dysfunction and brokenness.

We who are indwelt with the Spirit, followers of the Messiah, are the kingdom people, the future of humanity. God has privileged and commissioned us to give the world a foretaste of his kingdom through our actions and words, by modeling the way of restoration. Rather than allowing this age to squeeze our minds into its mold, we need to renew them according to God's transformative power (Rom 12:2). The kind of love and wholeness that will one day permeate the whole world can characterize our lives today!

What God plans to do then, he is already doing to his people now. He is healing us, redeeming us, and restoring us. We are appetizers, trailers, and signposts. The main meal awaits Christ's return, but we give the world a taste of the future. We can pique the interest of the masses with a preview of what life will look like when God reigns. We can point the way to the future by testifying in the present about what is to come like a sign on a highway. Our lives as individuals and as a community are prophetic. Just like Jesus, we too should look for ways to enact the kingdom in our own lives, from how we

---

10. See 2 Cor 1:22; 5:5.

do marriage and parenting to how we treat our enemies. Every action is an opportunity to reflect the glory of God's tomorrow into our lives today.

The future kingdom should affect how we live now by motivating us to do what is right as representatives of God's kingdom. The age to come, I was beginning to see, should change how I think and live.

I felt it changing me on the inside. I felt different, like I could relate to Jesus, like I could genuinely, though in my own limited way, carry on what he started. I felt like I understood God's heart, how it radiated through Jesus's ministry, and how it needs to shine through me today.

During the time of my kingdom journey, evangelicalism had ascended to the heights of power and many were associating Bible-believing Christianity with a certain political party, especially during the years immediately following the 9/11 attacks. I still didn't grasp what it meant to be a kingdom citizen. As a pastor, I received many emails urging me to publicly support one political candidate over another, warning of how the wrong president would destroy the United States. I didn't know it then, but I was about to discover how God's kingdom affected my patriotism and politics.

5

Kingdom Allegiance

Shane Claiborne was larger than life. A few friends and I went to Park Street Church in Boston to hear him speak.[1] He was like a modern-day John the Baptist, except instead of wearing camel hair and a leather belt, he sported homemade clothing and dreadlocks tied in a bandana. A cross between a prophet and a homeless man, he was the keynote speaker at a weekend of meetings focused on gratitude and creation care.

Many of the attendees and group leaders were Christian hippies. I met a girl there who didn't believe in washing her hair because it wasted water. Another woman shared a tip about using car fresheners in her kitchen to mask the odor of her composting biological waste. A third talked about how she never turned on the heat for an entire Boston winter, deriving warmth instead from the residual heat of the apartments surrounding hers. This was an interesting group—what Claiborne called "ordinary radicals."

At the event, Claiborne shared his gripping testimony of how following Christ had led him down a path of several social justice causes. He talked about a trip he made to Iraq just before the "Shock and Awe" military bombardment of Baghdad in 2003. With the help of Christian Peacemaker Teams, an organization that wages "nonviolent direct action to confront systems of violence and oppression,"[2] he linked up with the Iraq Peace Team so that he could visit homes, hospitals, and churches before and during the American offensive. In his book, Claiborne describes his reason for going:

1. For a nearly identical lecture, see youtube.com/watch?v=QPANKUHabx4

2. Community Peacemaker Teams, "About Us." They are now known as Community Peacemaker Teams.

> I went to Iraq to stop terrorism. . . . I went to Iraq to stand in the
> way of war. Thousands of soldiers have gone to Iraq, willing to
> kill people they do not know because of a political allegiance. I
> went willing to die for people I do not know because of a spiri-
> tual allegiance. I went to Iraq as a missionary . . . [to] stand by
> those who face the impending wrath of the empire and whisper,
> "God loves you, I love you, and if my country bombs your coun-
> try, I will be right here with you."[3]

I had never heard anyone talk like he did before. Living through the Iraq wars, I remember how inundated American culture was with slogans like "Support Our Troops," "Make the World Safe for Democracy," and terms like "The War on Terror." After the terrorist attack on the World Trade Towers in New York City on September 11, 2001, patriotism swelled and it felt like everyone was swept along by a powerful tide of God and country. But here was someone questioning the logic of retaliation—and doing so at the risk of his own life.

Claiborne went on to describe how he was playing with some kids in a park (a designated safe zone) when the bombs began to drop on Baghdad. He recalled how the children, already accustomed to it, met this latest round of bombing with indifference. Then he talked about what it was like to go to church in Iraq. He remembered telling one of the leaders how surprised he was that there were so many Christians there. The man replied, "Yes, my friend, this is where it all began. This is the land of your ancestors. That is the Tigris River, and the Euphrates. Have you read about them?"[4] Iraq was Abraham's native land; it really is where it all began.

Claiborne's story stunned me; I didn't realize that I had brothers and sisters in Iraq. Of course, I should have known that Christians would be there even if it was a majority Muslim country, but at that time, I had an oversimplified view of national homogeneity.

The man asked Claiborne about the church in the United States. He wondered how Christians there were standing against the bombing of his country. Claiborne's heart sank when he realized he could not give the answer this dear, foreign brother wanted. He explained what American Christians thought about "The War on Terror" and the search for weapons of mass destruction. The man shook his head and said, "We believe in the cross. . . . We will be praying for you. We will be praying for the church in the US . . . to be the church."[5]

---

3. Claiborne, *Irresistible Revolution*, 208.

4. Claiborne, *Irresistible Revolution*, 212.

5. Claiborne, *Irresistible Revolution*, 213.

That part of Claiborne's story hit me like a ton of bricks. I had never imagined that there were Iraqi Christians praying for us to stay faithful to Christ and his teachings regardless of what the government says. Claiborne explained that following Christ affects every aspect of our lives, even our politics. He was giving me a lot to think about.

I started to wonder how Jesus handled issues of allegiance and politics in his own day. By the time Jesus began his ministry, the Romans had ruled over the land of Israel for nearly a century. How Roman occupation must have aggravated the Jews of Jesus's day! They believed God had promised to give the land to Abraham and his descendants. Joshua led them into it over a millennium before the Romans came. They must have thought, "How dare these uncircumcised gentiles take God's land from his chosen people? Who do they think they are?"

Since religion and politics were not separate realms in Jewish culture, discussions about politics were inherently religious as well. They believed God had delivered them time and again—from Egyptian ethnic cleansing, from Persian genocide, and from Seleucid infanticide, to list just three examples. Each time God saved his people, they memorialized the event with a festival (such as Passover, Purim, and Chanukah). Celebrating these annual holidays ensured future generations would remember the remarkable feats of their covenant God.

Passover, in particular, became a rallying point for nationalism, a fact the Roman governors took seriously. The Roman soldiers looked down from their perch in the Antonia Fortress while countless pilgrims from all over the world brought lambs to slaughter in memory of when God brought the powerful Egyptians to their knees through the ten plagues. It's certain that pious Jews couldn't help but make the connection between their current masters and their time of slavery in Egypt. Looking up and seeing Roman soldiers at the ready must have provoked contempt.

In addition to their hunger for liberty and their belief in an almighty God who favored them, the Jews' scruples also made them difficult to govern. For example, while the second commandment forbids making images, the Roman world abounded with statues, idols, and standards.

Several incidents illustrate how this conflict played out. One night, Pilate had his legions bring their military banners, which had Caesar's image on them, into Jerusalem.[6] Outraged, the Jewish leadership sent a delegation to Pilate at Caesarea to protest the images, but he ignored them for six days. On the sixth day, Pilate ordered his soldiers to surround the delegates and draw their swords. Rather than backing down or fighting, the Jews fell to

---

6. Josephus, *Ant.* 18.3.1 (p. 575).

their knees, laid their necks bare, and cried out that they would rather die than transgress God's laws.

Pilate relented and had the standards removed.

Similar conflicts abounded between the Jews and their overlords. Once, the people rioted because Pilate had used funds from the temple treasury to build an aqueduct to supply water to Jerusalem. Pilate dispersed his soldiers into the crowd, dressed in plain clothes with weapons hidden. At a prearranged signal, the soldiers began stabbing and hitting people, instigating a stampede that left many dead. Incidents like these happened before, during, and after the time of Jesus, an extremely volatile period.

Incompetent Roman leadership, the constant pressure to pay taxes, and a belief that God had given them the land, prevented the Jews from submitting to the Roman boot on their neck. Over and over, protest movements flared up and revolutions broke out. For example, when Herod the Great died, Judah ben Hezekiah took over Sepphoris, a significant city very near the tiny hamlet of Nazareth. Judah armed his militia with the weapons he found there and robbed the city treasury as well. In response, the Roman governor Varus dispatched soldiers to crush Sepphoris. They burned the city and enslaved thousands.

When Jesus was growing up in Nazareth, Herod Antipas rebuilt Sepphoris, naming it Autocratoris, after the Roman emperor. Richard Horsley writes, "The Roman killing or enslavement of tens of thousands of Galileans and Judeans around the time Jesus was born must have left mass trauma among the people in its wake."[7] How must the villagers of Nazareth have whispered among themselves about Roman brutality during Jesus's childhood?

The Roman senator Quirinius precipitated another incident when he ordered a census of the region for tax purposes. Another revolutionary from Galilee, also named Judah, arose, saying that taxation was "no better than an introduction to slavery."[8] Judah called the people cowards if they submitted to the Romans instead of God. He, along with Zaddok, a Pharisee, stirred up the people to fight for freedom, arguing that God would not help them unless they committed to the cause. Judah's boldness garnered a great deal of support among the common people. In the end, he, too, failed to oust the Romans.

In addition to these incidents before Jesus's ministry, major movements arose after it as well. A decade or two after the crucifixion, a group of clandestine assassins came to prominence. They earned for themselves the

7. Horsley, *Jesus and Empire*, 30.

8. Josephus, *Ant.* 18.1.1 (p. 571). See also Josephus, *J.W.* 2.8.1 (p. 725).

name Sicarii from the curved daggers they hid in their garments. They identified and assassinated Roman sympathizers, mingling with the multitude
and slitting their throats in broad daylight. They even murdered Jonathan
the high priest, presumably for his compromising stand with the Romans.
Eventually, just thirty years after Christ, the whole Jewish nation got swept
into a revolutionary war for independence from Rome.

Josephus, a Jewish historian and Roman sympathizer, writes about this
war as follows:

> But of the fourth sect of Jewish philosophy, Judah the Galilean
> was the author. These men agree in all other things with the Pha-
> rasaic notions; but they have an inviolable attachment to liberty;
> and say that God is to be their only Ruler and Lord. They also do
> not value dying any kind of death, nor indeed do they heed the
> deaths of their relations and friends, nor can any such fear make
> them call any man Lord . . . and it was in Gessius Florus's time
> that the nation began to grow mad with this distemper, who was
> our procurator, and who occasioned the Jews to go wild with it
> by the abuse of his authority, and to make them revolt from the
> Romans.[9]

Indeed, the Jews did go wild, though the Christ-followers among them,
in obedience to Jesus, fled when they saw the armies coming.[10] To defeat
Jerusalem, it took the Romans seven years and five legions (sixty thousand
troops), resulting in a body count roughly twice the number of that in the
American Civil War.

When the Romans caught Jews deserting the city, they crucified them
in full view of Jerusalem, as many as five hundred in a day, making the air
thick with the stench of rotting flesh and cries of agony. When the Romans
finally broke through Jerusalem's mighty walls in AD 70, they burned the
temple and enslaved nearly one hundred thousand people.

One would think such a bitter defeat would put an end to Jewish as-
pirations for independence, but in fact, it did not. Only sixty years later,
the Jews again rebelled against the Romans. This time it took six legions
and troops from six other units, totaling as many as one hundred thousand
soldiers to crush the Jewish revolt. Upon the conclusion of the bloody saga,
the Romans demolished Jerusalem and built a pagan city on its foundation,
calling it Aelia Capitolina, even erecting a temple to Jupiter where the Jewish
temple once stood. They banned teaching the law of Moses and exiled the
Jews from their land for centuries.

9. Josephus, *Ant.* 18.1.6 (p. 753).
10. Eusebius, *Hist. eccl.* 3.5 (p. 82).

I bring all of this up because it helps us understand the tumultuous times in which Jesus carried out his ministry. Those of us who enjoy national stability typically assume that such was the case for Jesus as well. We imagine he lived in a period of religious freedom, when the church and state were separate realms. None of this is true.

Jesus lived during an immensely unstable period. During his time, the people chafed under Roman occupation and some voices already called for revolution. He carried out his ministry on the precipice of history. To prove the point, all we need to do is look to the cross. The Jewish leadership urged the Romans to crucify Jesus on the charge that he claimed to be the king of the Jews (Matt 27:37). Roman paranoia could not allow such a religiopolitical claim to go unpunished. Crucifixion made sense, not only because it demonstrated Roman superiority through humiliation, but also because it deterred other would-be messiahs from making such claims.

How did Jesus deal with the issue of Roman occupation? He had several options before him: he could join the underground resistance movement; he could petition Tiberius Caesar for independence; he could organize farmers to refuse to plant their crops until conditions improved.

He did none of these things. But he did fight evil: Jesus subverted the whole system of injustice person by person. He proclaimed a competing ideology, God's kingdom, and he called people to repent in light of its coming. He taught his followers how to love, not in a passive, safe way, but in a courageous, risky way. He brought signs of the kingdom wherever he went, raising the dead, healing the sick, and restoring the outcast.

His kingdom actualization efforts did not go unnoticed by the local ruler, Herod Antipas. Oscar Wilde portrayed Herod's response to Jesus's ministry with this dialogue:

> First Nazarene: The daughter of Jairus was dead. This man raised her from the dead.
> Herod: How! He raises people from the dead?
> First Nazarene: Yea, sire, he raiseth the dead.
> Herod: I do not wish him to do that. I forbid him to do that. I suffer no man to raise the dead. This man must be found and told that I forbid him to raise the dead. . . . Let them find him, and tell him, thus saith Herod the King, "I will not suffer thee to raise the dead!" To change water into wine, to heal the lepers and the blind . . . he may do these things if he will. I say nothing against these things. In truth I hold it a kindly deed to heal a leper. But no man shall raise the dead. It would be terrible if the dead came back.[11]

11. Wilde, *Salome*, 21–22.

Although this whole conversation is merely speculative (and a bit absurd), it gets to the heart of how Jesus's ministry must have unnerved the rulers. The final power of the state is the power to execute those who won't fall in line. If Jesus can raise the dead, he can undo the greatest weapon of all.

As a result of Herod's discomfort with Jesus, he sent to have him arrested (like John the Baptist before him). Before his cronies could capture Jesus, the Pharisees (of all people) warned him, saying, "Get away from here, for Herod wants to kill you" (Luke 13:31). Jesus replied, "Go and tell that fox, 'Behold, I cast out demons and perform cures today and tomorrow, and the third day I finish my course'" (Luke 13:32). Jesus eluded Herod up until he attended Passover in Jerusalem during the last week of his life.

It was during this final week that Jesus publicized his messianic claim by riding into Jerusalem in ostentatious fulfillment of Zechariah's prophecy (Zech 9:9), while crowds shouted, "Hosanna! Blessed is he who comes in the name of the Lord, even the King of Israel!" (John 12:13). Next, he turned over the money changers' tables and shooed the animals away in the temple courtyards, interrupting the central institution in Jerusalem. After that he took on the religious leaders, including Pharisees, Sadducees, and Herodians, outmaneuvering their stumper questions, resulting in their public embarrassment.

To publicly entrap Jesus, they asked him, "Is it lawful to pay taxes to Caesar, or not? Should we pay them, or should we not?" (Mark 12:14). Jesus asked them for a coin, which they handed to him. He inquired, "Whose likeness and inscription is this?" (Mark 12:16). They said it was Caesar's image on the coin. Jesus responded, "Render to Caesar the things that are Caesar's, and to God the things that are God's" (Mark 12:17). This answer dumbfounded Jesus's crafty opponents, probably because of how well it avoided the carefully laid traps on either side of their question.

Jesus endorsed giving Caesar his own money back, but he simultaneously taught that we should not compromise on giving God what we owe him. We see the same position on taxes later when Paul writes, "for the authorities are ministers of God. . . . Pay to all what is owed to them: taxes to whom taxes are owed . . . respect to whom respect is owed" (Rom 13:6–7). Peter likewise says, "Fear God. Honor the emperor" (1 Pet 2:17). Christianity does not oppose the ruling governments, but it does sublimate them to God's rule. So long as the government upholds justice, it is the servant of God, but when it makes demands that defy what God says, our ultimate allegiance must lie with our kingdom citizenship.

After Jesus's resurrection, the missionary, Paul, traveled to Thessalonica, spreading the kingdom gospel message over three weeks. He primarily preached in synagogues and was able to persuade a number of folks, both

Jews and Greeks, that "This Jesus, whom I proclaim to you, is the Christ" (Acts 17:3). Out of jealousy, some stirred up a mob that went to Jason's house, where Paul and Silas had been staying. Since they couldn't find them, they dragged Jason and some others to the authorities, shouting, "These men who have turned the world upside down have come here also, and Jason has received them, and they are all acting against the decrees of Caesar, saying that there is another king, Jesus" (Acts 17:6–7). Paul was preaching that Jesus was the Christ, and they equated that with saying Jesus was a king. Further, they correctly perceived that such a claim violated the decrees of Caesar.

I fear we have depoliticized Jesus because we have bought into the myth that religion and politics are two mutually exclusive realms. Perhaps this is because words like "Christ" and "Lord" have lost their zing. Many of us think Christ is Jesus's last name and Lord is synonymous with savior. However, Christ is just the Greek way of saying Messiah—the title for the one God anoints to rule the world as king. It is inherently political, and both the Jews and the Romans knew it.

In fact, this was precisely how the Sanhedrin forced Pilate's hand to order Jesus crucified.

> From then on Pilate sought to release him, but the Jews cried out, "If you release this man, you are not Caesar's friend. Everyone who makes himself a king opposes Caesar." . . .
> Now it was the day of Preparation of the Passover. It was about the sixth hour. He said to the Jews, "Behold your King!" They cried out, "Away with him, away with him, crucify him!" Pilate said to them, "Shall I crucify your King?" The chief priests answered, "We have no king but Caesar." So he delivered him over to them to be crucified. (John 19:12–16)

To be a king is to be a political leader. Thus, Jesus was and remains not only a religious man but also a political figure. Consequently, it should not surprise us when situations arise that force us to choose between God's kingdom and our earthly nation.

This has happened throughout the history of Christianity. The empire of the day executed Jesus for claiming to be the king of the Jews; it beheaded Paul for proclaiming Jesus as the rightful Lord of the world; it crucified Peter for preaching Jesus as resurrected Messiah. Though these did not threaten the empire's collection of taxes or foment disrespect towards the governing authorities, the empire still executed them. The blood of the martyrs flows deep and wide, from empires to monarchies to caliphates.

One early example worthy of mention is Polycarp, the overseer of the church of Smyrna in the second century. The government tracked him down and arrested him when he was already a very old man. He stood before the Roman proconsul in the arena while a mob was calling for his blood. Here is how the conversation went:

> Proconsul: "Have respect for your age. Swear by the genius of Caesar; repent; say, 'Away with the atheists!'"
> Polycarp: (Motioning toward the people in the stadium) "Away with the atheists!"
> Proconsul: "Swear the oath, and I will release you; revile Christ."
> Polycarp: "For eighty-six years I have been his servant, and he has done me no wrong. How can I blaspheme my king who saved me?"
> Proconsul: "Swear by the genius of Caesar."
> Polycarp: "If you vainly suppose that I will swear by the genius of Caesar, as you request, and pretend not to know who I am, listen carefully: I am a Christian. Now if you want to learn the doctrine of Christianity, name a day and give me a hearing."
> Proconsul: "Persuade the people."
> Polycarp: "You I might have considered worthy of a reply, for we have been taught to pay proper respect to rulers and authorities appointed by God, as long as it does us no harm; but as for these, I do not think they are worthy, that I should have to defend myself before them."[12]

What a fascinating exchange! How should we classify Polycarp? He is not a revolutionary, nor is he a loyalist. He will not swear by Caesar, nor will he deny that Jesus is his king. But he believes that the very man who is about to give the order to burn him alive *is appointed by God and should receive proper respect.*

Polycarp's allegiance was firmly with his heavenly king, but this loyalty had earthly ramifications. In the end, Polycarp faced torture and martyrdom because he couldn't hedge on his kingdom citizenship.

How should kingdom citizenship affect our lives today? I don't think it forbids patriotism, but it certainly limits it. It's proper to feel an attachment to one's homeland and gratitude for a country that enables human flourishing. However, at its heart Christianity is transnational, embracing believers from every tribe, nation, and language (Rev 5:9). A turban-wearing Arab who despises America but follows Christ is more my brother than

---

12. *Martyr. Poly.* 9.2—10.2 (pp. 316–17).

an apple-pie-eating, football-watching, flag-saluting American who doesn't care about God.

Christianity cripples nationalism and ethnocentrism in the heart of the believer precisely because it requires higher loyalty to Christ's kingdom than to our native countries. Although it may appear radical, what God's kingdom expects of us is no less than what modern countries require for citizenship. For example, here is the American oath of citizenship:

> I hereby declare, on oath, that I absolutely and entirely renounce and abjure all allegiance and fidelity to any foreign prince, potentate, state, or sovereignty, of whom or which I have heretofore been a subject or citizen; that I will support and defend the Constitution and laws of the United States of America against all enemies, foreign and domestic; that I will bear true faith and allegiance to the same; that I will bear arms on behalf of the United States when required by the law; that I will perform noncombatant service in the Armed Forces of the United States when required by the law; that I will perform work of national importance under civilian direction when required by the law; and that I take this obligation freely, without any mental reservation or purpose of evasion; so help me God.[13]

This declaration requires would-be citizens to renounce all other citizenships and allegiances to any foreign rulers. This makes good sense for a country, since it's in its best interest to maximize loyalty and eliminate potential conflicts of interest. But what about the confession "Jesus is Lord"? Doesn't that mean that he is sovereign? Jesus himself explains what he expects of his followers:

> Now great crowds accompanied him, and he turned and said to them, "If anyone comes to me and does not hate his own father and mother and wife and children and brothers and sisters, yes, and even his own life, he cannot be my disciple. Whoever does not bear his own cross and come after me cannot be my disciple. . . . So therefore, any one of you who does not renounce all that he has cannot be my disciple." (Luke 14:25–33)

The call to become a disciple of Christ is open to anyone, regardless of intelligence, success, wealth, fame, attractiveness, or fitness. Anyone can come to him, but they must commit to absolute loyalty.

Jesus is quite explicit here. He says that allegiance to him must come before one's family (Mark 3:31–35; Luke 11:27–28). Following him sometimes

---

13. Code of Federal Regulation, "Oath of Allegiance," para. 2.

causes family divisions (Luke 12:51–53), a fact he knew well: "For not even his brothers believed in him" (John 7:5). Jesus uses the strongest possible language, "hate his own father and mother," to communicate that he must be first. This Hebrew idiom does not literally mean to despise everyone but Jesus; rather, it communicates prioritization—one's family must take a backseat to him. Jesus says he must come before our fathers, mothers, spouses, children, brothers, and sisters. He must even come before *our own lives*.

This is Jesus's *sine qua non* of discipleship. If we do not commit to him over against all of this, we cannot be his disciples. We may go on having fond thoughts of Jesus and even attend church services, but we are not genuine disciples. Only if we take our king at his word, renouncing all and giving him absolute loyalty, will he accept us. He says we must bear our cross—be willing to die—or else we can't follow him. To those who won't commit, but still call him "Lord," Jesus asks, "Why do you call me 'Lord, Lord,' and not do what I tell you?" (Luke 6:46).

In summary, the kingdom affects our loyalties. It challenges our identity and limits our patriotism. As kingdom citizens, we submit to the governing authorities, pay taxes, and give proper honor to rulers, but we do not act against the interests of our king. Ultimately, our allegiance lies with Jesus as Lord.

This revelation means that "my country right or wrong" can't work for kingdom citizens. It means that we have to learn to think in tune with God's kingdom, rather than accepting blind patriotism. Believing in the kingdom really does change our whole outlook on life.

Now that I was grasping how central understanding the kingdom is to following Jesus, I couldn't help but ask: why was Christianity so silent on the kingdom? I needed to investigate the cold case of who killed the kingdom and why. I felt I had gone as far as I could on my own and needed to go back to school to study the history of Christianity. However, since I was married with two children and a mortgage, going to graduate school was going to take nothing short of a miracle. Nevertheless, that's exactly what happened next.

6

Quest for the Historical Kingdom

My wife and mother-in-law had just gone for a walk when the phone rang. I answered, "Hello, this is Sean."

"Hi Sean, this is Anastasia with Boston University's School of Theology."

Anastasia, I thought. *Doesn't that mean "resurrection"?*

She continued, "I am calling to congratulate you for being selected to receive our merit scholarship."

That sounded quite nice, but I had no idea what it was. "What's a merit scholarship?" I asked.

"It covers full tuition and fees, and for you, we are also offering a stipend of $1,000 per semester," she said.

Her words began to sink in.

"What? Are you serious?" I exclaimed. "Let me get this straight. You are saying that I don't have to pay any money to study at BU? Not only that, you are going to pay me to come there. Did I hear you correctly?"

"Yeah, that's right. Your tuition is covered, and the stipend can help you with your books and traveling expenses." Anastasia went on to invite me to a weekend visit to the school to be wined and dined by the university administration. I couldn't wait for Ruth to get back from her walk.

When I had first proposed the idea of going back to school, Ruth had replied, "Well, if God wants you to go back to school then God is going to have to pay for it." It had been a grueling process: filling out the applications, soliciting recommendations from old teachers, and studying endlessly for the GREs. I had done all of this in hopes that somehow, the financial aspect would work itself out.

Just then, Ruth and her mother came in. I told her what the school had said, my eyes full of wonder. She couldn't believe it. Who ever heard of winning such a scholarship, especially considering I had never even applied for it?

Just consider my situation for a moment. I was thirty years old with a mortgage on a house, a full-time job with benefits, and a family (including two little kids). How in the world was I going to afford grad school? Yet somehow, it was all working out.

I had already learned so much about the kingdom. I had a three-dimensional view of it now. I knew the kingdom was the age to come, when Jesus returns to make everything wrong with the world right. It was the message Jesus and his earliest followers preached as gospel from village to village. It was the way of life the church is called to embody in the present as a witness of what the future holds. However, one nagging question still rankled me: what happened? Why was it that I had to *discover* all of this about the kingdom? How come so many Christians, even biblical ones, still believe in the medieval myths of heaven and hell at death? Why do they believe the kingdom either refers to heaven or the church? If the kingdom is hope, gospel, and way, how in the world did we lose it? I had to find out what happened. I wanted to know when this teaching fell by the wayside and why. I wanted to investigate the story of who killed the kingdom.

I broached the subject of going back to school with the elders at my church. They supported the effort, and I worked out an arrangement where I could work for my home church on the weekends during the school year and come back for full-time work in the summers. Some fellow pastors and generous folks agreed to support me financially as they were able. Suddenly, going back to school seemed possible. Considering so many doors opened for me to return to school, I sensed that God was with me in this quest for the kingdom. So I took a leap of faith and packed up my family and we moved east to New England.

In my first semester at BU, I met Paula Fredriksen, the William Goodwin Aurelio Professor of the Appreciation of Scripture. From her title, one might conclude she held a very high view of Scripture like inerrancy. In fact, she was a critical scholar who approached the Bible from a historical rather than faith-based perspective—but that's beside the point. With degrees from Princeton and Oxford and years of painstaking research, publishing, and language training, Fredriksen was a powerhouse within historical Jesus scholarship and, to me at least, a seriously impressive woman.

From her confident poise and professional reputation to her fans, who sat in the back of the room behind her students, everything about this woman exuded authority. One time, I wanted to talk with her about a paper

I was writing for her class, and suggested we get lunch to discuss the matter (our class had just ended at noon). Without missing a beat, she quipped, "Lunch is for the weak. Let's talk while we walk." By the time we made it to her office, she had answered my questions and sent me on my way.

When Fredriksen returned my first paper, I was devastated. It contained dozens of corrections in electronic red ink with comments strewn throughout. I've never had another teacher, before or after, so scrupulously critique my work. I can't imagine, if she gave the same treatment to everyone in the class, how many hours she must have spent marking papers.

She would strike out entire sentences and write in the margin, "These do not contribute to the argument." When she handed back our papers, she expressed disappointment for how poorly written our essays were. The whole class was feeling pretty sorry for itself when she added, "But since I'm a liberal democrat, I'll allow you to revise and resubmit your papers." Suddenly our hearts took flight at the possibility of a second chance. Rewriting our papers to incorporate her copious suggestions, we would get a better grade. I've come to appreciate how much better of a writer she forced me to become.

Although she wasn't a Christian, I appreciated her scholarship and grew to genuinely like Fredriksen, despite my strong disagreement with some of her presuppositions. What I found so encouraging about her was how she spoke about the kingdom. For her, it was just obvious.

Here are two excerpts from her books where she describes the kingdom:

> Sayings and stories about marriage and divorce, drinking and eating in the kingdom, the position and authority within the kingdom of both Jesus and his disciples, the twelve tribes, and the new or renewed Temple—all point toward the traditional Jewish concept of a structured human society (albeit a morally transformed society) in a kingdom on earth (albeit a transformed earth).[1]

> The end time, which Paul also identifies as the establishment of God's kingdom, will be inaugurated by the return from heaven of the raised and glorious Christ. He will descend to the noise of celestial battle to defeat the enemies of God: rulers, authorities, powers, and finally even Death. The followers of Christ will also participate, both the quick and the dead.[2]

---

1. Fredriksen, *From Jesus to Christ*, 175.
2. Fredriksen, *Jesus of Nazareth*, 117.

As a convert to Judaism, Fredriksen had a keen eye for Hebrew perspectives and made sure we spent the first seven lectures of our "From Jesus to Christ" class covering what she called "remedial Hebrew Bible," as well as some background on Second Temple Judaism, before she even began talking about Jesus. I found her approach powerfully confirming what I had already learned. From an Old Testament perspective, it's not hard to argue that the Messiah is a political ruler over this world (Isa 11) and that God's kingdom amounts to him reigning upon the Earth (Dan 2), rather than a vague spiritual reality in people's hearts.

Not only did Fredriksen teach about the kingdom as the chief hope of Jews at the time of Jesus, but she also recognized that Jesus was a preacher of this kingdom message. Jesus, she pointed out, did not go around preaching to the masses to accept him into their hearts so they could go to heaven. Rather, "Jesus of Nazareth was a charismatic prophet who prophesied about the kingdom of God."[3]

Thus, I came to believe the historical Christian gospel included three elements: (1) Jesus the Messiah has come, (2) he died for our sins, and (3) he will come again in power.[4] But that was not all. Fredriksen also made much use of what's called "proleptic eschatology" (eschatology is one's understanding of the end times).

Here is how she put it in her book:

> Why would Jesus make such [ethical] demands of his followers? Why would they listen to him? *Because, as authoritative spokesman of the kingdom, Jesus created around himself a community of those who would live, proleptically, according to the "new" Torah written upon their hearts, the Torah according to which Israel would live when the kingdom came.* . . . Those who accepted him as the authoritative, final forerunner, and who therefore looked forward to the imminent restoration of Israel and redemption of the world, were in a privileged position: having received and accepted advance word, they could prepare for the event they knew was coming. And, accordingly, following the example of their master, they prepared themselves by already, in the last moments of the Old Aeon, living by the intensified, internalized precepts of the Torah that would order Jewish life in the New.[5]

---

3. Paula Fredriksen, "Historical Jesus 2." CAS 216, Department of Religion, Boston University, November 3, 2009.

4. Paula Fredriksen, "The Jesus Movement (Beyond Palestine)." CAS 216, Department of Religion, Boston University, 2009.

5. Fredriksen, *From Jesus to Christ*, 101 (italics in original).

Christ's followers, Fredriksen argued, live the kingdom way in the present as preparation for the end. According to her, gentile converts (called "God-fearers" in Acts) are supposed to become "eschatological pagans."[6] Instead of converting to Judaism, gentile Christ-followers were to remain gentile while acting like the kingdom of God had already arrived.

Sitting through her classes, I was seeing how Fredriksen was not some maverick, an outlier among New Testament scholars; on the contrary, she was the heir of a long series of academics who, beginning at the turn of the twentieth century, came to understand Jesus as an apocalyptic preacher of the coming kingdom.[7]

For me, this class was bittersweet. On the one hand, Fredriksen's commitment to naturalism drove her to dismiss miracles—especially the resurrection of Jesus. On the other, I remember feeling a sense of satisfaction, knowing that the research I had done had brought me to the same conclusions as not only Fredriksen, but also E. P. Sanders, Bart Ehrman, and several other well-known scholars.

Sadly, because these skeptical scholars don't believe God raised Jesus from the dead, vindicating his claim to be the Messiah, they are left with a false prophet who thought the kingdom was right around the corner but got it wrong.

In the words of one eminent Jesus historian, Dale Allison, the whole kingdom proclamation is either the most sublime dream or it is utter foolishness:

> And yet, despite everything, for those who have ears to hear, Jesus, the millenarian herald of judgment and salvation, says the only things worth saying, for his dream is the only one worth dreaming. If our wounds never heal, if the outrageous spectacle of a history filled with cataclysmic sadness is never undone, if there is nothing more for those who were slaughtered in the death camps or for six-year olds devoured by cancer, then let us eat and drink, for tomorrow we die. If in the end there is no good God to calm this sea of troubles, to raise the dead, and to give good news to the poor, then this is indeed a tale told by an idiot, signifying nothing.[8]

6. Paula Fredriksen, "The Jesus Movement "The Jesus Movement (Beyond Palestine)." CAS 216, Department of Religion, Boston University, 2009.

7. I'll return to the story of how biblical scholars recovered the kingdom doctrine in a later chapter.

8. Allison, *Jesus of Nazareth*, 219.

Either Jesus was a legitimate kingdom preacher, or he was a madman. Either the kingdom comes to heal our world, or we are foolish to believe such a tale. Either God will set everything right, judging the wicked, or else all of the blood shed through the eons will never be avenged. From Allison's perspective, heaven is not one of the options—it's the kingdom or nothing!

I couldn't help but marvel at the irony: throughout the world, so many thousands of honest-hearted pastors read Scripture as a holy text, but they miss the central message of Jesus, while agnostic and skeptical scholars, who treat the Bible as a mere collection of uninspired, partially-historical documents, get the kingdom right!

Sadly, these two realms seldom meet. Critical scholars spend a great deal of time sifting through the Gospels trying to determine which bits are historical and which are mythological while the Bible-believing scholars are so hampered with received tradition that they read into the Gospels their beliefs about heaven and hell. Is there another way? Can someone accept the authority and inspiration of Scripture and yet still interpret it historically instead of distorting the kingdom? This is precisely what I was after. I wanted to learn from both evangelicals and critical scholars and take the best from both worlds.

After taking Fredriksen's class, as well as interacting with more professors at BU, I solidified my previous findings about the kingdom as hope, gospel, and way. This only served to fuel my desire to investigate the cold case of who killed the kingdom. Why did Christian theology mutate from a renewed world of abundance to evacuating our world to play harps on clouds? I looked at the course offerings at BU but couldn't find any Christian history courses for the next semester except for one about early church leadership. Although I had no interest at the time in studying this topic, I signed up anyhow.

My first day of that class, I met a fellow student who was likewise interested in Christian history and, upon her recommendation, ended up in a class on Origen of Alexandria at Boston College, just a half hour down the road from Boston University.

Although I didn't know much yet about Origen, it turned out that he was one of the most influential anti-kingdom warriors of all Christian history. Learning about him and his philosophy was going to be one of the great keys to unlocking what happened to the kingdom and why.

7

Too Jewish

At Boston College, my class on Origen of Alexandria was like binge-watching a suspenseful TV show. Our professor would burst into the room several minutes late, a duct-taped briefcase in hand, hair disheveled. He made no apology for lateness, nor did he concern himself with frivolous introductory remarks. He started lecturing even before he reached the table at the front of the room and didn't stop for two and a half hours.

I never even thought to look at the clock; I never once concerned myself with the urge to take a break halfway through. We were there to learn about one of the most intelligent, prolific, eccentric, and influential Christian thinkers of all time.

Born in AD 186, he was one of the few in his generation to grow up in a Christian household. His father, Leonides, spent a good deal of time teaching him the Bible, requiring him to memorize much of it. He was a precocious boy who excelled in his studies, learning classical Greek grammar and philosophy, as well.

When Origen was sixteen, the Roman government seized his father and held him on account of his faith. Origen, undaunted by the horrors of torture and martyrdom, insisted he go and die for Christ with his dad. His mother pleaded with him not to go, but she couldn't dissuade him. The only way she avoided losing both her husband and her son was to hide young Origen's only clothes.

Naturally, the only situation a teenager fears more than torture and death is leaving the house naked. Origen's mother prevailed and he stayed home. He wrote his incarcerated father, exhorting him to keep the faith no matter what, saying, "Don't change your mind on our account."[1]

Once the Roman magistrates had executed Leonides, they seized his possessions for the royal treasury, leaving Origen's family destitute. Origen found financial support for his mother and six brothers with a wealthy woman who made possible Origen's further education. He studied under the preeminent philosopher of his time, Ammonius, the famed founder of Neoplatonism, a meditative and mystical take on Plato's philosophy. With this first-class education, Origen was able to make a living for himself teaching literature and philosophy. By the age of eighteen, he also took over the catechetical school, instructing those interested in becoming Christians in the rudiments of the faith.

New converts and those in training to become Christians were the most vulnerable people in that society. Oftentimes, neophytes wouldn't even make it as far as baptism before the Romans would arrest, torture, and execute them. Origen was on the front lines, bravely visiting these catechumens in jail, accompanying them up to the moment of death. For his remarkable courage he earned respect and fame among his fellow Christians in Alexandria, Egypt.

After some time at the catechetical school, Origen found himself in the good graces of a wealthy Christian patron named Ambrose, who funded him to write books in response to the most pressing issues of the day. And write he did. With seven stenographers taking dictation in turns he churned out an absurd number of books, many of which survive until today. Origen wrote commentaries, treatises on prayer and martyrdom, the first systematic theology, many homilies, the first parallel Bible (in six columns), and apologetic works defending the faith. Although Epiphanius later estimated Origen's output at six thousand rolls, the actual number was probably closer to one or two thousand.[2] Even the bookish Jerome admitted no one could read them all.[3]

Origen trained himself daily for the moment when the Roman authorities would seize and torture him. He never slept in a bed; he wore no shoes; he went years without wine or anything beyond the most basic food. He even went so far as to castrate himself, taking literally Jesus's remark, "there are eunuchs who have made themselves eunuchs for the sake of the kingdom of heaven" (Matt 19:12). Persecution flared up and then disappeared

---

1. Eusebius, *Hist. eccl.* 6.2 (p. 189).
2. Epiphanius, *Pan.* 64.63.8 (p. 216).
3. Jerome, *Letters and Select Works*, Letter 33 (p. 46).

intermittently throughout his life, but finally, when he was in his sixties, they came for him.

I bet Origen's tormentors were surprised at how well he endured the rack. Eusebius reports, "Day after day, his legs were stretched apart four paces in the stocks."[4] In the end, the Romans released him, and he died in obscurity some time later, presumably from wounds he suffered during his incarceration and torture.

It is hard for us to imagine today just how precarious third-century Christianity was. On one side, the government, both local and imperial, loomed like a storm cloud on the horizon, occasionally breaking out in squalls of persecution and public execution. On the other side, the synagogue constantly lured people away from the church with beautiful buildings, elaborate liturgy, and mystical powers to bless and heal. Under these two threats, the faith had spread rapidly among the lower classes, especially in urban areas. But the wealthy educated elites looked down on it as a crude superstition fit only for gullible peasants. Origen labored assiduously to present Christianity in a palatable way to the intelligentsia of his day.

Origen fought on the front lines of all three battles. To combat state-sponsored torture and public execution, he trained his new Christians in a robust theology of martyrdom. He told them stories of famous godly men and women who stood firm under heinous suffering. To defeat deviant forms of Christianity, like the gnostics, whom the literate elite found compelling, Origen showed a way of combining cutting-edge philosophy with the Bible that was more sophisticated and cohesive than their crude and confusing attempts. To head off the constant allure of the synagogue over against the church, not to mention their steady insistence that Jesus was not the true Messiah, he accused the Jews of misinterpreting the Bible by reading it too literally. It is this last facet of Origen's embattled life that I want to focus on here, since it had a massive bearing on why many later Christians rejected the plain meaning of the many kingdom texts throughout the Bible.

Before we see the kingdom as a casualty of the war with Judaism, we need to consider how the ancients interpreted holy texts. Although it may seem unusual to us today, employing allegory to interpret respected texts was all the rage in Origen's day. Here's how it worked: any time someone came across a passage that appeared absurd, immoral, or somehow unworthy of the divine, he or she would spin out a metaphorical meaning. Interpreters treated otherwise embarrassing portions of a text like loose threads to pull in order to unravel the hidden meaning. To them, the surface meaning of a text was like the part of an iceberg one sees above water. The

4. Eusebius, *Hist. eccl.* 6.39 (p. 212).

uninformed would think that's all there was, but the skilled reader would understand the majority of the iceberg remained under water like a massive frozen mountain.

The idea is that God hid the spiritual meaning to prevent those who are unprepared or unworthy from grasping insights fit only for the spiritual elite. Listening to my own professor, I could see why this way of thinking must have been so appealing to Origen's pupils while they listened to their eccentric and brilliant teacher with wide eyes and open ears, eager to learn sacred, hidden wisdom.

Modern sensibilities would express caution regarding allegory because the reader freely makes up a meaning on the spot, but for Origen, the opposite was the case. The danger he perceived was that those who refused to allegorize fell into error, like the Jews, who rejected Jesus as the Messiah, Marcion, who rejected the Old Testament entirely, and the gnostics, who concluded the God of the Jewish Scriptures was evil. From Origen's perspective, his interpretation strategy, or hermeneutic, enabled him to dig beneath the body of Scripture to its soul and Spirit. As a result, he could charge those who did not grasp these deeper more penetrating meanings with naiveté.

Before moving on to look at how competition with Judaism affected Christian theology about the kingdom, I will give just one example to illustrate Origen's allegory strategy in action. During the reign of Solomon, Israel's wealthiest and wisest king, the Bible narrates the visit of the queen of Sheba, who gave Solomon 120 talents of gold, along with other treasures. To understand this passage, Origen brings in two seemingly unrelated biblical facts: (1) that God had limited the lifetime of those living in the days of Noah to 120 years before the flood came; and (2) that Moses lived to be 120 years old. On the basis of these two other usages of the number 120, Origen concludes,

> So the church offers to Christ, in the semblance and weight of gold, not only the whole sum total of her faculties and mental powers; but the metaphor, inherent in this number that includes the span of Moses' years of life, denotes the further fact that her faculties are devoted to the Law of God.[5] (Origen, *Comm. Song*)

Reading according to the surface meaning leaves one thinking the Bible merely tells about a queen from a far land visiting a king and giving him 120 talents of gold, but according to Origen, the deeper spiritual meaning has to do with Christians committing the whole of their faculties to serve Christ.

5. Origen, *Song of Songs Commentary and Homilies*, 102.

Although such interpretational chicanery would easily prevent an aspiring minister from passing an entry-level preaching class in seminaries today, it seemed quite plausible to many ancient Christians. From Origen's time in the third century onward, this allegorical hermeneutic grew in influence until it became the primary way many read Scripture.[6]

For Origen, this was no matter of showing off—nor a process to be taken lightly. As I mentioned earlier, he was on the front lines of the battles against alternative forms of Christianity (like the gnostics and Valentinians) as well as Judaism, which constantly undermined the claims of Christianity. In these battles, Origen found in allegory a sharp weapon, and he wielded it relentlessly. For example, Origen explains how a literal interpretation gave the Jews the ammunition they needed to deny that Jesus was the Messiah:

> For the hard-hearted and ignorant members of the circumcision have refused to believe in our savior because they think that they are keeping closely to the language of the prophecies that relate to him, and they see that he did not literally "proclaim release to the captives" or build what they consider to be a real "city of God." . . . Further, they think that it is the wolf, the four-footed animal, which is said in prophecy to be going to "feed with the lamb" . . . and having seen none of these events literally happening during the advent of him whom we believe to be Christ, they did not accept our Lord Jesus, but crucified him on the ground that he had wrongly called himself Christ.[7]

Here we see how the Jews argued against the Christians. They pointed to the ancient prophecies that predicted not just the coming of a messiah but of an entire messianic age—a time when God would vindicate his people, when peace would reign over all nations, when even the wolf would feed *with* the lamb instead of *on* the lamb.

They were probably thinking of a section of Isaiah's prophecy that says

> There shall come forth a shoot from the stump of Jesse,
> and a branch from his roots shall bear fruit.
> And the Spirit of the LORD shall rest upon him,
>
> . . . .
>
> He shall not judge by what his eyes see,
> or decide disputes by what his ears hear,
> but with righteousness he shall judge the poor,
> and decide with equity for the meek of the earth;

6. In fact, Augustine of Hippo only gave Christianity a chance after he heard Ambrose of Milan expounding the allegorical meaning of Scripture during a sermon.

7. Origen, *Princ.* 4.2.1 (pp. 353–55).

> and he shall strike the earth with the rod of his mouth,
> and with the breath of his lips he shall kill the wicked.
> Righteousness shall be the belt of his waist,
> and faithfulness the belt of his loins.
> The wolf shall dwell with the lamb,
> and the leopard shall lie down with the young goat,
> and the calf and the lion and the fattened calf together;
> and a little child shall lead them.
>
> . . . .
>
> They shall not hurt or destroy
> in all my holy mountain;
> for the earth shall be full of the knowledge of the LORD
> as the waters cover the sea. (Isa 11:1–9)

It's not hard to see why Jews, reading this, anticipated paradise to arrive when the branch (messiah) came on the scene. But it would only take a second to confirm that snakes still bite, that the rulers of the world do not depend on God's Spirit to make decisions, or that the Earth remains full of ignorance about God. Thus, the Jews had a strong case that the Messiah could not have come, since this kingdom prophecy remains unfulfilled.

Origen's argument, however, was that the Messiah had come, but the Jews were reading Isaiah too literally—according to the letter—rather than grasping the text's true meaning by reading it according to the Spirit.[8] Essentially, Origen said God had already fulfilled this prophecy about the Messiah, and therefore, these other surrounding prophecies must likewise have come to pass, but in a figurative, or spiritual, sense, instead of a literal one.

Origen and others afterwards worked hard to find metaphorical meanings for the specifics in this and other similar biblical prophecies. Although Origen's *Commentary on Isaiah* has not survived, one of his successors, Eusebius (AD 263–339), gives a good idea of what Origen probably thought the prophecy meant. As for the wolves changing their nature, Eusebius writes, "even the rapacious and greedy wolves among people will turn from their depravity, and their souls will flock together as tame and meek lambs in one church."[9] So the wolves, bears, and snakes really refer to people. The prophecy pertains to the church, Eusebius says, not the world—to the present, not the future.

Before thinking through how this relates to the kingdom-believing Christians, we need to spend some time considering Jewish-Christian relations in the third century. It's important to keep in mind that even though

8. Rom 2:29; 7:6; 2 Cor 3:3–6.
9. Eusebius, *Commentary on Isaiah*, 63–64.

Christians far outnumber Jews today, in Origen's day, just the opposite was true. Christianity was an upstart faith in many people's eyes, and it didn't fit into Roman society very well. At least Judaism was both ancient and ethnic, but Christianity threatened to convert gods-fearing Roman subjects into atheist moralists.[10]

Beyond the social sphere, the Jews had several other advantages over the Christians. They had superior access to the Old Testament since they could read it in the original Hebrew, whereas Christians depended on the Greek translation known as the Septuagint.[11] Origen wrote,

> And I make it my endeavor not to be ignorant of their various readings, lest in my controversies with the Jews I should quote to them what is not found in their copies, and that I may make some use of what is found there, even though it should not be in our Scriptures. For if we are so prepared for them in our discussions, they will not, as is their manner, scornfully laugh at Gentile believers for their ignorance of the true reading as they have them.[12] (*Letter from Origen to Africanus*)

We get the sense that past encounters between Christians and Jews ended badly for the Christians. The Christians must have seemed foolish, reading a translation, thinking they knew better than the people who not only could read the original language but also had centuries of practice interpreting it.

But superior access to Scripture wasn't their only advantage. The Jews also possessed a much more developed liturgical calendar, better buildings, and far superior arts, making them the megachurches of antiquity.[13] Would someone rather meet in a dingy apartment above a butcher shop or in a cathedral, surrounded by vibrant mosaics depicting scenes from Scripture? What's more, Jews had a reputation for spiritual powers including blessings, curses, exorcisms, and even magic.

10. The Romans called the Christians atheists because they did not worship any statues.

11. Wilken compares the situation to "an American scholar living in Germany who knows only English yet claims to understand Goethe's Faust better than native-speaking German scholars" (Wilken, *Land Called Holy*, 68). Christian scholars like Origen (cf. his *Hexapla*) and Jerome (cf. his *Vulgate*) both took the time to learn Hebrew to varying degrees so as to overcome this deficiency.

12. Origen, "Letter from Origin to Africanus," 387.

13. One can easily perceive the contrast between Christian and Jewish places of worship by comparing the art recovered from Dura-Europos (a third-century city abandoned and covered with sand, preserving it). The Christian artwork is limited and crude, whereas the Jewish mosaics are both plentiful and well executed.

Even after the empire began favoring Christianity in the fourth century, the allure of Judaism continued to cause Christian leaders anguish. In Antioch, John Chrysostom felt it necessary to respond by preaching an eight-part sermon series called *Against the Jews.*[14] He was concerned that "Many who belong to us and say that they believe in our teaching, attend their festivals, and even share in their celebrations and join in their fasts."[15] In the first sermon, Chrysostom erupted with slanderous accusations, labeling the Jewish synagogue a theater full of effeminates and harlots. He goes on to say,

> Many, I know, respect the Jews and think that their present way of life is a venerable one. . . . If, then, the Jews fail to know the Father, if they crucified the Son, if they thrust off the help of the Spirit, who should not make bold to declare plainly that the synagogue is a dwelling of demons? God is not worshipped there. Heaven forbid! From now on it remains a place of idolatry. But still some people pay it honor as a holy place.[16] (*Adv. Jud.* 1)

In the sermon, Chrysostom continues on to tell a story that must have been the driving force for his thunderous, bitter, and abusive language. Three days earlier, he had come upon a man who, in order to make an oath, was forcing a woman to enter a synagogue. The preference of the synagogue over the church for oath-making enraged Chrysostom. After rebuking the man severely, he asked why the man had done this. The man replied that not only he, but many others, considered oaths made at the shrine of the Hebrews more binding than those made elsewhere.[17]

Perhaps it was their use of Hebrew, their foreign rituals, or the antiquity of their faith, but many Christians continued to hold Jews in high honor, sometimes even ascribing greater powers and respect to rabbis and synagogues than to pastors and churches.

Another example of this anti-Jewish reaction comes to us from the other side of the empire, in Elvira, Spain. In the early fourth century, the Christian bishops held a council and passed laws against Christians keeping the Sabbath or going to Jews for blessings on the fruits of harvest.[18] This law clearly forbade Christians from honoring Jewish mysticism and rites.

The allure of Judaism wasn't benign; "Jews and Christians actively competed for the allegiance of pagans," says Origen scholar Joseph Trigg,

14. Or *Against the Judaizers.*

15. Wilken, *Chrysostom and the Jews*, 67.

16. Chrysostom, *Discourses against Judaizing Christians*, 10–11.

17. Further, Jesus and James both prohibit the taking of oaths (Matt 5:34; Jas 5:12).

18. Dale, *Synod of Elvira*, Canons 26, 49.

"and, in Palestine, at least, the Jews did very well at it."[19] Beyond this, by their very existence, Jews confronted Christian thinkers with this question: If Jesus really was the prophesied *Jewish* Messiah, then why did the *Jewish* people, his own people, still reject him?

The Jewish rebuttal to Jesus centered on the biblical texts related to the future kingdom because their Scriptures prophesied the Messiah would play a determinative role in establishing God's reign in the world to come. By Origen's time, the Jews, excited by messianic possibilities, had twice attempted to retake Jerusalem from the Romans. Even after both failed attempts, they retained a vibrant faith in a traditional, political, this-worldly kingdom hope. On the Judaism of the period, Abba Silver writes,

> It should be borne in mind that Messianism was essentially a political idea. It was bound up with the restoration of the Davidic dynasty and with the reconstitution of the independence of Israel. Certain eschatological [end times] and supernatural features were combined with it, but essentially it remained a this-worldly, temporal, national idea.[20]

For example, Rabbi Yohanan, a contemporary of Origen's, wrote, "One day Jerusalem will be made into a metropolis for all nations and draw to her [all peoples] as a stream to honor her."[21] In light of the total lack of political fulfillment, the Christian claim that Jesus of Nazareth was the Jewish Messiah seemed preposterous to any biblically informed Jew. Simply put, since the prophecies about the kingdom had not come to pass, Jesus could not possibly be the Messiah.[22]

Of course, Christian theologians had a ready defense, but it's not what I would have expected. To answer this objection, many Christians employed allegory as a way of claiming that the great kingdom oracles of the Hebrew prophets had already found fulfillment in the church—but spiritually.

This is precisely where all of this relates to rejecting the kingdom. Studying the conflict between Christians and Jews during Origen's life gave me my first insight into how and why the core message of Christ fell out of favor with those who claimed to follow him. In their attempt to validate Jesus as the true Messiah, Christians reinterpreted the prophecies about the messianic age.

19. Trigg, *Origen*, 183.

20. Silver, *Messianic Speculation*, 13.

21. Wilken, *Land Called Holy*, 71.

22. Wilken, "Early Christian Chiliasm," 307.

This is how it worked: let's say an educated noblewoman converts to Christianity and reads Daniel chapter 7. She comes to believe that when God's kingdom comes, it will extend to all nations and languages, and it will last forever. In other words, she takes the messianic prophecy literally. She unwittingly sides with the Jesus-denying Jews, who say that the kingdom will be literal and physical rather than metaphorical and spiritual. To persuade her to read allegorically, Origen would take her under his wing and explain that, as a Christian, she should not read the Bible in a "Judaistic sense," but instead should grasp the deeper, *symbolic* meaning.[23]

Origen's followers continued to employ this way of thinking when dealing with kingdom believers. For example, Eusebius dismissed an Egyptian bishop, named Nepos, for interpreting the Scriptures in a more "Jewish fashion," resulting in his belief that "there would be a sort of millennium of bodily indulgence on this earth."[24] When Eusebius wrote his commentary on Isaiah, he said the grand vision where all the nations come to Zion to learn God's laws refers not to Jerusalem in the kingdom age but rather to the Roman Empire when Christ came. Eusebius noted that all nations had ceased to wage war against the Roman Empire since the time when Christ came and the word of the Lord radiated out from Jerusalem throughout the whole world.[25] Later interpreters like John Chrysostom and Basil of Caesarea followed in Eusebius's footsteps, arguing for a past fulfillment of Isa 2.[26] Christians went out of their way to massage and rework the prophecies, especially in Isaiah, to force them to fit with the church's history rather than the world's future.[27] But it did not stop here. As time went on, elite Christian thinkers came up with a way to slander kingdom believers for their "Jewish interpretations."

Let's return for a moment to our hypothetical noblewoman. Let's say she lived in the time of Jerome, in the fifth century (nearly two hundred years after Origen). As before, Christian leaders would try to persuade her to read kingdom prophecies as already fulfilled in the church, but if she refused, she would find herself charged not only with reading the Bible in a Jewish manner, but also with Judaizing.

The Judaizers of the apostle Paul's day were those who believed one needed to keep the law of Moses in order to be saved, but to these leaders, anyone who interpreted biblical prophecy literally received the label.

---

23. Origen, *Princ.* 2.11.1–2 (p. 185).

24. Eusebius, *Hist. eccl.* 7.24 (p. 241).

25. Eusebius, *Comm. Isa.* 9.15, 31–32, in Wilken, "In Novissimis Diebus," 5.

26. John Chrysostom, *Hom. Isa.*; Basil, *Comm. Isa.* 1–16.

27. Wilken, "In Novissimis Diebus," 7.

This is quite a leap! Our noblewoman was not interested in keeping the customs and precepts of Judaism, she merely came to believe in the kingdom from taking Scripture at face value. Nonetheless, she would be lumped in with the most ancient Christian heresy on the books.

Jerome, never one to hold back what he really thinks, puts it this way:

> If one of the Christians . . . reckons that the prophecy is not yet completed, let him know that he falsely bears the name of Christ and that he has a Jewish soul, lacking only circumcision of the body.[28]

> The wise Christian reader should retain this rule of prophetic promises: whatever the Jews and our Judaizers—or rather not ours—contend will happen carnally, we should show to have been accomplished already spiritually, so that we not be compelled to Judaize, according to the apostle, on account of these sorts of tales and tangled questions.[29]

In another place, Jerome notes that the Jews, along with "our Judaizers," believe Isa 54 refers to Jerusalem. He accuses them of loving the letter that kills (i.e., interpreting literally) and following after "Jewish ravings," since, he says, these readers seek to satisfy their gluttony, lust for marriage, and longing for circumcision, sacrifices, and the Sabbath.[30] Arguing that Jews who converted to Christianity should not keep the law, he writes,

> [Those] who assert that the ceremonies of the old Law should be observed in the Church of Christ by the stock of faithful Israel, those should also look forward to a golden Jerusalem for a thousand years, that they may offer sacrifices and be circumcised, that they may sit on the Sabbath, sleep, become sated, drunk, and rise to frolic, their amusement being offensive to God.[31]

Here Jerome flips the direction of the accusation. Those who want to keep the Jewish law might as well also just believe in the ludicrous kingdom idea, too. This tendency to slander literal interpretation, which began with Origen in the third century and continued with Eusebius and others into the fourth, had reached its peak under Jerome in the fifth.

By his time, the stereotype of a worldly, gluttonous, Judaizing Christian was so firmly entrenched that he freely used it to battle kingdom believers

---

28. Jerome, *Comm. Zeph.* 3:14–18 in Newman, "Jerome's Judaizers," 441.

29. Jerome, *Comm. Isa.* 11:15–16 in Newman, "Jerome's Judaizers," 437.

30. Jerome, *Comm. Isa.* 54:1–14 in Newman, "Jerome's Judaizers," 450.

31. Jerome, *Comm. Isa.* 53:12 in Newman, "Jerome's Judaizers," 432–33.

over interpretation. Of course, many Christians did not accept Jerome's crass oversimplifications; he even expressed a significant degree of anxiety in the preface to his commentary on Isaiah, owing to the fact that so many Christians in his day still held to a literal reading of the many kingdom prophecies in that book. (As is often the case, the harder and more absurdly one argues a point, the more it indicates significant opposition.)

Before moving on, I want to take a moment to return to the issue of competition between the church and the synagogue. Here's what I find so puzzling about this historical development. Why did the battle center on interpretation? Christians of the third, fourth, and fifth centuries could have accepted the Jewish understanding of a coming literal kingdom without denying Jesus as the Messiah. He is coming back after all, isn't he? Jesus came the first time to atone for sins and he will return to fulfill all of the kingdom prophecies. This is the perspective that most of us readily embrace when challenged by Jews today. I wonder why Christians didn't take advantage of this seemingly obvious strategy to rebuff Jewish arguments against Jesus.

Although learning about Origen at Boston College opened my eyes to the first major reason Christianity rejected the kingdom, I was far from done with my investigation. What I came to discover next was that in addition to being "too Jewish," the kingdom also grated on educated peoples' sensibilities. In order to get more answers, I had to learn more about the mindset of ancient intellectuals.

Where better for that than Harvard?

8

Too Crude

"You have two hours to complete your exam," said Anneweis Van Den Hoek in her usual cheery demeanor. The antique wood-paneling encased room quietly bore witness as another group of students anxiously worked through another grueling test.

Sitting in front of me on the table was a massive tome—the biggest book I had ever seen. With over two thousand pages of tiny print, the Liddel-Scott-Jones Greek-English Lexicon contained tens of thousands of ancient Greek words glossed with archaic English, maximally abbreviated for efficiency. Alongside the booster-seat-sized dictionary lay my final exam—a single, one-sided sheet, with a couple of paragraphs of classical Greek from one of Plato's books. My task was to come up with a correct English translation within the allotted time. With our hearts pounding and our legs nervously twitching, the students' anxiety was palpable.

The whole process was like putting together a puzzle without looking at the picture first. Van Den Hoek told us to begin and, for the next two hours, the sound of pages flipping filled the room as we scratched our way through the exam, trying to make intelligible sentences by first finding meanings for the words and then applying grammar rules to work out their function.

Van Den Hoek did not give credit for homework, class participation, or attendance. Our entire grade depended on the midterm and the final. If I bombed one or the other, that was it. My mind raced as I desperately flipped from definition to definition to translate and then rework my translation, untangling the knots of Greek lines into coherent English.

I was in my first semester of advanced Greek at Harvard Divinity School. My school had a cross-registration arrangement with the other theology programs in the Boston area. Once I had found out I could take classes at Harvard, I had to try. I had found a proverbial back door to access some of the world's leading researchers and thinkers.

Harvard has a beautiful, classic campus in a ritzy part of Boston called Cambridge. I remember strolling across the Harvard Yard—or as they called it, "the Hah-vahd Yahd"—thinking I was in way over my head. After walking from the subway all the way across campus, ten minutes later I arrived at Harvard's Divinity School—a gorgeous old brick building surrounded by biology buildings. I walked around to the back, looking for an entrance, and discovered a sand volleyball court in the center of a grassy quad. I entered the building, feeling somewhat like an impostor, and after getting some gourmet coffee (for free), I found the right classroom, settled into my seat, and got ready for an hour and a half of intense concentration and critical thinking.

No sooner did I meet Van Den Hoek than my fears melted away in the warmth of her cheery and gracious personality. She welcomed us cross-registered students with enthusiasm and treated us like regular Harvard students.

In preparation for each class, I would spend around six and half hours working on the assigned passage, looking up all of the words I didn't know, parsing each one that was unfamiliar, and applying the rules of grammar to untangle the word order. It was arduous, thankless work, but—kind of like going to the dentist—absolutely necessary. By the time I got to class each week, I was more or less ready to perform.

We would all sit around a large conference table and take turns translating a few lines each. I never knew which actual part of the passage would fall to me. But, when it came to be my turn, I would have to read the text in Greek and then translate it into English immediately. Usually, the professor interrupted here and there to ask questions or make corrections, and then the next person would go.

At first, class was terrifying, but eventually I got used to it. In my first semester of advanced Greek, Van Den Hoek chose Plato's account of the beginning of the universe, called *Timaeus,* for our text. This creation story had a massive influence on why some Christians rejected the kingdom idea. But before looking at the *Timaeus,* let's first situate Plato within the broader stream of classical philosophy.

Before Plato (428–424 BC), Greek philosophers had long puzzled over the basic substances underlying all of reality. They wanted to figure out both how our world came about (cosmogony) and how it is put together (cosmology). Before them, most premodern cultures just told stories about gods and battles to explain the physical universe. But now, these thinkers began looking at matters from a proto-scientific perspective.

One class of these early philosophers was the Milesians, who tried to uncover the unifying substance out of which all others could be derived.[1] Thales (624–545 BC), generally recognized as the first philosopher, thought water was the chief substance that either gave rise to all others or played a role in the other elements. He made huge strides in geometry and astronomy, even predicting when olive yields would be high and when an eclipse would occur. Anaximander (610–545 BC) likewise developed theories about our world, positing a new substance called the "boundless" that, he proposed, gave rise to the four elements: water, fire, earth, and air. He also developed a basic sundial and divided the hours of the day into twelve equal portions. Next, Anaximenes (546–528 BC) claimed that air was the original element that gave rise to all the others. He knew that air was intrinsic to fire and that air could turn into water (like when it rains), and so Anaximenes speculated that water could give rise to earth through a process he called rarefication.

Even though these presocratic philosophers seem rather primitive to our modern understanding of such matters, what's important here is that they initiated a tradition that applied reason to creation in an effort to figure out the workings of nature.

Pythagoras (570–490 BC) advanced the Greek understanding of numbers and ratios. His famous theorem about triangles can predict the length of the third side of any right triangle if one already knows the lengths of the other two. He found that geometric relationships like this don't just work for small triangles or large ones; they work everywhere and for all time.

Pythagoras relished the eternal perfection he found in geometry. He also studied musical harmony, learning the ratio between two string lengths and their respective sounds. For us today, these don't seem like headline revelations, but for Pythagoras, they were absolutely ground-breaking, winning him fame and a committed sect of followers—the Pythagoreans. We'll return to Pythagoras and his idea of reincarnation in the next chapter, but suffice it to say, his work massively influenced later philosophers like Plato.

We need to examine a particular pair of philosophers before we can delve into Plato and his account of creation. Heraclitus (540–480 BC) and Parmenides (515–450 BC) developed opposing views of the cosmos.

We'll begin with Heraclitus, who was a colorful figure, a loner, and a critic of those who came before him. Rather than seeking to find a unifying substance, he embraced the concept of change, averring that everything was

---

1. For more about the presocratic philosophers, see http://www.iep.utm.edu/presocra/.

in constant flux—going up and down, contracting and expanding, at war and at peace. To him, Plato credited the saying, "All things move and nothing remains still. . . . You cannot step twice into the same stream."[2] And yet, amidst all the ebb and flow of that river, through change it remains constant. Like a fire that is always flickering and consuming wood and moving with the wind, it finds its existence and stability amid constant flux. Thus, argued Heraclitus, change is what underlies all of reality.

In contrast to Heraclitus's theory, Parmenides taught a doctrine of radical stability. Hailed as the first metaphysician, Parmenides heavily prioritized rational argumentation over sense perceptions. He paired truth with being and opinion with non-being in his poem called *On Nature*, expressing an impenetrable division between what exists and what does not exist:

> Come now, I will tell you—and listen to my saying and carry it away—
> The only two ways of inquiry that can be thought of
> The first, namely, that "it is,"
> And that it is impossible for anything not to be,
> Is the way of conviction, for truth is its companion.
> The other, namely, that "it is not,"
> And that something must not be,
> That, I tell you, is a wholly untrustworthy path.
> For you cannot know what is not—
> That is impossible—nor utter it. (*Nat.* 2.1–8)[3]

According to Parmenides, one should not contemplate what does not exist, but only what does exist. What exists cannot at any time cease to exist, for that would create a contradiction, since "Only Being is, Not-Being is not and cannot be thought."[4]

This means that being not only cannot come into existence or go out of existence, but it cannot change, either. From the perspective of this philosopher, like a perfect sphere, being neither starts nor ends; it neither grows nor shrinks; it neither moves nor changes. Thus, the only way to perceive what is ultimately true and existing is through our internal mental faculties, not our external senses, which will only deceive us. To Parmenides, the world around us, with its constant generation, mutation, and destruction, only leads us into error and confusion.

---

2. Plato, *Crat.* 402a (p. 67).

3. Parmenides, *Nat.* 2.1–8. I've slightly edited Burnet's translation by updating his English to a more contemporary style.

4. Parmenides, *Fragm. Parm.* 6; Zeller, *Outlines of the History*, 65.

Plato built upon Pythagoras's ideas of eternal perfect realities and Parmenides's preference for stability over change in his famous theory of forms. In it, he posits that thought, as opposed to sense perception, focuses on generalities rather than particularities. Rather than seeing a tall pine tree, a short apple tree, and a crooked birch tree, Plato makes the move from the concrete to the abstract. He puzzles over "treeness" or, to put it as a question, he asks, "What makes a tree a tree?"

To Plato, "treeness" exists as an ideal form in his mind, thus making it inherently superior to all actual trees, since thought is immutable and perfect. Every actual tree, he says, is a mere shadow of the original form; some of them may be taller or shorter or lighter or darker, but they all reflect the essence of the form. For Plato, this pure, unadulterated reality of perfect prototypes actually exists in another dimension outside of our crude physical universe: the realm of the forms.

According to Plato, our souls once inhabited the super-celestial realm of the forms, and before coming into our bodies, were intimately familiar with all of the forms. Thus, argues Plato, the task of the philosopher is not discovery or speculation, but remembering these eternal realities as one does the hard work of contemplation.

In order to express this way of looking at the world, Plato used the allegory of the cave. In this illustration, Plato imagines prisoners who have lived in a cave since childhood, restricted with chains so they cannot even turn their heads away from looking at a wall. On that wall they see the shadows of people and objects cast by a pathway behind them backlit by a fire.

Such captives, Plato explains, would assume the shadows are the only reality that truly exists. In the allegory, Plato imagines that one of these prisoners gets out of the cave and sees the real world in the stunning vibrancy of a sunlit afternoon. According to Plato, at first his eyes will hurt and need to adjust to the sudden onslaught of the external word's radiance, but then, as he comes to see the real world, he will marvel at how colorful, sharp, and three-dimensional objects are. Perchance he will catch sight of his own reflection in water and come to an epiphany about his own appearance. Last of all, he may cast his gaze upon the sun and contemplate it as the source of all the delights of vision he now enjoys. With all of this knowledge, Plato's allegory predicts, the liberated man may return to the cave and try to communicate to his old comrades about the real world. But they will think he has gone mad, and that the trip above is to blame. They will not want to go and may even threaten to kill anyone who would bring them up to the surface.

In this allegory, the cave represents our present world which, due to our limited sense perceptions, we can grasp only as shadows and distorted sounds of what Plato regards as true reality. The philosopher, naturally, is the one who escapes the cave and perceives the genuine realm of the forms through meditation or, as Plato called it, "the ascent of the soul into the intellectual world."[5] Once thinkers taste and see the realm of the forms with their minds' eyes, they cannot content themselves with the shadows of this lower realm.

Plato put it this way:

> Moreover, I said, you must not wonder that those who attain to this beatific vision are unwilling to descend to human affairs; for their souls are ever hastening into the upper world where they desire to dwell; which desire of theirs is very natural, if our allegory may be trusted.[6]

In other words, truly enlightened people cannot find contentment in our lower realm of shadows and transience—not once they have ascended to the immutable realm.

This, finally, brings us to consider the book I was studying at Harvard—Plato's *Timaeus*. Written around 360 BC, the *Timaeus* is difficult to read in any language. It was Plato's attempt to describe the origin of the universe based on his understanding of the world. In it, Timaeus, a Pythagorean, goes into great detail about how a divine figure he calls "the craftsman" made our world on the basis of an eternal realm of perfect unchanging prototypes. Although it's hardly required reading today and may even appear "obscure and repulsive to the modern reader," Benjamin Jowett explains, the *Timaeus* "has nevertheless had the greatest influence over the ancient and mediaeval world."[7] As Timaeus begins to explain the creation of the universe, we encounter echoes of Parmenides and his bias against change:

> First then, in my judgment, we must make a distinction and ask, "What is that which always is and has no becoming; and what is that which is always becoming and never is?" That which is apprehended by intelligence and reason is always in the same state; but that which is conceived by opinion with the help of sensation and without reason, is always in a process of becoming and perishing and never really is.[8]

On the one side we have what always exists without change, which we can perceive with intelligence and reason, then on the other, we have what is

5. Plato, *Resp.* 7.517b.
6. Plato, *Resp.* 7.517c–d. (p. 260).
7. Plato, *Dial.* 341.
8. Plato, *Tim.* 27d–28a (p. 23).

always becoming, which we can apprehend by opinion and sense perception. The former, eternal realities are in another dimension, or realm—where the forms exist—whereas the latter, changeable objects are mere copies and shadows of the original. Timaeus argues that the craftsman created our world by copying the original eternal realm.

> Everyone will see that he [the craftsman] must have looked to the eternal; for the world is the fairest of creations and he is the best of causes. And having been created in this way, the world has been framed in the likeness of that which is apprehended by reason and mind and is unchangeable, and must therefore of necessity, if this is admitted, be a copy of something.[9]

If we imagine Earth as the center of the universe and draw concentric circles, each bigger than the last, we can get an idea of how the ancients thought about the universe. They thought of the Earth as the lowest realm, mired in flux, constantly changing from season to season, day to day, minute to minute. Moving outwards, we reach the moon, which is much more stable than Earth. Sure, it goes through the phases of its monthly cycle, but it's very consistent. The sun is even more superior, because its shape and color appear even more consistent than the moon. The sun is utterly predictable such that you can set time by it (hence sundials). As we move farther away, we get to the planets, which are more stable, but still not perfect. However, when we move to the outermost boundary of our realm, we get to the stars. These splendorous objects appear fixed with respect to one another and are the highest and best creatures in our realm. But, these philosophers thought, if we could travel beyond the stars, we would finally escape the cave and see the idealized forms that exist in perfect stability and eternity. Paula Fredriksen helpfully explains,

> In the imagined architecture of the ancient cosmos, the earth stood at the center of the seven planetary spheres, at the furthest remove—spatially and ontologically—from the regions of increasing stability and harmony that stretched from the moon upward toward the planets and the realm of the fixed stars. Such a worldview is prejudiced in favor of the "upperwordly" and spiritual.[10]

As we shall see, this view of the universe had a massive effect on how sophisticated Christian thinkers interpreted the kingdom. Philo of Alexandria

---

9. Plato, *Tim.* 29a–b (p. 24).

10. Fredriksen, "Apocalypse," 170n16.

(25 BC–AD 50), himself a Jewish philosopher, became the conduit for these ideas to enter Christian theology.

After my Harvard class had read through a generous portion of Plato's *Timaeus*, we began working on Philo's *On the Creation of the World*. Living at the same time as the apostle Paul, Philo had probably never heard of Jesus, though he certainly knew of Plato. As my class slowly made our way through his book, it became clear that Philo put himself to the task of harmonizing Moses's Genesis with Plato's *Timaeus*.

One might ask how Philo could accomplish such a task, considering the significant differences between these two creation accounts: one telling of a God who created the world and called it "very good," the other claiming this world is a shadowy copy of otherworldly perfection. But Philo did it by focusing on similarities between the accounts, and he did manage to mush them together, though not without significantly reshaping each. In Philo's work, no longer is Moses the prophetic mouthpiece; now, he is someone who "reached the very summits of philosophy and had learned from the oracles of God the most numerous and important of the principles of nature."[11]

Here is a brief sampling of how Philo worked the *Timaeus* and Genesis together:

> "In the beginning he created" is equivalent to "first of all he created the heaven;" for it is natural in reality that that should have been the first object created, being both the best of all created things, and being also made of the purest substance, because it was destined to be the most holy abode of the visible Gods who are perceptible by the external senses.[12]

Here Philo diverges from Genesis, which says, "In the beginning, God created the heavens and the earth" (Gen 1:1). Instead, Philo breaks this creation into two acts. First, he says, God formed the heavens where the "visible Gods" (i.e., stars) live, then he made our physical world. Philo believes God "conceived its form in his mind, according to which form he made a world perceptible only by the intellect, and then completed one visible to the external senses, using the first one as a model."[13]

Like a good Platonist, Philo imagines an unseen realm wherein more perfected realities exist without change. This, he says, is what God then used as a model to make our lower, physical world. In fact, he even taught that God made the first man as "an idea, or a genus, or a seal, perceptible

11. Philo, *Opif.* 1.8 (p. 2).

12. Philo, *Opif.* 1.7 (p. 27).

13. Philo, *Opif.* 1.4 (p. 19).

only by the intellect, incorporeal, neither male nor female, imperishable by nature."[14] This was how Philo understood the *imago Dei* (image of God). Since God is non-physical, the first human must have likewise existed in some idealized and immutable state as well.

Genesis, of course, militates against this wild cosmic perspective. It relates only one creation of the first man—when God reached down into the dust and shaped his body and then animated him with the breath of life. There is no hint of cosmic origins or incarnation for Adam in Genesis.

One more important aspect of Platonic cosmogony that affected Philo, along with countless other thinkers of his era, was the notion that God would not sully himself by directly creating the physical world. Philo writes, "God created everything, without indeed touching it himself, for it was not lawful for the all-wise and all-blessed God to touch materials which were all misshapen and confused, but he created them by the agency of his incorporeal powers."[15] As a Platonist, Philo is certain that since God is utterly perfect and transcendent, he's too different from our physical world to be directly responsible for its existence. In fact, Philo believes that "beyond the fact of his existence, we can understand nothing" about God.[16] However, as a Jew, Philo affirms that God is the creator of the heavens and the Earth, though asserting that he did so indirectly through intermediaries like his Word, his Wisdom, and his Spirit.

My interest here is not so much how Philo reworked Genesis to make it compatible with his philosophical sensibilities but the fact that he felt compelled to do this at all. He felt the pressure of Plato's cosmology squeezing him, but he couldn't bring himself to disavow the Torah and its sacred account of creation. He needed to preserve his Judaism but tried to update it in light of the philosophical understanding of his day. Philo may have even thought that Moses himself would have explained the creation differently if he were alive in Philo's time—or that perhaps Moses had intentionally hidden these truths beneath the surface of Scripture so as to reserve them for the enlightened readers.

Whatever his motivations were, Philo, the *Jewish* philosopher, became one of the most influential scholars for *Christian* thinkers more than a century after he died. This was especially true for Clement and Origen of Alexandria and their successors. In the words of Marian Hillar, Philo "laid

14. Philo, *Opif.* 1.46 (p. 134).
15. Philo, *Spec.* 1.329 (p. 565).
16. Philo, *Deus.* 1.62 (p. 163).

the foundations for the development of Christianity in the West and in the East, as we know it today."[17]

Of course, none of this way of thinking was much of an issue for Jesus in his ministry in Judea and Galilee. After all, he operated in a primarily Hebrew world rather than a Greek one. Jesus quoted Genesis freely and without offering correctives or employing metaphorical interpretations to harmonize it with reigning "scientific" paradigms of his day. Besides, neither Jesus nor his disciples had the kind of education that would introduce them to the complex and varied Greek philosophical traditions that held sway in many cities. Only a tiny percentage of the population had both the free time and the resources to acquire such instruction.

Jesus did not question that God created our physical universe and put people in it to enjoy the garden and care for the world, or that in the end, he intends to redeem creation from the corruption and chaos when the time of the kingdom arrives. The whole picture is one of restoration—not relocation. Rather than abandoning the world or demolishing it, God will transform it back to its original glory so that peace, justice, and wholeness reign supreme. Change, whether spatial or temporal, would naturally continue to be part of God's good world, just like it was in the beginning before the fall.

During Jesus's life, his and Philo's disparate worldviews did not meet. However, a century after Christ, Christianity began penetrating the higher strata of society and educated elites began to feel the pressure to show how their new faith held up under philosophical scrutiny. This pressure resulted in the emergence of the gnostics, who reworked Genesis to fit their own more philosophically mainstream view of creation.

"The formulation of the gnostic myth," says Bentley Layton, "ultimately drew on Platonist interpretations of the myth of creation in Plato's *Timaeus,* as combined with the book of Genesis."[18] The gnostics believed the fall was not the tarnishing of creation due to human sin (eating the forbidden fruit) but *the cause of our physical universe itself.*

The myth went like this: the monad—the high God of which almost nothing can be said since "it" is completely transcendent—is an immaterial mind. As it thinks, it generates aeons that correspond to the ideal forms of Plato's philosophy, with names like Intelligence, Truth, and Wisdom. These aeons are both independent beings and abstractions that enjoy radical stability in a perfect realm.

However, when Wisdom (Sophia) produced a thought without her male counterpart, the result was a misshapen creature named Yaldabaoth.

17. Hillar, "Philo of Alexandria."
18. Layton, *Gnostic Scriptures,* 5–8.

As an act of rebellion, Yaldabaoth created the physical universe on the pattern of the pleroma—the eternal realm—so he could be a god over lesser creatures. In creating people, he encased spirit within physical bodies such that some humans have a spark of the divine within them, but others do not. Thus, our world—and even matter itself—is the result of cosmic rebellion, designed to oppress and control these special humans by making them forget their divine beginnings. However, when people get special knowledge (*gnosis*), then they can not only perceive their august origin but also learn how to ascend back to the spiritual realm at death. Eventually, the gnostics say, the physical universe will come to an end, restoring balance to the higher sphere of immutable existence.

The gnostic reading of the Bible is utterly subversive. It says that the creator God is really the evil Yaldabaoth because he ensnares us in physical bodies, whereas the serpent is actually good since he leads Adam and Eve to the tree of knowledge (*gnosis*). Only those who descend through Seth have the spark of the divine, while the rest are little more than sophisticated animals. Throughout history, Yaldabaoth works to keep the true gnostics from discovering who they really are. Christ comes to bring us secret knowledge that can set us free, but Yaldabaoth has inspired certain false or non-spiritual gospels designed to confuse us about Christ—like the Gospels of Matthew and Luke. Only books like the *Gospel of Thomas* and the *Secret Book of John* provide the insider knowledge that Jesus entrusted to his real disciples.

It's easy to see why fighting the gnostics became such a major focus in the second and third centuries (as had fighting the Judaizers in the first). Although their ideology seems utterly bizarre and repelling to us today, people found it tremendously compelling in its own time, especially the elite.

By the late second century, educated Christians had a few options for dealing with the conflict between the Greek and Hebrew cosmologies: (1) like rabbinic Judaism, they could cling to Scripture over against whatever the top minds of their day said; (2) like the gnostics, they could concoct a pre-fall myth to resolve the tension; or (3) like Philo, they could find ways of interpreting Scripture (especially using allegory) to fit with Plato. As we will soon see, this last option gained traction first in Egypt in the third century and then spread rapidly in the fourth until it became the dominant mode of thinking in the early Middle Ages.

One of the first Christians who worked hard to develop this third option and harmonize the Bible with Greek philosophy was Clement of Alexandria, Egypt (AD 150–215). His influence through the school of Alexandria came to provide a lasting influence on later, key Christian thinkers. Only one of his sermons survives today, called "Who Is the Rich Man Who Is Saved?" In it, Clement discusses how the rich need the poor and vice versa. Thus, it is very likely that his congregation included a sizeable number of wealthy Christians. Such people in a metropolis like Alexandria, famous for its magnificent library, would have struggled to harmonize their newfound Christian faith with their traditional worldview inherited from Greek philosophy.

In addition to this pressure, Clement also had to rebuff the gnostics, who were offering a ready-made explanation to the biblical contradictions with Platonism. Clement had to find an explanation that satisfied his urbane listeners while simultaneously preventing them from joining up with the gnostics. Rather than rejecting Platonism, and the gnostic ideology with it, for contradicting Scripture, Clement decided to try a more subversive strategy with the gnostics. He did this by calling the ideal Christian a "gnostic" in his book, *Stromateis*. Rather than saying Gnosticism was bad, he stole back the term and claimed that a true gnostic (or "knower") thought the way he, Clement, did.

Other contemporary Christians dealt with this pressure differently. For example, Tertullian of Carthage (AD 155–240) once famously asked, "What indeed has Athens to do with Jerusalem? What concord is there between the Academy and the Church?"[19] Clement, however, saw no reason to let go of either ideology. Instead, he asserted that Plato had learned "laws that are consistent with truth" and "sentiments respecting God" from none other than "the Hebrews."[20]

Clement just couldn't imagine that God had not inspired Plato's masterful dialogues in some way.[21] He had no intention of letting go of either Plato or Christ, as Eric Osborn points out—"[he was] as deeply convinced of the world-view of Plato and Greek culture as he was of his Christian faith."[22] Thus, we should find it hardly surprising that he was one of the first to call heaven "home."[23] From a Platonic perspective, humans originated from the higher realm and would eventually return to it at death. Clement's bold synthesis between philosophy and the Bible, it turns out, was only the beginning.

19. Tertullian, *Praescr.* 1.7 (p. 246).

20. Clement of Alexandria, "Exhortation to the Heathen," 1.5 (p. 192).

21. Justin Martyr (*Dial.* 85.1; 88.8; 100.2) and Origen of Alexandria (*Cels.* 6.75) also taught Plato had access to the Old Testament.

22. Osborn, *Clement of Alexandria*, 26.

23. "They say, accordingly, that the blessed Peter, on seeing his wife led to death, rejoiced on account of her call and conveyance home, and called very encouragingly and comfortingly, addressing her by name, 'Remember thou the Lord.' Such was the marriage of the blessed and their perfect disposition towards those dearest to them." Clement of Alexandria, *Strom.* 541.

Following in his master's footsteps, Origen of Alexandria (AD 186–253) took Clement's project to a whole new level. By the dawn of the third century, both pressures had noticeably increased. On the one hand, more and more educated Alexandrians were joining the church, and on the other, the gnostics were making many converts. Clement's old strategy of taking back the name gnostic was no longer viable. Origen had to face the gnostic threat directly. However, once again, rather than challenging their insistence on combining the *Timaeus* and Genesis, Origen instead attempted to "out-gnostic" the gnostics. Their problem, argued Origen, was not that they were Platonists, but they weren't Platonic enough. If they had a better grasp of philosophy and Scripture, they could come up with a better synthesis of the two.

Origen had studied under Ammonius, a preeminent philosopher in Alexandria and the founder of Neoplatonism. Unlike many who came before him, Origen was an insider to both worlds. He grew up in a Christian home and studied cutting-edge philosophy under a well-known teacher. Origen's magnum opus, *On First Principles*, developed the first systematic theology in the history of Christianity, and definitively established a hybrid with an enduring legacy.

By now one might ask, "What in the world does all of this philosophical speculation about the beginning and nature of the universe have to do with the kingdom?" My short answer is: *everything!* Whatever we believe about the beginning profoundly shapes what we believe about the end. For example, here are three short statements by early Christians from completely different groups. They all intuitively "know" that the end will reflect the beginning.

> "The Lord says, 'Behold, I will make the last things as the first.'"[24]
> "For the end will be where the beginning is."[25]
> "For the end is always like the beginning."[26]

As a result of this common intuition, Origen believed our end goal is to return to the Platonic realm of the forms where the truest and most stable perfect realities existed. Thus, the notion of spending forever on Earth—the lower realm—constantly subject to change, seemed utterly absurd.

Believing God's kingdom would come on Earth, as we've seen in the Bible, would repel educated unbelievers and give the gnostics ammunition to say they were the true "knowers," while other Christians were locked into

---

24. Pseudo-Barnabas, *Ep. Barn.* 6.13 (p. 399).
25. Pseudo-Thomas, *Evang. Thom.* 18 (p. 383).
26. Origen, *Princ.* 1.6.2 (p. 53).

a primitive Jewish worldview. Origen derided kingdom believers, calling them "simpler Christians" for believing in "certain foolish stories and vain fictions, so that even after the resurrection they believe that physical foods must be used and drink taken not only from that true vine which lives forever, but also from vines and fruits of wood."[27] Origen wanted to make it clear that true Christians interpret Scripture allegorically, in a manner that harmonizes with accepted knowledge of the day.

Well after he died, Origen's influence continued through his successors. For example, Dionysius of Alexandria (AD 200–265) called those who believed in an earthly hope "simpler brethren" who were incapable of having "high and noble thoughts, about the glorious epiphany of our Lord or about our own resurrection from the dead."[28] A century later, Eusebius of Caesarea (AD 263–339) called Papias "a man of very limited intelligence" for teaching that "the kingdom of Christ will be established on this Earth in material form."[29] By his time, Augustine of Hippo (AD 354–430) could say without hesitation that those who believe "the first resurrection is future and bodily" were holding to "ridiculous fancies."[30] Furthermore, Augustine worried that pagan philosophers would think Christians were "speaking boldy and rashly" if they believed "our bodies are going to be victorious on a new earth and not in heaven."[31]

Paula Fredriksen summarizes this trend of thought with the following words:

> Many thinking Christians from the second century onward could not take seriously the proposition that lower, material reality was the proper arena of redemption. . . . Their grasp of the principles of philosophy made claims to physical redemption seem incoherent and ignorant; these Christians repudiated the idea of a fleshly resurrection and a kingdom of God on earth.[32]

Today the sophisticated thinkers of the first few centuries are forgotten and the cosmology they espoused is totally passé. No one thinks the planets are living organisms comprised of finer, less mutable matter, nor does anyone believe they orbit the Earth rather than the sun. So why should Christians continue to believe the afterlife will be in an otherworldly, immutable realm of heaven instead of the biblical hope of a renewed paradise on Earth?

27. Origen, *Comm. Cant.* Prologue (p. 222).
28. Eusebius, *Hist. eccl.* 7.24 (p. 242).
29. Eusebius, *Hist. eccl.* 3.39 (113).
30. Augustine, *Civ.* 20.7 (p. 426).
31. Augustine, *Sermons,* 245.5 (p. 31).
32. Fredriksen, "Apocalypse," 154.

To be honest, replacing the promises God made to Abraham with the pontifications of Plato is nothing short of a betrayal. We've traded our birthright for a mess of pottage. We've spurned our real inheritance for a fairy tale of Jack and the Beanstalk, climbing up and wandering around in the clouds, heedless that Jesus promised us the whole world. Instead of believing Daniel's vision of a Son of Man who comes to inherit all the kingdoms of this world, we've allowed ourselves to be sweet-talked by Origen and his allegorizing deceptions about our soul ascending to the pleroma. We've turned our back on Isaiah's prophecies of a healed, renewed creation, in which peace pervades, and embraced Parmenides's fantasy of changeless tedium. Instead of being wooed by God's dream for our world, we arrogantly defy him, siding with Clement, the gnostics, and Pythagoras and adopting their counterfeit gospel.

One wonders, what can we do? But ancient science is only part of the picture. There's more to the story of why ancient people rejected the kingdom. A whole other movement had a major impact on why Christians began favoring heaven over the kingdom. The issue came down to bodily pleasures, especially sex.

9

Too Hedonic

THE SPEAKER, A SCHOLAR of early Christian history, began his comedy spiel at our formal dinner by noting that the International Mister Leather competition began the same year as the conference we were now attending. To the roaring laughter of his colleagues, mostly college professors from universities around the United States and Canada, he playfully suggested a connection between the two organizations. He went on to show pictures of that year's female conference president's tattoos, revealing—to the delight of the scholarly onlookers—a sultry snake slithering down the flesh of her naked back. One might think I was attending a conference on human sexuality. In fact, I was at my first North American Patristic Society (NAPS) Conference in Chicago.

The keynote address was titled "'Fleeing the Uxorious Kingdom': Augustine's Queer Theology of Marriage." While I was there, I met a fellow graduate student who hunts for evidence of historical gay saints, mostly through iconography. A good portion of the talks also addressed feminist concerns.

What I witnessed at the conference was an exaggerated focus on sexuality and gender. Of course, this was nothing new or really shocking to me, since I had been pursuing graduate education at Boston University. Jennifer Knust, one of my professors, released her book *Unprotected Texts: The Bible's Surprising Contradictions about Sex and Desire* while I was attending. Sex, sexism, gender roles, homosexuality, and gender identity were all the rage among the humanities, and the school of theology was no exception. It was like academia had just hit puberty and had begun interpreting everything through the lens of sexuality.

Today, we live in a liberated society where anything goes so long as all parties consent (and are of age). How different this is to what I kept reading about in early Christian sources, where the opposite was the case: even as early as the second and third centuries, some Christians had already begun promoting an ideal of denying any bodily pleasure.

To illustrate: in one Christian document, called *The Proto-Gospel of James*, we read Mary's alleged backstory—a subject the New Testament never mentions. However, this "Gospel," written nearly a century after the biblical Gospels, claims that when Mary was young, she grew up as a temple virgin who served in purity, weaving the temple veil. In this account, the temple elders assigned Joseph, already an old man, to look after Mary. He "married" her, but never had relations with her.

In this Gospel, not only is Mary a virgin before she gives birth, but she retains her virginity afterwards, as well.[1] Here is a brief excerpt, stressing Mary's miraculous perpetual virginity:

> And the midwife went forth out of the cave, and Salome met her. And she said to her: Salome, Salome, I have a strange sight to relate to thee: a virgin has brought forth—a thing which her nature admits not of. Then said Salome: As the Lord my God lives, unless I thrust in my finger, and search the parts, I will not believe that a virgin has brought forth. And the midwife went in, and said to Mary: Show thyself; for no small controversy has arisen about thee. And Salome put in her finger, and cried out, and said: Woe is me for my iniquity and my unbelief, because I have tempted the living God; and, behold, my hand is dropping off as if burned with fire.[2]

In the story, Salome—her hand apparently melting after contacting Mary— immediately repents. Mary tells her to touch the baby; when she does, God restores her hand.

Another Christian book that enjoyed extensive popularity in the late-second century was *The Acts of Paul and Thecla*. Early on in the story, the apostle Paul preaches a series of blessings. He begins with Jesus's classic blessing on the pure in heart, but then quickly adds new material, like, "Blessed are they who have wives, as though they had them not, for they shall be made angels of God."[3] In the story, Paul gets in trouble for his

---

1. This flatly contradicts Matt 1:24–25, where we learn Joseph kept Mary a virgin only until she gave birth to Jesus. The Bible plainly and unapologetically talks about Jesus's other brothers and sisters in Mark 3:32; 6:3.

2. *Infancy Gospel of James*, 19.18—20.4 (pp. 375–76).

3. *Acts of Paul and Thecla* 5 in Elliot, *Apocryphal New Testament*, 365.

message, since "he deprives young men of their intended wives, and virgins of their intended husbands, by teaching, there can be no future resurrection, unless you continue in chastity and do not defile your flesh."[4] Thecla, a young woman, eavesdrops on Paul's marvelous teaching for three days from the window of a neighboring house. She bribes the guards so she can visit Paul in prison, sitting at his feet and listening to his teaching all night. The story tells us that eventually, Thecla decides to leave her fiancé and follow Paul on his journeys, embracing a life of celibacy.

A third text from the same period is *The Acts of John*, where we read about a godly Christian wife, Drusiana, who is so holy that she stops sleeping with her husband. Drusiana's husband is not a Christian and, infuriated at her refusal, locks her up in a tomb, saying, "Either I must have you as the wife whom I had before, or you shall die."[5] Drusiana chooses death over sullying herself with marital sex and (somewhat miraculously) convinces him to become a Christian and have a sexless marriage.

But that's not the end. In the story, Drusiana must possess a rare beauty, because an admirer named Callimachus begins lusting after her, seeking an opportunity to pursue an affair. When she finds out, she feels so overwhelmed with shame and sadness that she could have inflamed such sinful desires in a man that she falls ill and dies. Callimachus does not want Drusiana to escape his desires so easily, so he pays off a servant to gain access to her tomb so that, even if he could not have her alive, he can at least have her now that she is dead. Before he can violate the dead heroine, a huge snake comes out and bites the servant—and then an angel strikes Callimachus dead. On the third day, the apostle John enters the tomb with Drusiana's husband and raises them all from the dead. Callimachus repents and joins Drusiana and her husband in following Christ, adopting abstinence for himself thereafter

These texts show us that some early Christians thought holy people shouldn't enjoy bodily pleasures, especially sex (even within a lawful marriage). Although such sensibilities began as a minority, they influenced a wide swath of Christianity in the second century. Before long, the idea of celibacy within marriage, as illustrated by Joseph and Mary, Paul and Thecla, and Drusiana and her husband, became the ideal for serious Christians.

Even more moderate Christians of the time, like Clement of Alexandria, admired "those who have adopted an austere life, and who are fond of water, the medicine of temperance, and flee as far as possible from

---

4. *Acts of Paul and Thecla* 12 in Elliot, *Apocryphal New Testament*, 366.

5. *Acts of John* 63 in Elliot, *Apocryphal New Testament*, 329.

wine, shunning it as they would the danger of fire."[6] Although Clement approved of sexual intercourse within marriage, he was careful to say, "Pleasure sought for its own sake, even within the marriage bonds, is a sin and contrary both to law and to reason."[7] He taught one should hold a "noble contempt" for "all that belongs to the creation and nutriment of the flesh."[8] In short, Clement said, "It is absolutely impossible at the same time to be a man of understanding and not to be ashamed to gratify the body."[9]

Other Christian thinkers afterwards likewise disparaged the indulgence of any kind of fleshly pleasures.[10] By the early fourth century, the Council of Elvira unequivocally outlawed sexual relations for clergy:

> It has pleased the whole to prohibit bishops, presbyters, and deacons indeed all established clergy in the ministry to abstain themselves from their own wives, and not to beget sons: whoever has done so shall be driven out from the office of the clergy.[11]

Such a statement represents a transitional period in what would become the Roman Catholic Church. During this time, not only deacons and priests but even bishops could marry, but they were expected to forego the marriage bed. As time went on, the church would forbid marriage to clergy altogether.[12]

Encountering these Christian documents while I was at Boston University really made me question from where this anti-pleasure attitude arose. As I continued to study, I came to see that this was not at all a view native to Christianity but was a dominant stream of thought within the Greco-Roman world. The story of how that came to be, once again, originates from Greek philosophy, specifically how they thought about the body.

Before the rise of the philosophers, Greeks were not overly worried about bodies or bodily pleasures. They did not look forward to the afterlife, since they believed after death they would descend into Hades: the realm of

6. Clement of Alexandria, *Paed.* 2.2 (p. 112).

7. Clement of Alexandria, *Paed.* 2.10 (p. 170).

8. Clement of Alexandria, *Strom.* 7.12 (p. 546).

9. Clement of Alexandria, *Strom.* 3.43 (p. 281).

10. For the second century, see Athenagoras and Justin Martyr. For the third, see Tertullian and Origen. For the fourth, see Eusebius, Anthony, Athanasius. For the fifth, see Augustine and Jerome.

11. Dale, *Synod of Elvira*, Canon 33. This translation is my own.

12. See Canons 3 and 21 of the First Lateran Council (AD 1123). Sometimes the Catholic Church makes exceptions for married Anglican priests who wish to convert to Catholicism while keeping wives.

shadows. But once Pythagoras (570–495 BC) put forward the idea of cycles of rebirth, everything changed.

It's hard to say if Pythagoras himself heard of the immortality of the soul from the Egyptians or the Hindus (perhaps via Orpheus), but what is clear is that his followers, the Pythagoreans, desired to escape an endless series of births and deaths by renouncing what is sensual and earthly.[13] They fasted from meats and beans in an effort to purify themselves. But their greatest focus was on mental work—pondering eternal realities like mathematics and music so that their soul could lift itself beyond the realm of sense-perceptions.

These Pythagorean notions made their way into Plato's philosophy, as well. In fact, in Plato's book on creation (written ca. 360 BC), Timaeus, the main speaker, is himself a Pythagorean. As such, we should not find the following account of reincarnation surprising:

> And he that has lived his appointed time well shall return again to his abode in his native star, and shall gain a life that is blessed and congenial; but whoso has failed therein shall be changed into woman's nature at the second birth; and if, in that shape, he still refrains not from wickedness he shall be changed every time, according to the nature of his wickedness, into some bestial form after the similitude of his own nature; nor in his changings shall he cease from woes until he yields himself to the revolution of the Same and Similar that is within him.[14]

Apart from the obvious chauvinism in Timaeus's categorization of womanhood as cosmic punishment, what sticks out here is that the end goal is to escape the body and return to the heavenly realm.

What happened to descending to Hades? In the *Timaeus*, Plato has reconfigured the afterlife to be a matter of escaping endless cycles on Earth in order to flit off to the higher eternal realms.

Another of Plato's dialogues played a crucial role in how his intellectual successors would think about bodily pleasures. In the *Phaedo*, Plato tells the story of Socrates's last moments before death. In the story, the city of Athens has condemned Plato's master on the charge of disbelieving in the city's gods and corrupting the youth. Before Socrates drinks the hemlock designated for his execution, he converses at length with his close philosopher friends. The *Phaedo* records that dialogue.

With his death just hours away, the topic of conversation naturally turns to the afterlife, and Socrates presents four arguments that the soul

13. Zeller, *Outlines of the History*, 33.
14. Plato, *Tim.* 42b–c (pp. 91–92).

survives the death of the body. While discoursing on the soul, Socrates makes repeated disparaging remarks about the body.

Socrates explains that true philosophers shouldn't concern themselves with pleasures like eating, drinking, or wearing costly garments. In fact, they should despise "anything more than nature needs" and should be "entirely concerned with the soul and not with the body."[15] The problem, he says, with the human body is that it's always insisting on having its needs met, "interrupting, disturbing, distracting, and preventing us from getting a glimpse of the truth."[16] Furthermore, it fills with "loves and desires and fears" so that "we literally never get an opportunity to think at all about anything."[17] Socrates even goes so far as to blame the body for armed conflict, since wars occur to acquire wealth which, in turn, the victors spend on their own bodies. As true seekers of wisdom, Socrates posits, thinkers should undergo a "purification" by which they isolate their souls, endeavoring to be "freed from the chains of [their] bod[ies]" in anticipation of death.[18]

Furthermore, Socrates says, no one should fear death, since it is no more than the separation of the soul from the body. In the end, death, for Socrates, is not the end of life nor even a sad event, but something to look forward to and embrace, since death liberates the soul from the body. After death, the philosopher can finally contemplate and meditate and apprehend the true nature of the world without hindrance or interruption. For his part, Socrates does not resist his demise. In the *Phaedo*, he even takes the poison before the sun has fully set, since he sees no reason to delay his departure from this lower realm. When Socrates takes the poison, his friends begin weeping and wailing. Rather than comforting them, he rebukes them: "What is this strange outcry? he said. I sent away the women mainly in order that they might not misbehave in this way, for I have been told that a man should die in peace. Be quiet, then, and have patience."[19] At these words his comrades restrain their tears and wait patiently for the poison to work its way up Socrates's body, from his feet to his legs to his torso. When the hemlock finally reaches his heart, he dies. He does not struggle, complain, or whimper. He welcomes death.

This view—the body as prison and death as freedom—came to dominate many subsequent schools of thought in the Mediterranean world. As time went on, philosophical schools embraced different ways to train

15. Plato, *Phaed.* 64d–e.

16. Plato, *Phaed.* 66b, d.

17. Plato, *Phaed.* 66c.

18. Plato, *Phaed.* 67c.

19. Plato, *Phaed.* 117d–e.

themselves to live *according to nature*, as Socrates had done in his last moments. These schools debated how people should best conduct their lives. Though they disagreed on what the ultimate good was, they all agreed that everyone should train themselves to strive continually after the Good. This "training" in Greek is *askesis*, whence we have the English word "ascetic," meaning training oneself to deny certain pleasures.

By the time Christ arrived on the scene, the Stoics were the most influential of these ancient schools, often holding significant positions in city governments. The Stoics believed that it was futile to resist the course of the universe.[20] Their founder, Zeno of Citium (334–262 BC), had instructed his followers to avoid four negative emotions: desire, fear, pleasure, and pain. Life, the Stoics taught, is like a dog tethered to the back of an ox cart. Whether the dog sits or pulls with all its might, it cannot help but go in the direction that the larger, stronger ox is going. Instead of resisting fate, the enlightened need to train themselves to detach from bodily and emotional desires so that when bad things happen, they can accept them while retaining equilibrium.

Writing in the latter half of the first century, Musonius Rufus, a well-known Roman philosopher, advised training (*askesis*) the body and soul to "adapt to cold, heat, thirst, hunger, plain food, a hard bed, abstinence from pleasure, and endurance of strenuous labor."[21] In the first century, the Cynic Pseudo-Crates advised his disciples, "Practice needing little, for this is nearest to God."[22]

Around the same time that Rufus was advising asceticism, he called the body a tomb for the soul and compared the stomach to swine.[23] In his book, *On the Contemplative Life*, Philo, the Jewish philosopher from our last chapter, describes a community of ascetics called the Therapeutae who lived simply, denying themselves carnal desires. "No one of them may take any meat or drink before the setting of the sun," he says, since such matters belong to the body and are not worthy of daylight.[24] Some would go up to three days forgetting to eat. Even at their banquets, Philo says, "wine is not introduced, but only the clearest water," along with "bread for food and salt

---

20. Interestingly, they called the force pervading and animating everything in the universe the "*logos*."

21. Musonius Rufus, *On Training*, disc. 4 (Vaage, "Musonius Rufus," 131).

22. Pseudo-Crates, *Cynic Epistles*, 11 (Vaage, "Cynic Epistles," 119).

23. Philo, *Spec.* 1.148 (p. 548); Philo, *Leg.* 1.108 (p. 37); Philo, *Deus.* 1.50 (p. 71).

24. Philo, *Contempl.* 1.34 (p. 701).

for seasoning," since "wine is the medicine of folly, and costly seasonings and sauces excite desire, which is the most insatiable of beasts."[25]

Second-century sensibilities were little different in this regard. Celsus, in his *True Doctrine*, rails against the Christians, deriding our belief in resurrection, since, he says, the flesh "is full of those things which it is not even honorable to mention."[26] In addition, the gnostics called the body a bond, bondage, a fetter, and a prison of the soul, which it merely wore as a garment.[27]

In the third century, Plotinus calls the soul a stranger to the body, which needs to turn "towards the exact contrary of earthly things."[28] Plotinus's student, Porphyry of Tyre, who lived into the early fourth century, taught one should live with frugality, including "no wine, little food, small, hard bed, little sleep . . . to allow the ascent of the soul."[29] In fact, Porphyry says, "if it were possible, we should abstain from all food," but since it is not, we should content ourselves, "granting to nature what is necessary, and this of a light quality," and "reject whatever exceeds this, as only contributing to pleasure."[30] I could go on, multiplying more examples of leading intellectuals in the Roman era who taught against physical enjoyment, but these should be enough for the point at hand.

As a result of the influence of these ideas in their society, educated people in antiquity tended to believe the virtuous life was one that avoided pleasure. Of course, that didn't mean the old Roman Empire was full of disciplined saints, but that the educated elite held in common a kind of sense that bodily pleasures such as eating luxuriant foods, drinking alcohol, indulging in the comfort of a soft bed, and especially sex, were at best suspect and at worst shameful. Consequently, as Christianity began to spread beyond the Jewish world into the Roman one, converts combined their old sensibilities about pleasure with their newfound Christian faith, resulting in the kinds of aversions we've already seen at the top of this chapter.

Such asceticism was totally foreign to the Hebrew culture of Jesus and his Jewish forbearers. In contrast to the philosophers and the pagan myths, the Hebrew Bible portrays God's creation of bodies as a result of his generosity and goodness. After surveying his creation and repeatedly declaring it good, the first fact that displeases God is that Adam is alone (Gen 2:18).

25. Philo, *Contempl.* 1.73–74 (p. 705).

26. Origen, *Cels.* 5.14 (p. 549).

27. Layton, *Gnostic Scriptures*, 18.

28. Plotinus, *Enneads*, 3.6.5 (232).

29. See Kolenkow, "Chaeremon the Stoic," 388.

30. Porphyry, *Abst.* 1.38 (pp. 46–47).

After carefully forming the first woman and presenting him to the first man, we read,

> Therefore a man shall leave his father and his mother and hold fast to his wife, and they shall become one flesh. And the man and his wife were both naked and were not ashamed. (Gen 2:24–25)

God's mandates in the garden of Eden ("Eden" means pleasure, by the way) are not "abstain from sex," "eat only tasteless grains," and "submit." Rather, God's commands are "be fruitful," "eat freely," and "have dominion." God so loved his first two humans that he wanted them to reproduce and fill the new world with many more people. The Earth was not an exercise in testing people for some other realm but a home for his own crowning achievements to delight in and rule over. Although he forbade eating from one tree in the garden, the rest of the trees were for Adam and Eve's enjoyment—their pleasure.

The God of Genesis is more an Epicurean than a Stoic. He does not design bodies without pleasure sensors, but instead squeezes onto the human tongue ten thousand taste buds. He does not make reproduction an onerous or bland affair but loads human genitals with thousands of erotogenic nerve endings. In his extravagant kindness, he engineered eating and intercourse to give us pleasure and then commanded his first two humans to engage in both.

It's no wonder the first two chapters of Genesis declare creation "good" seven times over. The second chapter of the Bible concludes with two naked humans in a garden of delight who are commanded to be fruitful and multiply, eat of the garden, and rule the world.

Not only does God's design of the body shout to us that he engineered us to experience pleasure, but the law he gave Israel on Sinai likewise indicates his promotion of enjoyment. Consider the holy days built into the Torah: the Feast of Unleavened Bread; the Feast of Weeks; the Feast of Trumpets; the Day of Atonement; and the Feast of Tabernacles. Although the Day of Atonement is a single day of fasting and repentance, the rest of these are multi-day celebrations or festivals. The Feast of Unleavened Bread follows on the heels of the Passover meal, when families roast lambs, enjoy wine, and tell stories of God's deliverance from Egypt. The rule for the rest of the week is no work other than preparing food.

The Feast of Weeks commemorates the first fruits of the harvest. According to the Mishnah, the festival is "accompanied by a large celebration, in which pilgrims gather in the towns of their district and go as a group with their ripe produce to Jerusalem. There they are greeted by Levitical singing and celebration."[31]

Christians sometimes misinterpret the law as some terrible straitjacket strapped onto the people of God until Christ could free them from it. In reality, it was a way of life God provided for his people to live equitably and joyfully.[32]

Beyond the created order and the holy days instituted in the Mosaic law, the Old Testament unapologetically accepts physical pleasure as not only normal but a gift from God. Here are a few quick examples:

> Let your fountain be blessed,
> and rejoice in the wife of your youth,
> a lovely deer, a graceful doe.
> Let her breasts fill you at all times with delight;
> be intoxicated always in her love. (Prov 5:18–19)

> Go, eat your bread with joy,
> and drink your wine with a merry heart. . . .
> Enjoy life with the wife whom you love,
> all the days of your vain life that he has given you under the sun,
> because that is your portion in life and in your toil at which you
> toil under the sun. (Eccl 9:7–9)

> I know that there is nothing better for them than to be happy
> And enjoy themselves as long as they live;
> Moreover, it is God's gift that all should eat and drink
> And take pleasure in all their toil. (Eccl 3:12–13)

Proverbs encourages young married couples to enjoy each other's bodies—after all, finding a wife is not a curse, but a gift from God (Prov 18:22). Far from forbidding alcohol, Ecclesiastes flatly affirms the goodness of drinking wine and eating food. Even wealth is not inherently evil but a blessing from God (Eccl 5:18–19). Where is the meditation of Socrates, the fasting of the Therapeutae, the vegetarianism of Porphyry? The Hebrew view sits in sharp contrast to these, accepting eating, drinking, work, and even sexual relations as goods.

But all of these examples pale in comparison to the lofty manner in which the Song of Solomon rejoices in bodily pleasures. This elaborate

---

31. Neusner and Green, *Dictionary of Judaism*, 573.

32. Two more quick examples from Torah are that the first year of marriage qualified a soldier for exemption from service, so that he may "be happy with the wife whom he has married" (Deut 24:5). Secondly, if someone had just planted a vineyard, he was likewise excused from duty until he could enjoy its fruit (Deut 20:6).

collection of poems brims with sexual imagery. The book opens with the words, "Let him kiss me with the kisses of his mouth! For your love is better than wine" (Song 1:2). For the author, wine is obviously good, but the kisses of her lover are better still. By the time we reach the fourth verse we read, "Draw me after you; let us run. The king has brought me into his chambers" (Song 1:4).

In another riveting scene, the woman awakes in the middle of the night with an intense desire to find her lover. She gets out of bed and begins searching through the city streets and squares. She encounters the night watchmen and inquires where he might be, but they are no help. Finally, she finds him and consummates her desire (Song 3:4).

Later on, we encounter the following picturesque love poem:

> Your stature is like a palm tree,
> and your breasts are like its clusters.
> I say I will climb the palm tree
> and lay hold of its fruit.
> Oh may your breasts be like clusters of the vine,
> and the scent of your breath like apples,
> and your mouth like the best wine.
> It goes down smoothly for my beloved,
> gliding over lips and teeth.
> I am my beloved's,
> and his desire is for me.
> Come, my beloved,
> let us go out into the fields,
> and lodge in the villages;
> let us go out early to the vineyards
> and see whether the vines have budded,
> whether the grape blossoms have opened
> and the pomegranates are in bloom.
> There I will give you my love. (Song 7:7–12)

Such words as these would never be allowed in a book that is at its core against sensual pleasure. In fact, marriage is the norm throughout the Scriptures. Sure, eunuchs and prophets like John the Baptist practiced celibacy, but these are exceptions, not the rule.

The Bible celebrates weddings right from creation onwards. When Jesus went to a wedding and they ran out of wine, he did not scold them for their merriment, rather he turned 120 gallons of water into wine—and not just any wine, quality wine (John 2:1–11). In fact, Jesus had a reputation for indulging in food and drink, as evidenced by his critics calling him a "glutton and a drunkard" (Luke 7:34).

Now, let me be clear. The Bible no more endorses hedonism (living for pleasure) than it does asceticism (denying all pleasure). Rather, it affirms the goodness of God's designed bodily pleasures while simultaneously placing clear boundaries on them. God limits sex to marriage, eating to bodily needs, and alcohol to moderation. Taking these indulgences outside of their respective boundaries results in adultery, gluttony, and drunkenness. Thus, unlike Bacchic hedonism or the lechery of Mardi Gras, God reins in the pleasures we should indulge in to safeguard us from ruin.

Many Scriptures convey the importance of restraining the flesh from its lustful drive, but too often these texts are taken to the extreme of abstaining from all physical appetites.[33] In fact, when one early Christian congregation began swerving into asceticism, the apostle Paul corrected them with the following words:

> If with Christ you died to the elemental spirits of the world, why, as if you were still alive in the world, do you submit to regulations—"Do not handle, Do not taste, Do not touch" (referring to things that all perish as they are used)—according to human precepts and teachings? These have indeed an appearance of wisdom in promoting self-made religion and asceticism and severity to the body, but they are of no value in stopping indulgence of the flesh. (Col 2:20–23)

Furthermore, when some Christians in Corinth likewise began advocating celibacy—even within marriage—the same apostle commanded husbands and wives to give each other their conjugal rights, rather than depriving themselves (1 Cor 7:3, 5). Rather than conveying embarrassment about God's gift of sex for married couples, he expresses concern that those who abstain for extended periods of time will fall prey to Satan's temptations. The entire Bible offers a different way from the Greco-Roman traditions of looking at physical gratifications: it insists on their goodness while cautioning against their abuse.

Within the first few centuries of Christianity, two opposing views on bodily pleasures emerged: the Hebrew and the Greek. Educated Christian teachers tended to lean toward the Greek view, since that was the more common stream of thought in their world. In fact, this very issue became a major battleground for rejecting the idea of the kingdom. As it turned out, the Christians who preferred more allegorical interpretations of the future argued that those who believed in literal resurrection bodies living in a literal kingdom on Earth were motivated by their desire for physical pleasure.

---

33. Heb 11:25–26; 2 Thess 2:12; 1 Tim 5:5–6; 2 Tim 3:3; Jas 5:5; 1 Cor 7.

For example, in the early second century, Gaius accused Cerinthus of believing that "after the resurrection . . . the kingdom of Christ will be on earth, and humanity living at Jerusalem will again be enslaved to lusts and pleasure."[34] Although today we might ask, "What's wrong with that?" in their world, such an accusation could immediately discredit someone's idea.

A century later, Origen likewise took great offense at the idea of experiencing bodily pleasure in eternal life. In a comment dripping with outrage that anyone could even believe such nonsense, he accuses his opponents of "giv[ing] way to their own desires and lusts" because they think that after the resurrection, "they will never lack the power to eat and drink and to do all things that pertain to flesh and blood."[35]

A generation later, Bishop Dionysius also opposed a physical hope when he criticized a kingdom believer because he was "in love with his own body and thoroughly sensual."[36] Dionysius claims his opponent really wants "endless gluttony and sexual indulgence at banquets."[37]

This stream of criticism continued to grow in popularity throughout the fourth century until it met its peak with Jerome in the early fifth century. He writes,

> I do not envy them, if they love the earth so much, that they desire earthly things in the kingdom of Christ, and if after an abundance of foods and the gluttony of their gullet and belly, they seek that which is below the belly.[38]

Even Augustine stooped to this ignoble strategy in his famous *City of God*, when he says,

> But, as they assert that those who then rise again shall enjoy the leisure of immoderate carnal banquets, furnished with an amount of meat and drink such as not only to shock the feeling of the temperate, but even to surpass the measure of credulity itself, such assertions can be believed only by the carnal. They who do believe them are called by the spiritual Chiliasts, which we may literally reproduce by the name Millenarians.[39]

34. Eusebius, *Hist. eccl.* 3.28 (p. 103). For a fascinating reconstruction of Cerinthus's theology, harmonizing both strands of polemic later writers aimed at him (that he was a chiliast Judaizer and that he was a gnostic) see Hill, "Cerinthus, Gnostic or Chiliast?," 135–72.

35. Origen, *Princ.* 2.11.1–2 (p. 184).

36. Eusebius, *Hist. eccl.* 3.28 (p. 103).

37. Eusebius, *Hist. eccl.* 7.25 (p. 243).

38. Jerome, *Comm. Isa.*, Prologue to Book 18 (Newman, "Jerome's Judaizers," 440).

39. Augustine, *Civ.* 20.7.1 (p. 426).

This smear tactic was as simple as it was effective; the "carnal" Christians, these writers argued, want a fleshly resurrection with physical bodies that can experience pleasure. However, they claimed, the "spiritual" Christians know that such notions are beneath God, so they interpret the biblical passages about the coming kingdom in a metaphorical sense (i.e., eating spiritual food).

Christians like Origen, who refused to use a bed, endured extreme poverty, and walked without shoes, and Jerome, who thought the only benefit of marriage was the production of more virgins,[40] could not stomach the Hebrew vision of the age to come, which features a messianic banquet replete with choice pieces of meat and refined wine.[41] No: instead they radically reimagined the resurrection body, remaking it as completely impervious to any normal desires and appetites. Origen, for example, accepts a resurrected body but believes it is "no longer hindered by its former carnal senses."[42] Augustine believes "the flesh will rise again" but then quickly adds that God will transform it into "a celestial and angelic body."[43] Thus, the future Christian hope gradually lost its physicality and gave way to a picture of spiritual bodies in heavenly realms.

Drawing together the threads of this investigation, the following story comes into focus: the Hebrew background expressed in the Old Testament held a high view of the body, owing to its august origin. The Jews did not disparage bodily pleasures such as enjoying food, drink, sex, and work, but accepted them as God-ordained so long as they remained within his appointed boundaries. The New Testament documents do not challenge or innovate on this basic understanding. In fact, the Gospels portray Jesus as someone who attends dinner parties often, consumes alcohol, and discourages fasting. That his enemies called him a drunkard and a glutton would be unthinkable if he were an ascetic.

But as Christianity spread beyond the thought-world of Judaism into the Greco-Roman matrix, new converts to Christianity in Colossae and Corinth advocated a much more austere attitude toward the body's desires. Paul confronted these issues head on, advocating a balanced perspective that shunned hedonism on the one hand and asceticism on the other. However, as more and more gentiles became Christ-followers, the desire to abstain from physical pleasures grew. By the second and third centuries, key

40. "I praise wedlock, I praise marriage, but it is because they give me virgins. I gather the rose from the thorns, the gold from the earth, the pearl from the shell." *Letter 22 to Eustochium* in Jerome, *Letters and Select Works*, 20 (p. 30).

41. For Origen, see Eusebius, *Hist. eccl.* 6.3.9–12.

42. Origen, *Princ.* 2.11.7 (p. 192).

43. Augustine, *Seasons*, 264.6.

Christian thinkers found themselves embarrassed by the kingdom hope, especially bodily, physical resurrection, since it militated against the mores of the time. As a result, they rejected the Christian hope of embodied humans living in paradise and mutated it by imagining a new, less corporeal resurrection body in a new, less terrestrial, ultimate reality.

Sadly, even today, many Christians react so strongly against the lewdness of our own time that we tend to fall back into quasi-ascetic restrictions. Rather than promoting Christianity as a holistic, fulfilling, joyous, and satisfying experience, we sell it short by portraying it as a restrictive religion that evacuates fun and enjoyment from the human experience. Christians don't dance, don't drink, and don't play cards. We feel guilty about eating filet mignon, going on vacation, or living in a nice house. We abstain from sex unless for procreation, alcohol unless for communion, and film unless it supports a Christian agenda. To top it all off, we preach a gospel of disembodied heavenly worship, where, we say, we will spend eternity locked in a tractor-beam gaze staring at a white glow without sleep, without change, without individuality. Is it any wonder that outsiders take one look at us and run the other way?

This is not to say that we should embrace whatever lusts and physical appetites well up inside of us; we certainly should control our impulses. God has graciously put boundaries in place to protect us while facilitating human flourishing. It's like a tomato plant in the wild, which can only grow so tall before it bends over on itself; its freedom limits its ability to produce and reach its full potential. But if a farmer comes along and stakes it—essentially limiting its direction of growth—the plant flourishes, growing much bigger and producing much more fruit. So it is with God. He gives us boundaries not to suppress us, but to help us grow.

Although the ancient, "enlightened" thinkers of the Roman Empire rejected the biblical kingdom because it allowed for the enjoyment of physical pleasures, our age, as it turns out, is just the opposite. Rather than rejecting God's dream for our world because it involves carnal gratification, many people today would instead reject it on the grounds of it not being enough "fun." In a time such as this, we are tasked with presenting the gospel to our own generation in a way that is maximally palatable without succumbing to the seductive temptation to reimagine the kingdom as a theme park or a debauched soirée.

We'll return to how the kingdom affects our world in a later chapter, but for now, I was getting to the end of my investigation about the kingdom. On the cold case of "who killed the kingdom," I was narrowing not only a list of suspects, but their motives as well. Finally, I was in a position to synthesize what I had learned into a clear account explaining how we lost the kingdom.

10

Kingdom Lost

Naturally, I found myself drawn to those authors who agreed with and promoted the kingdom idea, but I came to see that only by locating and carefully analyzing the arguments of the powerful, elite Christians who thought it was wrong would I find why Christianity had discarded it. This led, of course, to countless hours in the library of the School of Theology at Boston University, digging up historical sources, researching, and writing. By now, I had clarified the three main reasons I presented in the recent three chapters: the kingdom was considered to be too Jewish, too crude, and too hedonic.

I felt both satisfied and saddened; I had gotten the answers I was seeking, but the fact that Christ's church had rejected such an integral aspect of Christ's message overwhelmed me with grief. How could this have happened?

One particularly dreary day, sitting at one of those little cubicle duplex desks with walls on either side, I was studying book 5 of Irenaeus's work, *Against Heresies*—a cheery read—when I came to chapter 31. My reading slowed, but as I realized what Irenaeus was saying, I got so excited I sped up again, holding my breath in anticipation of what he would say next. I flew through two more chapters, sat back, and erupted into tears.

When Christians study church history, we look for ourselves, our tribe, our people. I had spent the last two years seeking out and contemplating the writings of those responsible for killing the kingdom, but when I came face to face with one of my own, giving a thorough, biblical, and well-reasoned argument for the kingdom on the basis of the promises God made to Abraham, the prophecies of the Hebrew Bible, and the teachings of Jesus, I was unprepared for the emotion. It gushed up like a bubbling spring.

I sat, sobbing with joy: I wasn't crazy; I wasn't latching onto some obscure, sectarian view; I was tapping into the mainstream teaching of the early church. Irenaeus was not some fringe radical, but a bishop with ties to Smyrna, Rome, and Gaul—a powerhouse in second-century Christianity. At once, I felt like I was home. Separated by eighteen centuries, thousands of miles, and a language, Irenaeus was one of my people.

And he wasn't the only one.

The first Christian authors who wrote about the kingdom outside of the New Testament are referred to as the "Apostolic Fathers." These were not apostles, but those whose lives overlapped with them, writing in the second half of the first century and the first half of the second. Many of them did not personally know the apostles, but they were the earliest mainstream Christian authors. As we would expect, we can find all three dimensions of the kingdom Jesus taught, as future hope, gospel preached, and way of life, in their writings. For example, Clement of Rome (AD 35–99) wrote about the first generation of Christ followers who "went out preaching as gospel that the kingdom of God was about to come."[1] Another early author taught that Jesus had "given us a foretaste of things to come,"[2] making the link between the future kingdom and how we need to live in anticipation of its arrival.

Generally, the Apostolic Fathers do not spend much time on theology; instead, they focus on pastoral concerns, especially living righteously. Even so, by carefully observing what they do and do not write, we can get a decent understanding of their theological framework. This approach yields important details: these authors do not write about each person flitting off to heaven after an individual judgment. Rather, they argue that if the church as a whole is "doing what is right in God's sight, we will enter his kingdom and receive the promises" (2 Clem. 11.7). They tie eternal life to "rest in the coming kingdom" (2 Clem. 5.5), which, they claim, arrives at the day of Christ's appearing, when he rewards his people, and his enemies "see that the kingdom of the world belongs to Jesus" (2 Clem. 17.5).

These early Christian authors think from a temporal perspective. Rather than talking about "being in a better place" or "going home to be with the Lord," they speak of awaiting "the revelation of the kingdom of Christ" (1 Clem. 50.3), and how "the righteous person not only lives in

---

1. 1 Clem. 42.3, translation my own from Greek: "ἐξῆλθον, εὐαγγελιζόμενοι τὴν βασιλείαν τοῦ θεοῦ μέλλειν ἔρχεσθαι."

2. Barn. 1.7. Unless otherwise indicated, all quotes of Apostolic Fathers are from *APF*.

this world but also looks forward to the holy age to come" (Barn. 10.11) To them, the goal is not to go to heaven, but to "enter the kingdom of God" or "inherit the kingdom of God" (2 Clem. 5.5).

The author of the Epistle of Barnabas (AD 70–130) writes that the Lord will "make the last things as the first" and that the saints "will live and rule over the earth" at the time when "we ourselves have been made perfect" (Barn. 6.13, 17, 19). Polycarp (AD 69–155) can hardly put it more clearly than when he says,

> If we please him in this present world, we will receive the world to come as well, inasmuch as he promised that he will raise us from the dead and that if we prove to be citizens worthy of him, we will also reign with him—if, that is, we continue to believe. . . . Do we not know that the saints will judge the world, as Paul teaches? (*Poly. Phil.* 5.2; 11.2)

However impressive these little snippets of kingdom theology seem, they pale in comparison to what Papias of Hierapolis (AD 60–130) wrote. Although it's plain to see that he did not invent the kingdom, later anti-kingdom authors accused pro-kingdom believers of following Papias.[3] However, he was no originator; just the opposite, he was very concerned about getting to the exact truth of what Jesus said. According to him, he was writing down "everything I carefully learned then from the elders and carefully remembered, guaranteeing their truth."[4] He was not interested in "those who have a great deal to say," rather he wanted to know what actually happened.[5]

Since significant roads passed through Papias's home city of Hierapolis, he had ample opportunity to interview various second-generation Christ-followers. He wanted to know what "Andrew or Peter said, or Philip or Thomas or James or John or Matthew or any other of the Lord's disciples."[6] Living at the close of the first century, Papias had access to secondhand knowledge about Jesus's teachings. In fact, he wrote, "I did not think that information from books would profit me as much as information from a living and abiding voice."[7]

After a lifetime of collecting Jesus's sayings from those who knew the original disciples, Papias composed a book called *The Exposition of the*

---

3. For example, Jerome says that Irenaeus, Apollinaris, Tertullian, Victorinus, and Lactantius all got the idea that "after the resurrection the Lord will reign in the flesh with the saints" from Papias. See Jerome, *Letters and Select Works*, 18 (p. 367).

4. Papias, *Fragments of Papias*, frag. 3 (p. 735).

5. Papias, *Fragments of Papias*, frag. 3 (p. 735).

6. Papias, *Fragments of Papias*, frag. 3 (p. 735).

7. Papias, *Fragments of Papias*, frag. 3 (p. 735).

Sayings of the Lord, which is now lost except for fragmentary quotations in later authors. Thankfully, we do have one lengthy excerpt about the kingdom, which was preserved by Irenaeus, who wrote around fifty years later. Here is what Papias wrote:

> The blessing thus foretold undoubtedly belongs to the times of the kingdom, when the righteous will rise from the dead and reign, when creation, too, renewed and freed from bondage, will produce an abundance of food of all kinds from the dew of heaven and from the fertility of the earth, just as the elders, who saw John the disciple of the Lord, recalled having heard from him how the Lord used to teach about those times and say:
> The days will come when vines will grow, each having ten thousand shoots, and on each shoot ten thousand branches, and on each branch ten thousand twigs, and on each twig ten thousand clusters, and in each cluster ten thousand grapes, and each grape when crushed will yield twenty-five measures of wine. And when one of the saints takes hold of a cluster, another cluster will cry out, "I am better, take me, bless the Lord through me." Similarly a grain of wheat will produce ten thousand heads, and every head will have ten thousand grains, and every grain ten pounds of fine flour, white and clean. And the other fruits, seeds, and grass will produce in similar proportions, and all the animals feeding on these fruits produced by the soil will in turn become peaceful and harmonious toward one another, and fully subject to humankind.[8]

This is quite a grandiose vision of the future. Whether Jesus actually uttered these words or not isn't my focus here so much as the fact that this statement shows us what Papias believed. Although some later Christian writers dismissed Papias as "a man of very limited intelligence,"[9] since they thought he believed in talking grapes and grain, this prophecy actually fits quite nicely with Amos's prophecy about the plowman overtaking the reaper, the mountains dripping sweet wine, and Isaiah's prophecy about the taming of the animals. Obviously Papias didn't think grapes would literally shout out "I am better" in the kingdom age. The language is prophetic hyperbole describing an age of spectacular abundance and harmony.

Thus, Papias, a man dedicated to carefully preserving sayings of Christ, provides us with an early second-century witness to the physicality of the Christian hope, very similar to what we read in the Hebrew prophets.

8. Papias, *Exposition of the Sayings of Our Lord*, frag. 14, quoted from Irenaeus of Lyons, *Haer.* 5.33.3–4 (pp. 751, 753).

9. Eusebius, *Hist. eccl.* 3.39 (p. 113).

As we move along into the second half of the second century, we encounter two powerful kingdom defenders: Justin Martyr (AD 100–165) and Irenaeus of Lyons (AD 130–202). Justin wrote a fascinating dialogue with a Jew named Trypho, in which the two discussed a myriad of Jewish-Christian issues. The setting of the dialogue is shortly after the Romans had destroyed Jerusalem in AD 135.

At one point in the dialogue, Trypho asks Justin, "Do you really believe that this place Jerusalem shall be rebuilt, and do you actually expect that you Christians will one day congregate there to live joyfully with Christ, together with the patriarchs?"[10] Justin's response to this question gives us some of our best insight into what Christians in the 160s believed about the kingdom. He replies, "With many others, I feel that such an event will take place." He quickly adds that there are "pure and pious Christians who do not share our opinion." His tone changes dramatically as he describes a third group of so-called Christians who are "godless, impious heretics." Here, Justin tells Trypho, is what they believe:

> [Those who] blaspheme the God of Abraham and the God of
> Isaac and the God of Jacob by asserting that there is no resur-
> rection of the dead, but that their souls are taken up to heaven
> at the very moment of their death, do not consider them to be
> real Christians; just as one after careful examination, would
> not acknowledge as Jews the Sadducees or the similar sects. . . .
> Whereas I, and all other wholeheartedly orthodox Christians,
> feel certain that there will be a resurrection of the flesh, followed
> by a thousand years in the rebuilt, embellished, and enlarged
> city of Jerusalem, as was announced by the prophets Ezekiel,
> Isaiah and the others.[11]

Thus, in Justin's time, we have three groups of Christians with respect to the kingdom of God. The first group includes Justin and those who agree with him: the so-called orthodox. These agree with Trypho and the Jews that there will be a resurrection, and that God will restore Jerusalem in a period lasting for a thousand years. The third group thinks that upon death they will go to heaven, thus, Justin asserts, denying the resurrection and the kingdom.[12]

The second group is harder to pin down. They seem to believe in resurrection, but not that their souls float up to heaven at death nor that there will be a millennium in Jerusalem (or that the city will be rebuilt). Regardless,

10. Justin Martyr, *Dial.* 80 (p. 125).

11. Justin Martyr, *Dial.* 126 (p. 126).

12. We know from an earlier chapter the groups he had in mind, including Marcion-ites, Valentinians, Basilidians, and Saturnilians (Justin Martyr, *Dial.* 35).

they believe in some sort of a terrestrial inheritance following the resurrection from the dead.

Justin recognized some diversity on this issue, but he drew a strong boundary: the difference between best and good Christians on the one hand and false Christians on the other was singular. For him, those who believed their souls went to heaven at death were heretics. Outsiders.

About twenty years later, Irenaeus of Lyons took the business of combating deviant Christian beliefs to a whole new level in his massive treatment of every heresy known at his time in his book *Against Heresies*.

In it, most of the groups Irenaeus describes and refutes are gnostics of some sort or another. At the end of this tome, he lays out a positive case for Christian teaching, including a solid exposition of the kingdom doctrine, and in doing so, he proposes an explanation for why some mainstream Christians have given up on the kingdom idea.

He argues that some who are reckoned among the orthodox have come to despise God's handiwork, including the salvation of the flesh, since they believe that immediately upon their death they will pass above the heavens and the creator and go to the highest God. These Christians, Irenaeus argues, have allowed gnostic perspectives to invade and colonize their thinking to such a degree that they no longer believe in the resurrection of the whole person. Irenaeus goes on to claim that Christ's experience—death, descent into the Earth, and then resurrection which brings life—is the pattern for all who follow him.

According to Irenaeus, Jesus himself said he didn't go to heaven during the intermediate state, so why should we (John 20:17)? He waited in the tomb until the third day, when God restored him to life in the resurrection. Here, Irenaeus lays out his position:

> Inasmuch, therefore, as the opinions of certain orthodox persons are derived from heretical discourses, they are both ignorant of God's dispensations, and of the mystery of the resurrection of the just, and of the kingdom which is the commencement of incorruption, by means of which kingdom those who shall be worthy are accustomed gradually to partake of the divine nature; and it is necessary to tell them respecting those things, that it behooves the righteous first to receive the promise of the inheritance which God promised to the fathers, and to reign in it, when they rise again to behold God in this creation which is renovated, and that the judgment should take place afterwards. For it is just that in that very creation in which they toiled or were afflicted, being proved in every way by suffering, they should receive the reward of their suffering; and that in the

creation in which they were slain because of their love to God, in that they should be revived again; and that in the creation in which they endured servitude, in that they should reign.[13]

We can see that by the time of Irenaeus (approximately AD 180), the gnostic belief in escaping the body and floating up past our physical universe into the eternal realm had already begun to take a strong foothold among mainstream Christians. On the contrary, Irenaeus taught that the righteous will receive the promise of inheritance at the resurrection, when God restores the world back to paradise.

Here we note two clear differences: timing and location. Whereas the gnostic scheme teaches that the individual's soul escapes and ascends at death, the biblical view says that the resurrection occurs at the end of time, to all the righteous at once: timing. Whereas Irenaeus's heretics believe the goal is to escape the physical realm and inhabit a celestial, immutable space, Irenaeus explains that Christians will reign in creation—in the very same place we endured servitude: location.

Between Justin and Irenaeus, the battle had intensified. Irenaeus does not even mention honest-hearted Christians who believe in resurrection but not the kingdom. He sees only two groups: those who believe in the kingdom and those who believe the lies of the gnostics.

Before moving on to look at the third-century kingdom advocates, I want to mention one last point about Irenaeus. Earlier, when we considered how some Christians rejected the kingdom, the allegorical method of interpretation played a significant role. With allegory, one can take the kingdom prophecies symbolically as references to the church. Much of what we saw here developed in the third century, but Irenaeus had already anticipated this tactic in the late second century. For example, after quoting Isaiah's prophecy about the wolf dwelling with the lamb, he wrote,

> I am quite aware that some persons endeavor to refer these words to the case of savage men, both of different nations and various habits, who come to believe, and when they have believed, act in harmony with the righteous. But although this is true now with regard to some men coming from various nations to the harmony of the faith, nevertheless in the resurrection of the just the words shall also apply to those animals mentioned. For God is rich in all things. And it is right that when the creation is restored, all the animals should obey and be in subjection to man, and revert to the food originally given by God (for

13. Irenaeus of Lyons, *Haer.* 5.31.1.

> they had been originally subjected in obedience to Adam), that
> is, the productions of the earth.[14]

Knowing the subsequent battle with "Jewish interpretation" that would rage on for the next two centuries, Irenaeus's words are a clear light in the midst of a fog. If only the third-century Christian theologians would have listened to Irenaeus on this point, history may have turned out differently!

Now we enter the third century and consider Hippolytus, Commodian, and Nepos. Hippolytus (AD 170–235) was by far the most influential of the three. He was a bishop and theologian who enjoyed considerable sway in Rome, though only a fraction of what he wrote survives today. Like Justin and Irenaeus before him, he was quite aware that some of his fellow Christians had taken on the belief that heaven was the destination of the righteous.

In his book on the six days of creation in Genesis, he says he is writing "in order to disprove the supposition of others."[15] He names the objectionable teaching: "Some choose to maintain that paradise is in heaven, and forms no part of the system of creation." Hippolytus goes on to explain that paradise in fact was once a place upon Earth. Although one might ask what the location of the original paradise has to do with the kingdom, as we've already seen, people tend to expect the end to be like the beginning. Hippolytus is deeply committed to the teaching of the Old Testament; he knows that humanity originated on Earth and God's dream is to renew it, not evacuate it, in the end.

What's unusual about Hippolytus is that he employs allegory extensively, especially in his interpretation of Genesis, yet this does not affect his belief in a coming physical kingdom. He steadfastly believes that the righteous had not yet received their reward—not even the apostles—but that all have to "wait for their time of redemption, when they shall be called into a kingdom which cannot be moved, when Christ addresses them with the word, 'Come, you blessed of my Father.'"[16]

In that day, Hippolytus writes, God promises "the blessing and the hope of a kingdom to come, in which the saints shall reign with Christ"[17] and he will "subvert the whole dominion and power of the adversary."[18] In one place, Hippolytus allegorizes the Sabbath as a symbol of the kingdom, not unlike what we find in Heb 4:9, "there remains a Sabbath rest for the

14. Irenaeus of Lyons, *Haer.* 5.33.4.

15. Hippolytus, "On Six Days Work," 163.

16. Hippolytus, *Comm. Gen.* 49.16–20 (165–66).

17. Hippolytus, *Jerome's Epistle 36 to Pope Damasus*, 3.6 (p. 168).

18. Hippolytus, *Scholia on Daniel*, 7.22 (p. 190). See also *Antichr.* 65.

people of God." He writes, "The Sabbath is the type and emblem of the future kingdom of the saints, when they 'shall reign with Christ,' when he comes from heaven."[19] Hippolytus thinks of the world on the pattern of a week of years, with each day lasting a millennium. Thus, he argues, all of history will run six thousand years and then the Sabbath age, when our toil ends and humanity enters into rest, will begin.

The next third-century kingdom believer is Commodian (AD 250) who wrote in Latin and probably lived in or around Carthage in North Africa. His placement is significant; it shows that, at that time, the kingdom belief was widespread. From the Apostolic Fathers in the Middle East to Justin and Hippolytus in Rome to Irenaeus in Gaul to Commodian and Nepos in Africa, the message is everywhere attested.

By Commodian's time, Clement and Origen of Alexandria had already written their thousands of works, spreading their ideas like a virus throughout the body of Christ, starting from northern Egypt. Would the kingdom defenders be able to stand against these antigens? Or would they underestimate the three-pronged attack upon our Lord's gospel? We will see.

At this historical moment, Commodian stands tall, proclaiming that God will "give us back again ourselves in a golden age" when the dead "may live and may rise in his kingdom, when there shall be the resurrection of the just."[20] Not at death, but when the golden age arrives, then "you will begin to live always an immortal life."[21] At one point Commodian describes in detail how the heavenly city will descend to the Earth and what life will be like as a result. No longer will there be grief or groaning, but God will make the saints incorruptible and immortal. This city will be free from sieges and rapines. Just like Isaiah, Amos, and Papias, Commodian writes, "The earth renewed without end pours forth abundantly."[22]

Around the same time and on the African continent, but more than 1,700 miles east of Commodian, Nepos (AD 255) exerted a great deal of influence in Arsinoe, a small oasis community about 175 miles south of Alexandria, Egypt. Nepos was an exemplary bishop, known for his faith, industry, and diligence in the Scriptures. He even wrote a collection of hymns for the saints that became quite popular throughout the region.

Nepos found the tendency of interpreting Scripture metaphorically so egregious that he wrote a book called *Refutation of the Allegorizers*, in

19. Hippolytus, *Comm. Dan.* 2.4 (p. 179).

20. Commodian, "Instructions of Commodianus," 29, 33 (p. 209); altered to modernize the English text.

21. Commodian, "Instructions of Commodianus," 34.

22. Commodian, "Instructions of Commodianus," 44.

which he strongly defended the kingdom against the new "spiritual" ideas about ascending to heaven. Sadly, this book is now lost—no one can say how long it was or find out what kind of arguments he made. However, we do know that after his death, people in the region clung to it in order to bolster their faith against an onslaught of spiritualizing that loomed on the horizon. Dionysius, a later critic of Nepos, said of the book that the Christians there relied on it confidently, "as indisputable proof that Christ's kingdom will be on the earth."[23] Sadly, this same Dionysius was the most powerful bishop in Egypt. He extended his influence to Arsinoe through a personal visit and fought to persuade the people that their former bishop's interpretation was simple-minded and literal. In this way, by the end of the third century, the great anti-kingdom theologians had begun to turn the tide against the kingdom believers.

By the time we arrive at the fourth century, the main three arguments against the kingdom had gained considerable traction. Alexandrian theology had infiltrated a significant portion of the church, partly because of Origen's fame and partly due to the popularization of his followers like Eusebius of Caesarea and the Cappadocian fathers.[24] Even so, we encounter a couple of bright spots early on, including Victorinus and Lactantius.

Victorinus of Petau flourished in the late third century and gave his life for his faith during the Great Persecution of Diocletian in the year 304. He wrote commentaries on at least nine books of the Bible, a book combating heresy, and another about creation. Sadly, only two of his works have survived to our day. Fortunately for our investigation, one of them speaks about creation and the other offers commentary on the book of Revelation.

In Victorinus's work on creation, he interprets the original week to correspond to God's plan for the ages, equating each day to a thousand years. He writes, "That true Sabbath will be in the seventh millenary of years, when Christ with his elect shall reign."[25] But oddly, in his other work, the text strongly disavows any belief in a literal thousand years of reigning upon the Earth. Instead, it reads, "they are called a thousand, according to that mode of speaking, wherein a part is signified by the whole. . . . I do not think the reign of a thousand years is eternal."[26]

The text goes on to claim that we are now living in the "millennium" and that Satan is bound with respect to the saints. This is a complete reversal

<hr>

23. Eusebius, *Hist. eccl.*, 7.24 (p. 242).

24. The Cappadocian fathers include Basil of Caesarea (AD 330–379), Gregory of Nyssa (AD 335–395), and Gregory of Nazianzus (AD 329–389).

25. Victorinus, "On the Creation of the World," 342.

26. Victorinus, *Comm. Rev.* 20.1–3, 6.

of what he said earlier. Still, I did not expect foul play until I came to the closing lines of his book, which read,

> Therefore they are not to be heard who assure themselves that there is to be an earthly reign of a thousand years; who think, that is to say, with the heretic Cerinthus. For the kingdom of Christ is now eternal in the saints, although the glory of the saints shall be manifested after the resurrection.[27]

Cerinthus was a stock heretic who had lived two centuries earlier, and anti-kingdom Christians had developed a strategy of lumping pro-kingdom believers in with Cerinthus in an effort to discredit the kingdom idea by association. Finding this at the end of Victorinus seemed awfully strange. Of course, he could have changed his mind on the kingdom between the time he wrote these two books, but that seems unlikely, since later Christianity remembers him as a staunch kingdom advocate—on par with Papias and Irenaeus.[28]

How did Victorinus get the reputation for believing in the kingdom while simultaneously teaching not only that the millennium is figurative, but that Christ's kingdom is already "now eternal in the saints"? As I continued to investigate this matter, I started to suspect that someone had monkeyed with Victorinus's book. I read it again, more carefully this time, and found the smoking gun in his comments on Rev 14:15. Here is what he says:

> "Thrust in your sharp sickle, and gather in the grapes of the vine," he signifies it of the nations that should perish on the advent of the Lord. And indeed in many forms he shows this same thing, as if to the dry harvest, and the seed for the coming of the Lord, and the consummation of the world, and the kingdom of Christ, and the future appearance of the kingdom of the blessed.[29]

Here, Victorinus unequivocally affirms that the final judgment of the nations is the very time of the "future appearance of the kingdom of the blessed" and "the kingdom of Christ"![30] How could the same person contradict himself in the same book, teaching in one place that the kingdom is already eternal and in another that it is yet future?

---

27. Victorinus, *Comm. Rev.* (*ANF*) 21.21.

28. Jerome, *NPNF*, 18.

29. Victorinus, *Comm. Rev.* (*ANF*) 14.15 (p. 357).

30. See also *Comm. Rev.* 1:15, where he says, "Because where they first of all stood and confirmed the Church, that is, in Judea, all the saints shall assemble together, and will worship their Lord." Victorinus, *Comm. Rev.* (*ANF*).

As it turns out, more than a century later, Jerome, the most vociferous of all kingdom deniers, went through Victorinus's book and edited it to conform to his beliefs! In his letter to Anatolius, Jerome writes that Victorinus's explanation of Revelation is "dangerous and opens to the barkings of detractors."[31] He admits to "erasing from there those things which he [Victorinus] perceived according to the letter."[32]

Jerome disliked Victorinus's kingdom interpretation so much that he *changed his book*, sanitizing it so that it would be suitable to his celestial sensibilities. He extinguished Victorinus's witness from the annals of history, snuffing it out like a candle.

Thankfully, both versions of Victorinus have survived, though the original is not very easy to get access to, owing to the fact it is locked away in a top-notch scholarly collection called *Source Chrétiennes*, containing the original Latin of both versions along with French translations by Martine Dulaey.[33] Back in 2006, Kevin P. Edgecomb, a keen Greek Orthodox seminary student, took it upon himself to offer good English translations of both versions on his website. The differences are staggering. For example, Victorinus writes,

> Therefore, however many were not previously to rise in the first
> resurrection and to reign with Christ over the world, over all
> nations, will rise at the last trumpet, after the thousand years,
> that is, in the last resurrection, among the impious and sinners
> and perpetrators of various kinds.[34]

Whereas in Jerome's edited version of Victorinus's work, the resurrection is a present reality for all Christians, in the original, the resurrection will occur at the end of the age, when Christ returns to reign with the saints over the world. Victorinus goes on to quote Isa 60, Dan 2, and 1 Cor 6, three of the strongest biblical texts teaching the future physical kingdom.[35] He continues to describe the reversal of fortunes in the kingdom, where those who have suffered will be rejoicing. Victorinus takes the Hebrew prophecies literally, believing the saints will receive gold and precious stones, serve God as priests, drink wine, and receive anointings.[36] Jerome's absurd ending, dis-

---

31. Jerome, *Letter to Anatolius*, in Edgecomb, "Victorinus: In Apocalypsin," para. 101.

32. Edgecomb, "Victorinus: In Apocalypsin," para. 101.

33. Dulaey, *Sur l'Apocalypse*.

34. Victorinus, *Comm Rev.* 20.2.

35. Victorinus, *Comm Rev.* 20.3.

36. Victorinus, *Comm Rev.* 20.5.

avowing the millennium, is completely missing from the original. Instead, Victorinus concludes with the words, "They will judge the world."[37]

The astonishing fact that Jerome expurgated Victorinus's work shows how disputed the kingdom came to be in the late fourth and early fifth centuries. Jerome must have known that Victorinus, a man of impeccable character and heroic memory, would influence others to retain the old kingdom idea, so he bowdlerized his work. Sadly, to this day, the most accessible version of Victorinus is the false one, and there are no footnotes indicating that anything is wrong with it.

Before continuing with Jerome, we need to look at one last kingdom defender, Lactantius (AD 240–320). Writing in the early part of the fourth century, Lactantius was an educated man with significant influence. The emperor Diocletian had appointed him as the official professor of rhetoric in Nicomedia. However, once Lactantius converted to Christianity, he resigned from his post shortly before Diocletian began severely persecuting Christians. After Constantine came to power and began favoring Christianity, Lactantius became an adviser and eventually a tutor to the emperor's son, Crispus.

As to the kingdom, Lactantius represented a rare combination of high education with a very traditional view of the age to come. He recognized the difference between the two comings of Christ, saying that the first time, Christ came "to announce to the nations the one God," and the second time, he comes "to reign."[38]

This is the perfect answer to the Jewish criticism that Jesus could not be the Messiah since he did not bring the kingdom. Lactantius recognized that Christ would return to fulfill his messianic role, so his lack of stereotypical messianic activity did not in any way defeat his claim. Lactantius looked to prophecies like Daniel's, which spoke of the Son of Man receiving a kingdom to reign over all nations without end. Although the anti-kingdom theologians typically claimed these types of prophecies had already found their fulfillment in the church, Lactantius recognized both the present and future aspects. Commenting on Dan 7, he writes,

> This is understood in two ways: that even now he has an everlasting dominion, when all nations and all languages adore his name, confess his majesty, follow his teaching, and imitate his goodness: he has power and glory, in that all tribes of the earth obey his precepts. And also, when he shall come again with majesty and glory to judge every soul, and to restore the

37. Victorinus, *Comm Rev.* 20.6.
38. Lactantius, *Inst.* 4.12.

> righteous to life, then he shall truly have the government of the
> whole earth: then, every evil having been removed from the af-
> fairs of men, a golden age (as the poets call it), that is, a time of
> righteousness and peace, will arise.[39]

Lactantius's nuanced understanding not only holds to the biblical teaching about the future kingdom, but also recognizes that Christ has already inaugurated his reign over those who voluntarily subject themselves to the way of the kingdom.

Lactantius also believed that after Jesus returns in judgment, he will raise the righteous to rule for a thousand years.[40] During this time he will bind the devil in chains, while regular people—those who happen to be alive when Christ returns but aren't believers—will not die but continue to have children until they become a multitude. At the end of the millennium, the final judgment will take place and God will plant his holy city in the middle of the Earth. Then, Lactantius says, in this eternal state, the sun will become brighter and the Earth will produce abundantly.

Here is how he describes the final condition of the Earth:

> The earth will open its fruitfulness, and bring forth most abun-
> dant fruits of its own accord; the rocky mountains shall drop
> with honey; streams of wine shall run down, and rivers flow
> with milk: in short, the world itself shall rejoice, and all nature
> exult, being rescued and set free from the dominion of evil and
> impiety, and guilt and error. Throughout this time beasts shall
> not be nourished by blood, nor birds by prey; but all things shall
> be peaceful and tranquil. Lions and calves shall stand together
> at the manger, the wolf shall not carry off the sheep, the hound
> shall not hunt for prey; hawks and eagles shall not injure; the
> infant shall play with serpents. . . . The earth shall be subject to
> God. . . . Therefore men will live a most tranquil life, abounding
> with resources, and will reign together with God; and the kings
> of the nations shall come from the ends of the earth with gifts
> and offerings, to adore and honor the great king, whose name
> shall be renowned and venerated by all the nations which shall
> be under heaven, and by the kings who shall rule on earth.[41]

Such a beautiful vision of the future hearkens back to the great Hebrew prophets like Isaiah and Amos, as well as other kingdom believers like Papias and Irenaeus. Lactantius, though late in time, sounds just like the early

---

39. Lactantius, *Inst.* 4.12.
40. Lactantius, *Inst.* 5.24.
41. Lactantius, *Inst.* 7.24 (p. 215).

Christians, who longed for an age when God will make everything wrong with the world right.

In the end, I came to see that those who believed, taught, and defended the kingdom comprised a considerable force in the first three hundred years of Christianity. Sadly, each successive century saw fewer and fewer of these kingdom believers. In the first century, John the Baptist, Jesus Christ, and his many followers all held to a belief in the coming kingdom as put forward by the Hebrew prophets. In the second century, a great majority of the Christian authors continued to write about the kingdom, even declaring that those who believe in going to heaven were heretics. However, the third century saw a reduction in kingdom teachers, until the fourth century came and only a couple of authors remained.

In the end, the deniers won the day, arguing that the old kingdom idea was too primitive, too hedonic, and too Jewish. Still, even as late as Jerome, who lived into the fifth century, we find evidence of a sizeable number of kingdom believers. In his *Commentary on Isaiah*, written between AD 406 and 416, Jerome admitted that his "spiritual" interpretation would "contradict the opinions of many earlier [interpreters]" and that in his own day he knew that his anti-kingdom approach would cause problems. He wrote, "I already perceive with foreboding that the anger of many will be aroused against me."[42] Thus, at the opening of the fifth century, even a man with Jerome's braggadocio worried how a substantial group of Christians would receive his book.

But even if scores of kingdom believers persisted into the fifth century, the church's view of the kingdom (at least in the West) was destined to rest upon the shoulders of one man. Easily the most influential Christian of the first five hundred years—apart from Jesus and Paul—Augustine of Hippo

---

42. Jerome, *Comm. Isa.* prologue to book 18, in Newman, "Jerome's Judaizers," 440. Here is the full quotation: "If we treat it spiritually, as it is written, we will be found to contradict the opinions of many earlier [interpreters]: from among the Latins, Tertullian, Victorinus, Lactantius; from among the Greeks, passing over others, I mention only Irenaeus bishop of Lyons, against whom a most eloquent man, Dionysius the bishop of the church of Alexandria, wrote a fine book mocking the tale of the millennium, as well as the golden and bejeweled earthly Jerusalem, the restoration of the temple, the blood of sacrifices, the idleness of the sabbath, the injury of circumcision, nuptials, childbirth, child-rearing, the delights of feasting, and the servitude of all nations, and once again wars, armies, and triumphs, and the slaughter of the vanquished, and the death of the hundred-year-old sinner [cf. Isa 65:20]. Apollinaris responded to him in two volumes, and he is followed not only by men of his own sect, but also by a great multitude of our own, at least in this matter, so that I already perceive with foreboding that the anger of many will be aroused against me. I do not envy them, if they love the earth so much, that they desire earthly things in the kingdom of Christ, and if after an abundance of foods and the gluttony of their gullet and belly, they seek that which is below the belly."

not only gave medieval theology its defining shape, but he also lived on in the minds of the most influential reformers of the 1500s.

Strangely enough, Augustine started out as a partial kingdom believer, but then changed his mind. Like several others before him, Augustine likened all of time to eight days. Since Christ came, he said, we've been on the sixth day, awaiting the Sabbath, when "the Lord will reign on earth with his saints"[43] for a thousand years. He also believed that on the eighth day, the world will return to the beginning: "For just as when seven days have passed, the eighth becomes the first [of a new week], so after the seven periods of this transitory world have been spent and completed, we shall return to that immortal blessedness from which man fell."[44]

It appears that Augustine, at this time in his life, thought the kingdom was only a temporary reign upon the Earth—until the saints could "return" to heaven. This view, though an unusual hybrid, is what many still believe today. It's a way to have the kingdom and heaven without picking a side. But Augustine was not content to straddle the fence. Over time, his allegorical interpretation technique enabled him to rethink even his millennial view. In his later (and much more influential) work, *City of God*, he writes,

> Those who . . . have suspected that the first resurrection is future and bodily, have been moved, among other things, specially by the number of a thousand years, as if it were a fit thing that the saints should thus enjoy a kind of Sabbath-rest during that period, a holy leisure after the labors of the six thousand years since man was created. . . . I myself, too, once held this opinion. . . . They who do believe them are called by the spiritual chiliasts.[45]

Augustine went from a partial kingdom believer to a kingdom denier. In the words of the translator Robert Wallis, "Augustine had now given the death-blow by his famous retraction."[46] Richard Landes summarizes the result:

> These closing years of the 4th century also marked a crucial moment in the history of millenarianism, since during this period Augustine repudiated even the allegorizing variety he himself had previously accepted. From this point on he dedicated much of his energy to ridding the church of this belief. Modern historians hold that he was so successful that millenarianism disappeared from Christianity for the eight centuries until Joachim

43. Augustine, *Seasons*, Sermon 259.

44. Augustine, *Seasons*.

45. Augustine, *Civ.* 20.7 (p. 426).

46. See Wallis's comment in endnote 4 of Victorinus, "Commentary on Revelation," 360.

of Fiore [twelfth century]. After Augustine "only cranks and heretics dared to put forward an eschatological [i.e., future] interpretation of the millennium."[47]

Now, Augustine's efforts to destroy the kingdom interpretation didn't mean that Christianity as a whole lost Christ's message completely. It remained present in the Scriptures whenever and wherever they were read, whether individually or publicly. Although we have slender evidence during the medieval period, we find several denouncements and controversies over this issue in both the Eastern[48] and Western[49] churches.

As Christians came to focus more on the saints—memorializing their deaths, venerating their relics, praying to them, and carving statues in their honor—questioning heaven as the abode of the righteous came to be seen not merely as unconventional, but disrespectful and even scandalous. After all, if the righteous are already in heaven, it's hard to see why the kingdom matters. However, if the righteous dead are "asleep," as Paul taught,[50] then the return of the Messiah to establish the kingdom on Earth moves to the very center of our hope.

Sadly, the Christendom of the Middle Ages obdurately clung to Augustine rather than Paul, even when challengers and Bible students defied the status quo. Alas, by the fourteenth century, Dante Alighieri could exegete the afterlife in painful and mind-numbing detail, enumerating the levels of hell, purgatory, and heaven in his *Divine Comedy*. Alighieri's literary masterpiece gave expression to the triple-decker geography of the afterlife that remains influential to this day.

We've ended our tour on a low note. But it's important to keep in mind that the story doesn't end here, in the murky dimness of the Middle Ages. Thankfully, three major unconnected movements over the last five hundred years have brought the kingdom back to the fore. We'll turn now to look at the great kingdom restorations of the Anabaptists, the Adventists, and New Testament scholars.

47. Landes, "Lest the Millennium," 156.

48. See the writings of Eustratios of Constantinople (6th century), Anasatasios of Sinai (8th century), John the Deacon (11th century), Niketas Stethatos (11th century), Philip Monotropos (11th century), and Michael Glykas (12th century). For a brief synopsis, see Constas, "To Sleep, Perchance to Dream," 95.

49. In 1312, Clement V decreed at the council of Vienne that anyone who diverged from his view of the soul was a heretic (Decree 1, second paragraph). Then, in 1513 at the Fifth Lateran Council, Leo agreed with Clement V, asserting unequivocally that the soul is immortal. These Roman Catholic declarations would not have occurred, had not others questioned the soul's inherent immortality.

50. 1 Cor 15:6, 18, 20, 51; 1 Thess 4:13–18.

11

Kingdom Found

It was coming to the end of class, and my church history professor was droning on and on. Eyes were heavy as we neared 10:30 a.m., when the class would finally come to an end.

Regardless of the boredom in the air, I was not the least bit tired; in fact, I was hyperattentive. I had seen on the class notes that the professor planned to talk about the Anabaptists.

I had a keen interest in this group of Christians from the sixteenth century. The Anabaptists advocated believers' baptism (as opposed to infant baptism), voluntary assemblies (as opposed to state churches), and radical obedience to Christ's teachings (as opposed to merely believing in him).

However, the closer we got to the end of our time, the more nervous I became. When there were only five minutes left, I said to myself, "Well, I guess he'll just have to cover the Anabaptists at the beginning of the next lecture since there's no time left." But then, with only two minutes left in the period, the teacher rushed through the Anabaptist movement, summarizing it with a few dismissive comments.

I sat in utter disbelief as students began getting up to leave the classroom all around me. The Anabaptists planted the seeds that later blossomed into religious freedom, especially in America, and they were only given two lousy minutes? And that's not all. The Anabaptists, as disorganized and bold as they were, also happened to be the ones who rediscovered the kingdom way back in the 1500s.

In this chapter we'll begin with the Anabaptists before looking at two more movements that likewise found the lost kingdom, the Adventists and the scholars.

During the Renaissance of the fourteenth to the sixteenth centuries, thinkers across Europe, disillusioned with the medieval accretions which had settled like dust over the classical world, wanted to scrape away the layers of traditions and get back to the sources. This desire affected a great many fields, including rhetoric, history, philosophy, architecture, and theology.

Applying these principles to Christianity meant forsaking the church's Latin translation for the original Hebrew and Greek of the Bible. This research had a profound result, not only because of how it shook people from their complacent confidence, but also because Johannes Gutenberg's printing press (1440) made mass distribution possible during this time.

A flurry of Bible translations followed. After Desiderius Erasmus printed the Greek New Testament (1516), Martin Luther produced a German translation in 1522, putting the sacred text of Scripture into the hands of the people in their own language. Later he managed to translate the Hebrew Scriptures, resulting, in 1534, in a complete German Bible. That same year, William Tyndale published the New Testament in English, instantly earning it a top spot on the Catholic Church's banned books list. Suddenly, a great many people no longer depended on the church to give them little bits of Scripture in carefully crafted homilies; instead, they could read large chunks of it for themselves without the church's filter.

Once the Bible came into the hands of the people, differing interpretations began to emerge, resulting in three broad approaches to Christianity: Roman Catholics, Protestants, and Radical Reformers. The first two continued the practice of working with and through the government, resulting in state churches. However, the Radical Reformers, especially the Anabaptists, generally believed in voluntary assembly and had little resistance to new biblical ideas.[1]

At the time, the main competitor to the kingdom was the idea of immediate judgment at the moment of death. With so many now reading the Scriptures in their own languages, it didn't take long before some Bible students began to question the medieval doctrines of the afterlife.

Luther had sparked the reformation by questioning the sale of indulgences—certificates purchased from the church to shorten how long someone endured purgatory before entering heaven. Indulgences only made sense alongside the belief in a conscious soul that survived death. As it turned out, both Luther and Tyndale came to question a conscious intermediate state in light of how the Bible talked about death and resurrection.

---

1. Apart from the Anabaptists, other groups also discovered the kingdom, including the Huguenots and the Bohemian Brethren.

Instead of heaven, hell, or purgatory at death, they came to believe the dead were asleep until the resurrection.

In commenting on Ecclesiastes, Luther writes,

> But the dead know nothing, and they have no more reward. Jerome has clumsily distorted this passage to apply to the reward of the dead in purgatory. Solomon seems to feel that the dead are asleep in such a way that they know nothing whatever. . . . But when Jerome raises the quibble that although the dead do not know anything of what goes on in the world, they do know other things, namely, those that go on in heaven, this is an error, and a foolish one at that. . . . The dead lie there without counting days or years; but when they are raised, it will seem to them that they have only slept for a moment.[2]

Likewise, Tyndale writes,

> *More:* Item, that all souls lie and sleep till doomsday.
> *Tyndale:* And ye, in putting them in heaven, hell, and purgatory, destroy the arguments wherewith Christ and Paul prove resurrection. What God doth with them, that shall we know when we come to them. The true faith putteth the resurrection, which we be warned to look for every hour. The heathen philosophers, denying that, did put that the souls did ever live. And the pope joineth the spiritual doctrine of Christ and the fleshly doctrine of the philosophers together; things so contrary that they cannot agree, no more than the spirit and the flesh do in a Christian man. . . . And again, if the souls be in heaven, tell me . . . , what cause is there of the resurrection?[3]

Should we be surprised that these two men, both of whom had spent countless hours reading the Bible, especially the New Testament, in their original languages, came to see the importance of resurrection over against the immortal soul? This is significant for our topic, because if the soul escapes the body to enjoy conscious heavenly bliss, the kingdom hope no longer matters much. Just like the moon blocks the sun in a solar eclipse, so an instantaneous afterlife hides the biblical hope. At best, heaven-at-death relegates the future kingdom to a mildly intriguing theological footnote.

But when we see death as no more than a temporary state of resting in peace, the focus moves from the moment of death to the coming of Christ, when he will resurrect the faithful, waking them up as he himself said:

2. Luther, *Luther's Works*, vol. 15, loc. 2760.
3. Tyndale, *Answer to Sir Thomas More's Dialogue*, 180.

> Do not marvel at this, for an hour is coming when all who are
> in the tombs will hear his voice and come out, those who have
> done good to the resurrection of life, and those who have done
> evil to the resurrection of judgment. (John 5:28–29)

What these two massively influential men discovered was simply this: "life after death conditional on the coming resurrection was the position of [the] New Testament," as George Williams puts it.[4] This revelation undermined then-pervasive Catholic Church doctrines like prayer to saints (most notably Mary), sale of indulgences, endowing of masses for the dead, and a great deal of spiritualism.

Although Luther and Tyndale made huge strides in the direction of the kingdom, the task of continuing down the path to find the biblical hope would fall to the Anabaptists.

Arising from conflict with the established church in Zürich, Switzerland, Anabaptists believed that regular people could read the Bible and put its teachings into practice. One of their first discoveries was that the Bible did not condone infant baptism, so they began baptizing adults, which resulted in their expulsion from the city. Undaunted, they carried on obeying the teachings of Jesus no matter what consequences came their way.

Once this group started reading their Bibles without "professional" guidance on what it was supposed to mean, discovering the return of Christ was inevitable. A number of Anabaptists began to fixate on the future coming of Christ as the momentous event of all human history, with a few even setting dates. They oriented their lives in light of Christ's return and made every effort to prepare themselves for his arrival on Earth.

Tragically, a horrific incident early in the movement's history would typecast Anabaptists for centuries to come. In the early 1500s in Münster, a subset of Anabaptists, spurred on by the prophetic splutterings of Melchior Hoffman, took over the city and went about establishing a utopia. It quickly descended into a dystopian nightmare, complete with polygamy, coercion, communism, and a final battle that left many dead.[5]

At this time, Protestants and Catholics, who were ensconced at the highest levels of government, took the Münster fiasco as a warning: if they tolerated Anabaptists in their territories, the same thing could happen. Suddenly, teaching about Christ's kingdom coming to Earth seemed subversive and dangerous, not only because it went against the reigning heaven-and-hell ideology, but also because it broke the magistrates' monopoly on power.

---

4. Williams, *Radical Reformation*, 65.

5. However, as Karl Kautsky pointed out, our information about this comes from the enemies of the Anabaptists who had a motive to justify their bloody sack of the city.

As Jerome smeared kingdom believers as Judaizers in the fifth century, now, a millennium later, mainstream Protestants condemned all Anabaptists as dangerous radicals for whom governments should have no compassion. While ironically, nearly all Anabaptists held to strict Christian pacifism, especially after Münster,[6] it didn't stop the powers that be—whether Catholic or Protestant—from persecuting them relentlessly, executing hundreds. Even this was not enough; the dominant mainstream Protestant denominations wanted to make sure their own people would not adopt this belief themselves, so they included denunciations about belief in the kingdom in their sixteenth-century confessions.

Here are a few examples:

> Augsburg Confession (1530)
> We condemn the Anabaptists who think the punishment of demons and those people whom God condemns will not last forever. We also condemn all others who are now spreading the Jewish idea that before the dead are raised, the godly will rule this world and everywhere the ungodly will be overcome.[7]

> 42 Articles of Religion (1552)
> They that go about to renew the fable of heretics called Millenarii are repugnant to Holy Scripture, and cast themselves headlong into Jewish dotage.[8]

> The Second Helvetic Confession (1566)
> We further condemn Jewish dreams that there will be a golden age on earth before the Day of Judgment, and that the pious, having subdued all their godless enemies, will possess all the kingdoms of the earth.[9]

Whereas Augustine and Jerome reduced the kingdom belief to a thousand-year reign upon the Earth at Christ's coming, these later polemicists only conceived of it as something that will occur before the coming of Christ. The result is a false dichotomy: either the righteous go to heaven at death or the righteous should conquer the ungodly and forcibly establish a Jewish kingdom on Earth now.

---

6. See the *Schleitheim Confession* of 1527.

7. Melancthon, *Unaltered Augsburg Confession*, Art. 17.4–5 (p. 9).

8. Article 41. The 42 articles were written under the direction of Thomas Cranmer during the short reign of Edward VI (Henry's sole male heir). Queen Elizabeth later revised the articles down to 39, omitting this one.

9. Bullinger, "Confessio Helvetica Posterior," 404.

The trouble with false dichotomies is that they hide the third option from view. Had anyone cared to read the Jewish Scriptures, they would have learned that the golden age predicted by the Hebrew prophets is to happen on the last day, when the Messiah comes.

It's alarming to see how the ghosts of fifth-century anti-kingdom rhetoricians continued to haunt the church, even a thousand years later. Once again, the kingdom was obscured and confused; once again, for believing what the Bible teaches, Christians were accused of being too Jewish.

Thankfully, as we'll see, this old polemic was finally turned on its head in the early twentieth century, but in the sixteenth, the accusation was still quite dangerous.

Although the Protestant Reformation made much headway in rolling back certain medieval innovations, they managed to miss the very gospel Jesus preached from town to town. As a whole, Protestantism diverged from Luther and Tyndale, returning to the old idea of an instantaneous afterlife at death.

For example, John Calvin (1509–64), perhaps the most influential Protestant of the sixteenth century, wasted no time in castigating and dismissing kingdom believers. In 1534 he wrote his first theological book, *Psychopannychia*, which called out the "dregs of Anabaptists" for their belief that at death the soul is asleep.[10] In his later work, *The Institutes of the Christian Religion*, Calvin not only rebuked his theological opponents because they "limited the reign of Christ to a thousand years," but he dismissed them by calling their position a "fiction too puerile to need or to deserve refutation."[11]

Calvin did not even consider, much less refute, the teaching of the Hebrew prophets, that paradise will be on Earth for God's people to enjoy forever. As the Anabaptist movement waned, leaving in its wake the Hutterites, Amish, Schwarzenau Brethren, and Mennonites, Christendom remained mostly united on heaven as the ultimate destination of God's people—until the Adventist movement of the nineteenth century burst onto the scene.

Although in the intervening three centuries between the Anabaptists and the Adventists, some believed in Christ's coming to establish God's kingdom, it's in the first half of the 1800s that disparate sparks set ablaze a fire that continues burning to this day.[12]

---

10. Calvin, *Psychopannychia*.

11. Calvin, *Institutes of the Christian Religion*, 657.

12. For example, Joseph Priestley (1733–1804) believed "We have no promise of any reward, or any threatening of punishment, after death, but that which is represented as taking place at the general resurrection." Priestley, *Corruptions of Christianity*, 132.

The religious climate of the nineteenth century was complicated. Although there had been a massive revival in America before the Revolutionary War, afterwards, American religiosity sank to a new low, with only 10 percent of the population formal members of any church.[13] The situation was much worse on the ever-expanding western frontier, where settlers moved out in such a hurry to stake their claims that they often encountered no Christian influence whatsoever. Lastly, among the educated, the Enlightenment was in full swing, resulting in severe skepticism towards miracles of any kind, not least the idea of Jesus physically returning to Earth. Many sophisticated Christians were leaving the faith for either rationalistic deism (the belief that God exists but is uninvolved in human affairs) or liberal universalism (the belief that everyone will be saved eventually regardless of belief or behavior).

Onto this dry and parched land fell the reviving waters of heaven in the form of camp meetings, especially in Kentucky. Initially led by the Presbyterian minister James McGready in Logan County in the spring of 1801, these gatherings included preaching, singing, and communion services over a single weekend. By August, revival of historic proportions broke out in Cane Ridge. Many thousands of people attended meetings, coming from Kentucky as well as the neighboring states. Barton Stone (1772–1844), one of the lead preachers there, writes about what it was like when he arrived.

> The roads were literally crowded with wagons, carriages, horsemen, and footmen, moving to the solemn camp. The sight was affecting. It was judged, by military men on the ground, that there were between twenty and thirty thousand collected. Four or five preachers were frequently speaking at the same time, in different parts of the encampment, without confusion. The Methodist and Baptist preachers aided in the work [alongside the Presbyterian organizers], and all appeared cordially united in it—of one mind and one soul, and the salvation of sinners seemed to be the great object of all.[14]

After six or seven days, when the Cane Ridge camp meetings ended, thousands of zealous new converts and reinvigorated believers went to their homes, eager to share the good news. This sparked both a revival in Christianity as well as interdenominational participation. Stone, for his part, dissolved his own presbytery in an effort to eliminate organizational divisions

---

13. Noll, *History of Christianity*, 166.

14. Stone and Rogers, *Biography*, 37–38.

and help Christians find unity.[15] Although this was not a new idea, Stone was able to popularize it, co-founding the Restoration Movement.

Stone and Alexander Campbell (1788–1866) urged people to cling to Scripture as their only standard rather than the human creeds and traditions which had caused so much division in Christianity. As a result of the tireless labors of these restorationists, early-1800s Christians throughout the United States took an interest in Bible study. Once people were eagerly reading their Bibles again, it wasn't long before they discovered the kingdom of God.

One such man was William Miller (1782–1849), the father of the Adventist movement. Raised in Low Hampton, New York, in a Baptist home, his parents taught him "to reverence the Scriptures as a revelation from God to man."[16] Later, he became a deist, believing that God was uninvolved in human affairs; but after miraculously surviving the battle of Plattsburg (1813), he returned to his Christian faith.

In response to the challenge of a friend, Miller set out on a two-year quest to lay aside his presuppositions and diligently compare Scripture with Scripture, starting in Genesis and continuing verse by verse, not moving on until he was satisfied with his understanding of each verse. In the course of this study, he discovered the kingdom. He wrote,

> I found it plainly taught in the Scriptures that Jesus Christ will again descend to this earth, coming in the clouds of heaven, in all the glory of his Father: that at his coming the kingdom and dominion under the whole heaven will be given to Him and the saints of the Most High, who will possess it for ever, even for ever and ever. . . . All the affairs of our present state would be wound up; that all its pride & power, pomp and vanity, wickedness and oppression would come to an end; and that in the place of the kingdoms of this world, the peaceful and long desired kingdom of the Messiah would be established under the whole heaven. . . . The glory of the Lord would be revealed, and all flesh see it together, the desert bud and blossom as the rose, the fir-tree come up instead of the thorn, and instead of the briar the myrtle-tree, the curse be removed from off the earth, death be destroyed, reward be given to the servants of God—the prophets and saints and them who fear his name, and those be destroyed that destroy the earth.[17]

15. See *The Last Will and Testament of the Springfield Presbytery.*

16. Miller, "Mr. Miller's Apology and Defence," 1.

17. Miller, "Mr. Miller's Apology and Defence," 2.

All it took was someone reading through Scripture—without overlaying it with the church's tradition—and he came away with the kingdom!

Miller's passion for the return of the Messiah led him to a tragic mistake; he calculated the timing of the end, concluding that Jesus would come back in 1843, some twenty-five years in the future. This prediction got the attention of a certain influential Boston pastor, Joshua Himes, who published a great deal of Miller's material, distributing his teaching about Christ's return far and wide across the United States. This Millerite Movement got the attention of tens of thousands of Americans. It brought the idea of Christ's return to the forefront of many peoples' minds. Some even sold their houses in the belief that they wouldn't need them once Christ returned.

It didn't happen. Miller's predicted date came and went, leaving disappointed Christians to figure out where they would go from here. Some of Miller's followers returned to traditional churches, while others gathered in Albany, New York, in 1845 to determine the future of the movement. Still others claimed the prediction date was right, but that it referred not to Christ's coming to Earth, but him entering a new stage of work in heaven.[18]

Out of the defunct Miller movement emerged Ellen G. White (The Seventh-Day Adventists), Jonathan Cummings (Advent Christian Church), John Thomas (Christadelphians), and Joseph Marsh (Church of God of the Abrahamic Faith). Although these groups continued to develop in their own directions, they all retained Miller's discovery about Jesus's second advent. To this day, they bear the label "Adventist."

Each of these groups, which are still present in our time, collectively represent only about 1 percent of Christianity. Our story does not end here, though. Another completely independent movement among sophisticated scholars at the turn of the twentieth century resulted in the same conclusions.

The third major kingdom movement began among liberal Protestant New Testament scholars in Germany.[19] At the close of the nineteenth century, some thought the kingdom of God was the present community of those who live by Christ's teaching of love, i.e., the church.[20] Others saw the kingdom in an individualistic sense: as God reigning in each believer's heart.[21] Into this milieu came Johannes Weiss, who initiated a quiet revo-

18. Hiram Edwon, quoted in Knight, *Seventh-Day Adventists*, 30.

19. For this section, I am indebted to the helpful book *The Kingdom of God in 20th-Century Interpretation*. Especially the first chapter: "The Discovery of the Eschatological Kingdom: Johannes Weiss and Albert Schweitzer."

20. The foremost example of this was Albert Ritschl (1822–89).

21. An example of this line of thinking was Wilhelm Herrmann (1846–1922).

lution in scholarship with his landmark work, *Jesus' Proclamation of the Kingdom of God* in 1892, when he was just twenty-nine years old. One of his observations was that "Jesus proclaimed the kingdom of God without generally defining this conception more closely for his hearers."[22] Although this may seem like a rather obvious fact, it allowed Weiss to import the various kingdom prophecies from the Old Testament into his understanding of the historical Jesus.

Weiss concluded,

> The kingdom of God as Jesus thought of it is never something subjective, inward, or spiritual, but is always the objective messianic kingdom, which usually is pictured as a territory into which one enters, or as a land in which one has a share, or as a treasure which comes down from heaven. . . . The land of Palestine will arise in a new and glorious splendor, forming the center of the new kingdom. Alien peoples will no longer rule over it, but will come to acknowledge God as Lord. There will be neither sadness nor sin; instead those who are in God's kingdom shall behold the living God, and serve him in eternal righteousness, innocence, and bliss. . . . Jesus and his faithful ones will rule over this newborn people of the twelve tribes, which will include even the Gentiles.[23]

Next came Albert Schweitzer in 1906 with his *Quest of the Historical Jesus*, in which he reviewed the various "lives of Jesus" books that had come out in the nineteenth century and condemned them for domesticating Jesus, producing a Jesus that looked suspiciously like a liberal nineteenth-century Protestant. Schweitzer thought Weiss was right, that Jesus really did believe the kingdom would be a real future apocalyptic event that would drastically and irreversibly change our world.

But here's the problem: whereas Weiss believed the Jewish leadership's rejection of Jesus postponed the coming of the kingdom, Schweitzer concluded Jesus was a heroic, but ultimately failed, prophet.[24] He wrote,

> There is silence all around. The Baptist appears, and cries: "Repent, for the kingdom of heaven is at hand." Soon after that comes Jesus, and in the knowledge that he is the coming Son of Man lays hold of the wheel of the world to set it moving on that last revolution which is to bring all ordinary history to a close. It refuses to turn, and he throws himself upon it. Then it does

22. Weiss, *Jesus' Proclamation*, 101.

23. Weiss, *Jesus' Proclamation*, 130–31, 33.

24. On Weiss's postponement theory, see Weiss, *Jesus' Proclamation*, 86–87.

turn; and crushes him. Instead of bringing in the eschatological conditions, he has destroyed them. The wheel rolls onward, and the mangled body of the one immeasurably great man, who was strong enough to think of himself as the spiritual ruler of mankind and to bend history to his purpose, is hanging upon it still. That is his victory and his reign.[25]

This conclusion is incredibly disappointing. It leaves the reader with a healthy admiration for Jesus, but nothing like historic Christianity. Schweitzer believed Jesus was an apocalyptic prophet who proclaimed the kingdom's arrival in his own lifetime but got it wrong.

Schweitzer's view still dominates much of historical Jesus scholarship today. But despite his popularity, his hypothesis had painted Jesus as a failed prophet.[26] As we might expect, it wasn't too long before Christian scholars reacted to his position in various ways.

One challenger who took the kingdom pendulum and swung it back the other way was C. H. Dodd. He could not accept the burgeoning consensus among scholars that Jesus wrongly prophesied a future event, so he parried with a theology that saw the kingdom as an entirely present reality.

"The kingdom of God," wrote Dodd in 1926, "means God reigning, reigning in the hearts of men, and reigning in the whole sphere of their outward life as well, individual and corporate."[27] Dodd thought of Jesus's sayings about the kingdom as "realized eschatology"—a future that is already reality. This is no small matter, for "Dodd was probably the most influential Anglo-Saxon NT scholar of the twentieth century."[28] Furthermore, he wasn't just inventing a theory out of whole cloth, he pointed to several kingdom texts, like when Jesus said, "But if it is by the Spirit of God that I cast out demons, then the kingdom of God has come upon you" (Matt 12:28) as proof that "the sovereign power of God has come into effective operation."[29]

Dodd's challenge to Weiss and Schweitzer wasn't widely accepted; most "agreed that he had a point, but overplayed it."[30] Nevertheless, he drew attention to the "kingdom now" sayings[31] in the New Testament and in so doing, paved the way for more moderating approaches.

---

25. Schweitzer, *Quest of the Historical Jesus*, 368–69.

26. Zarrella and Oppmann, "Pastor with 666 Tattoo"; Associated Press, "Miami Church."

27. Dodd, *Gospel in the New Testament*, 19.

28. Hiers, "Pivotal Reactions," 23.

29. Dodd, *Parables of the Kingdom*, 28.

30. Sanders, *Jesus and Judaism*, 131.

31. For "kingdom now" sayings, see Matt 12:28; Luke 16:16; 17:21; Rom 14:13; 1

Dodd reimagined the kingdom to be a present, but only spiritual, reality, and while his "kingdom now" theology successfully rescued Jesus from Schweitzer's failed prophet hypothesis, it did so only at the cost of losing the progress made towards recovering the Bible's teaching about the future kingdom.

Some scholars gravitated towards Dodd's approach because it was a way to save Christianity and retain Jesus's relevance. However, most of New Testament scholarship sailed right on with the apocalyptic prophet approach, which went hand in hand with naturalistic presuppositions in vogue at that time. Many historical Jesus scholars either dismissed miracles altogether or reinterpreted them as allegories or myths owing to their philosophical commitments. Sadly, this resulted in a rather awkward conclusion: on the one hand, scholars heartily affirmed that Jesus's kingdom was when "God was going to extend his rule from the heavenly realm . . . down here to earth," but on the other, they didn't believe one lick of it, because their worldview had already excluded miracles as a possibility.[32] After all, it's hard to believe that Christ is coming back to establish God's kingdom on Earth if the resurrection is merely a metaphor and his corpse is moldering in a grave somewhere. Without the resurrection, Jesus's atoning death collapses into a noble suicide and his "reign" reduces to little more than a positive example.

Other scholars, like the Lutheran pastor Dietrich Bonhoeffer and the Canadian Baptist professor George Eldon Ladd, incorporated the conclusions of these skeptical scholars into their more traditional approaches to Christianity. Ladd, in particular, was concerned that conservatives were not engaging with critical scholarship in general nor studying the kingdom in particular. His own work aimed to fill that gap, providing a conservative and critical treatment of the kingdom of God.[33] Ladd recognized that "the kingdom of God is a present spiritual reality" (Rom 14:17), while also seeing it as "an inheritance which God will bestow upon his people when Christ comes in glory."[34] Here is how he made sense of it:

> *Before the eschatological appearing of God's Kingdom at the end of the age, God's Kingdom has become dynamically active among men in Jesus' person and mission. The Kingdom in this age is not merely the abstract concept of God's universal rule to which men must submit: it is rather a dynamic power at work among*

Cor 4:20; Col 1:13.

32. Ehrman, *Jesus*, 143.

33. Ladd wanted to offer a non-dispensationalist approach to the whole topic of eschatology that also took into account the findings of critical scholarship.

34. Ladd, *Gospel of the Kingdom*, 16–17.

men. . . . The Kingdom of God involves two great moments: fulfillment within history, and consummation at the end of history.[35]

In this way, Ladd synthesized Weiss (future kingdom) and Dodd (present kingdom) into a package that recognized the truth of both, sometimes dubbed the "already-not yet" perspective.

In this view, the kingdom is already here, as Jesus reigns in the hearts and lives of his followers, but not yet here *en toto* until the consummation on the last day. Ladd influenced a generation of American pastors through his long tenure at Fuller Theological Seminary as well as his book *A Theology of the New Testament*. In 1986, one poll even dubbed Ladd "the most widely influential figure on the current generation of evangelical Bible scholars."[36] Unusually, since Ladd published in the scholarly world, he had a significant impact among critical scholars as well; through this man's influence, many Bible-believing scholars and pastors came to grasp the kingdom as both the biblical hope and a way of life.

At the turn of the twenty-first century, N. T. Wright emerged as a leading voice who, like Ladd, straddled the divide between skeptical and evangelical scholarship on Jesus. Deeply influenced by the work of both Schweitzer and Dodd, Wright has written extensively, both about Jesus's very real expectation of a coming kingdom as well as his own self-understanding as God's anointed one through whom God inaugurated that kingdom in three events: (1) the return from exile; (2) the defeat of evil; and (3) the return of God to Zion.[37] Wright has been on his own quest to challenge the old heaven ideology and replace it with kingdom language. He writes,

> When the New Testament speaks of God's kingdom it never, ever, refers to heaven pure and simple. It always refers to God's kingdom coming *on earth as in heaven,* as Jesus himself taught us to pray. We have slipped into the easygoing language of "the kingdom of heaven" in the sense of God's kingdom *being* "heaven," but the early church never spoke like that.[38]

While retaining the future aspect of God's kingdom as "the long-awaited rule of Israel's God on earth as in heaven," in his *Jesus and the Victory of God*

---

35. Ladd, *Presence of the Future*, 139, 218.

36. Noll, *Between Faith and Criticism*, 112.

37. Wright, *Jesus and the Victory*, 477.

38. Wright, "On Earth as in Heaven."

(1996), Wright boldly puts forward a historical case for Jesus's kingdom-conscious work.[39] He writes,

> Jesus . . . *believed that the kingdom was coming in and through his own work.* . . . Jesus saw himself as a prophet announcing and inaugurating the kingdom of YHWH; he believed himself to be Israel's true Messiah. . . . Jesus applied to himself the three central aspects of his own prophetic kingdom announcement.[40]

Wright, like Dodd before him, is easily the most influential Anglican scholar of his time. He's written more than seventy books, published his own eighteen-volume commentary on the New Testament, and produced nearly four thousand pages in his Christian Origins series alone.

Although Wright has done much to promulgate the biblical definition of the kingdom, he's also presented a rather muddled view of the intermediate state. He's uncomfortable both with Plato's immortal soul and the notion that the dead are unconscious. As a result, he tries to strike a middle position, where the dead are awake in some way, but their temporary status is not nearly as good as their lives will be when Jesus returns to resurrect his church. He has used the awkward phrase, "life after, life after death" to move the emphasis from what happens at death to the excitement of kingdom activity that will happen later.

Wright's unwillingness to give up a conscious intermediate state weakens his case for the kingdom's importance. The simple fact is that people care much more about what's next for them than what will happen one day long in the future. If a little girl asked, "Is my grandmother in heaven now looking down on me?" Wright would not say, "No, she's asleep in her tomb until Jesus comes to wake her," but rather would provide a weak affirmation, immediately followed by, "but that's not what's most important, the kingdom is." What if, instead, we told the little girl that she will see her grandma again when the kingdom comes? She would be driven to seek first the kingdom of God, rather than asking speculative questions about the state of the dead.

Even with his fuzzy intermediate state, Wright's contributions about the kingdom are still a breath of fresh air to countless professors, pastors, and pupils.

As a result of these three movements (the Anabaptists, Adventists, and scholars), the kingdom that once was lost has now been found. Time

39. N. T. Wright, "Imagining the Kingdom: Mission and Theology in Early Christianity," inaugural lecture delivered at University of St Andrews, St Mary's College, October 26, 2011.

40. Wright, *Jesus and the Victory*, 417, 612, 52 (italics in original).

would fail me to mention all of the excellent kingdom books written for popular audiences in the last thirty years. While many languish in medieval categories of thought, some popular preachers are now on board with the biblical kingdom, too. One positive example is the late Timothy Keller, the founder of a Presbyterian church in New York City. Though he's an heir to John Calvin and the various Reformed creeds that have splashed up in that stream over the last five hundred years, creeds that specifically condemn millenarian beliefs, Keller has completely embraced the kingdom. In a 2005 sermon, Keller said,

> In the future you have all these cultural activities going on. Why? Because our future is a material future. The book of Revelation makes it very clear. At the end of time, the end of history, we do not see us as individuals leaving the material world and going off into some ethereal realm, a disembodied spiritual realm. Instead we see the power of God coming down to cleanse and perfect this material world. So if you want to see the future of the human race, you look at Jesus after the resurrection when he had his absolutely perfect glorified body but he could eat a fish. You could put your hand through the nail prints and you could feel him. Now contrary to everything you've ever heard through Star Trek, the evolutionary future of the human race will not be balls of light or points of consciousness. We are going to hug and be hugged. We are literally going to eat, drink, and dance in the kingdom of God.[41]

This is such an impressive correction from the old idea of sitting on a cloud with a harp in an eternal sing-along. Keller's description is radically tactile and immensely interesting—a hope we can sink our teeth into, a hope that draws us forward and gives us something to live for.

Now that we've made it through twenty centuries of history, including how the kingdom was lost and then found again, it's time to take stock and ask the big questions about what this means for us today.

<hr>

41. Keller, "Culture," sermon given at the Redeemer Presbyterian Church in New York on October 30, 2005.

12

Ambassadors

IT IS TIME FOR us to take stock. We've seen how the writers of Scripture weave the golden thread of the kingdom from Genesis to the kings to the Prophets to the Psalms, right through the Gospels, Acts, and the Epistles to the last book of the Bible, where we find humanity on a renewed Earth, enjoying the presence of God. We've seen how the kingdom is not only God's vision for the future, but also the gospel Jesus tirelessly heralded from village to village—the same good news he commissioned his followers to carry far and wide, right up until the end of the age. It's a message that demands allegiance and total commitment from those who become kingdom citizens. We've seen how Christianity lost this precious truth owing to cultural, philosophical, and religious pressures, including that it seemed (1) too Jewish, (2) too crude, and (3) too hedonic.

Although these three reasons for rejecting the kingdom were compelling in antiquity, they no longer are today. On the first reason—that the kingdom is too Jewish—so much has changed. Owing to the work of several important New Testament scholars, notably E. P. Sanders, attempting to interpret Jesus as anything but a Jew today is tantamount to academic suicide. Wright explains:

> The Old Quest [to understand the historical Jesus] was determined that Jesus should look as little like a first-century Jew as possible. . . . The renewed "New Quest," following this line, has often played down the specifically Jewish features of Jesus, stressing instead those which he may have shared with other Mediterranean cultures. . . . The present "Third Quest," by and large, will

have none of this. Jesus must be understood as a comprehensible
and yet, so to speak, crucifiable first-century Jew.[1]

This new insistence on the Jewishness of Jesus has demolished the old
strategy of calling those who believe in the kingdom "Judaizers," as if they
were trying to make Christianity Jewish. Christianity is a tree with Jewish
roots (Rom 11:16–24). Not only the Hebrew Bible but most, if not all, of
the New Testament came from the children of Israel. Since the late twentieth century, anyone seeking to understand Jesus apart from his Jewishness
would suffer the ignominious accusations of, at best, ignorance, or at worst,
anti-Semitism.

The second reason why Christianity ultimately rejected the kingdom
is also archaic. Due to the cosmology inherited from Greek philosophy and
their assumption that perfection necessitated immutability, ancient people
thought the Earth was inherently inferior to the lights they observed in the
heavens and thus an unsuitable location for eternal life. However, in 1543,
when Nicolaus Copernicus published his landmark book, *On the Revolutions of the Celestial Spheres*, he showed that the Earth is not the center of the
universe. Still, Copernicus kept the stars in orbit around the sun, albeit the
farthest out, and labeled them *stellarum fixarum sphaera immobilis* "the unchanging sphere of fixed stars"; it wasn't until Galileo Galilei looked through
his telescope and observed the supernova of 1604 and sunspots in 1612 that
he definitively disproved the old idea that stars were unchanging, perfect
bodies. As astronomy continued to develop, the modern view of the cosmos
slowly came into view.

Now, the mere thought of an object that never changes is laughable,
regardless of how close or far away it is. We've learned that even the most
distant and seemingly stable objects in the sky are in constant flux, as ther-
monuclear fusion converts hydrogen to helium, radiating energy into space.
What is more, because scientists today understand how incredibly precise
conditions must be for life to exist, it's impossible to deny how incredibly
special Earth is. The list now includes over two hundred independent fac-
tors that all must coincide for a planet to support life. While the stars have
fallen from their privileged position at the pinnacle of cosmic hierarchy,
our own planet has risen to new heights of importance. In sum, not only do
scientists completely reject the old Greek models of the universe that put
the Earth on the bottom of the cosmic totem pole, but modern science has
elevated our world to the very zenith of all known cosmic bodies.

The last reason I discovered for rejecting Scripture's kingdom vision—
that it was too hedonic—applies least in our day. Ascetic sensibilities of the

---

1. Wright, *Jesus and the Victory*, 85–86.

Stoics, Jesuits, Puritans, and the Victorian era no longer feel compelling to most of us. We live in a liberated society that sees repressing one's desires as unhealthy. How different is this culture from theirs? Today, a commercial advertising a hard bed's lack of comfort would fail spectacularly, though many in antiquity would have considered such austerity a major selling point. Advertisements inundate us with messages about how we deserve to buy ourselves fancy chocolates or how the latest gadgets will make our lives easier and more enjoyable. We feel that a life with more leisure, more adventure, more pleasure is better. Whether we think of vacations, visiting the spa, or a million other ways to treat ourselves, our society is much more hedonic than ascetic in its orientation. Consequently, very few today would reject the kingdom hope on the grounds that it allows for the satisfaction of bodily pleasures.

So, the three reasons Christianity rejected the kingdom are no longer convincing. It would be difficult to find a single Christian who holds even one of them.

Where does that leave us now?

In the academy, whether among evangelicals or liberal scholars, New Testament professors and historical Jesus specialists know about the kingdom and how important it was to Jesus. However, in Christianity today, it's far from the dominant understanding. Attending any funeral can easily disabuse us of the notion that the scriptural hope has overtaken the old medieval categories. Obituaries routinely read along the lines, "She is now having a joyous reunion and dancing with her loved ones in Heaven."[2]

Even with all his influence through books, interviews, and viral videos, N. T. Wright laments his ineffectiveness to break through "the thick wall of traditional thought and language that most Christians put up."[3]

Currently only a minority of pastors, preachers, and teachers know about God's kingdom from a biblically grounded perspective—and very few know anything about the history of its loss or recovery. Among the few of us who do know about the kingdom, we are sometimes too timid to rock the boat. When we hear traditional language about heaven and hell, we wince and awkwardly remain silent. What can be done?

I'm convinced that the kingdom is *not* just another interesting doctrine to be checked off in classes for church membership or systematic theology. It's incredibly important—more like the meat of the sandwich than the bread; but if we're going to convey why the kingdom matters, thinking through some of the most compelling reasons is essential.

2. See "Geraldine T. Scharoun."
3. Wright, *For All the Saints?*, 21.

Firstly: Jesus said the kingdom matters. This point comes out loud and clear in his parables, specifically the sower, the treasure in the field, and the pearl of great price. Although many of us can recite the parable of the sower with its four soils—the path, the rocky ground, the thorns, and the good soil—we fail to notice what Jesus means by the seed. In fact, when Jesus explains the parable to his inner circle, he tells them the seed is "the word of the kingdom" (Matt 13:19). This drives the entire parable. It's not about how people respond to Jesus in general, or even to the Scriptures, but how they understand, accept, and hold fast to the message about the kingdom, the same kingdom that he and his disciples preached tirelessly throughout Galilee and Judea. Furthermore, he likens the kingdom to a man who finds a treasure hidden in a field who quickly covers it up and sells all of his possessions so he can buy the field (Matt 13:44). Jesus attaches so much value to the treasure that it is worth giving up everything else to acquire. Or, in his next parable, Jesus tells about a pearl merchant who sold everything just to acquire one fine pearl of great value (Matt 13:45–46).

How much clearer could he have been? Jesus wants his followers to value the kingdom as something so precious that in comparison, all of our possessions are accounted as expendable. Rather than fussing over what we eat or what clothes we wear, we should "seek first the kingdom of God and his righteousness" (Matt 6:33).

We dare not relativize or demote the kingdom in light of Jesus's clear statements on the matter. We should not say, "Oh, well, it's fine if they don't know about the kingdom. So long as they know that Jesus died for their sins, they'll be fine." Speaking this way is not only presumptuous, but outright contradicts the importance Jesus regularly attached to his message about God's kingdom. Who are we to change the gospel? Of course, understanding Jesus's death and resurrection is of paramount importance as well. Let's embrace a "both-and" approach rather than "either-or." The biblical gospel is about the kingdom *and* what the Messiah has done for us so we can enter into it.

Secondly, how could we possibly say we know Jesus if we don't understand the most significant fact about him—that he is the Messiah, the one destined to reign over the world in the age to come? To say, "I know Jesus," or "Jesus is all the world to me," or "Jesus is my everything" and not understand the most significant role God has assigned him, is as unthinkable as saying one is close friends with Elizabeth Windsor without knowing that she is the queen of England. For Elizabeth, being the queen is not just something she does occasionally, it is her very identity—the one role that far outshines everything else she does. If someone claimed to be friends with Elizabeth II and didn't know she was the queen, we would say that person didn't really know her. In the same way, knowing Christ entails knowing about his kingdom. It's what he talked about, what he manifested through his miracles, what he longed for, and what he is coming back to establish. We cannot possibly say that the core of Jesus's identity—his role in the kingdom as king—is disposable or trivial.

Additionally, we cannot understand the great overarching metanarrative of Scripture apart from the kingdom. Nancy Pearcey's outline of the four stages in redemption history includes creation, fall, redemption, and restoration.[4] The kingdom is that last stage, when God restores our world to its original, glorious, pre-fallen state, a work he has already begun in believers' lives as we allow his Spirit to transform us. It is the ultimate goal toward which the entire biblical narrative arc bends.

Losing sight of the kingdom is like blindfolding someone throwing darts. Would we expect good aim from a blindfolded person? No, aim depends on clearly seeing the target. The kingdom is that target—and as we've seen, it's not merely a future reality, but something that Christ has made available to experience in the present. It is not a peripheral biblical sub-theme, but the bullseye to which all of Scripture points, from Genesis to Revelation. The whole Bible explains what went wrong and how God has worked through creation to redeem and restore everything back to its original beauty and glory, with every creature in harmony with him and each other. That's the kingdom.

As we allow the kingdom to pull us towards it, we experience change in how we think and live. In a previous chapter, I mentioned the example of the Corinthian believers who were suing each other. Paul rebuked them with the words, "Do you not know that the saints will judge the world?" (1 Cor 6:2). If they are going to rule the world, shouldn't they act like it now—at least to some degree? He wanted them to figure out their own business issues rather than appealing to outsiders to make judgments for them.

Indeed, we should avoid the kinds of behaviors today that have no place in the kingdom age. But there's more to proleptic ethics than that. Having a clear vision of the future enables us to find fresh ways to embody the future in the present. For example, Jesus's commands about love—to love God, love our neighbors, love as he loved, and love our enemies—are all ways that we can anticipate the coming time, when God's love will permeate all of creation and harmony will reign supreme.

One intriguing example of this is RAWtools, Inc., a blacksmithing organization founded by Michael Martin based on the prophecy of Micah.

4. Pearcey, *Total Truth*, 49.

> They shall beat their swords into plowshares, and their spears
> into pruning hooks; nation shall not lift up sword against na-
> tion, neither shall they learn war anymore; but they shall sit ev-
> ery man under his vine and under his fig tree, and no one shall
> make them afraid. (Mic 4:3b–4a)

Martin's group collects guns, especially from urban areas, and literally beats them into garden tools in an effort to live out the future that Micah prophesied and help those affected by gun violence to heal.

They don't melt weapons down with the naïve assumption that doing so will provide a quick fix to the disturbing bloodshed all too common in America today, but to be true to their calling to shine as lights in a dark world by embodying God's beautiful tomorrow in the present. This example is just one way of allowing God's vision for our world to so infiltrate and woo our hearts that we find ways to prophetically live out wholeness and love in the midst of our cold, dark world.

The kingdom is our north star, but our moral compasses too easily read magnetic north rather than true north. We live in a fallen age, surrounded by people who are alienated from God and actively rebel against what he says is right. Isaiah's condemnation feels eerily relevant today:

> Woe to those who call evil good
> and good evil,
> who put darkness for light
> and light for darkness,
> who put bitter for sweet
> and sweet for bitter!
> Woe to those who are wise in their own eyes,
> and shrewd in their own sight! (Isa 5:20–21)

In such a context we can easily get confused about what is right and wrong. We need some way of finding true north, and this is precisely what the biblical teaching about the kingdom does for us. We look to the age to come and see a healed world, full of God's *shalom*—his peace, wholeness, and harmony—where sickness, suffering, and death are no more, where we are in right relationship with our God and each other. Once we get God's dream for our world crystal clear in our hearts, we can judge our own world by *that* standard and see what aligns with it and what is out of order. We can, like Jesus, reach out to the marginalized, sick, outcasts, and vulnerable.

Of course, we cannot solve all our world's problems; after all, Jesus himself said, "you always have the poor with you, and whenever you want, you can do good for them" (Mark 14:7). However, that's not our primary goal. Christ-followers have started hospitals, hospice services, homeless shelters, food pantries, anti-human trafficking agencies, medical missions, micro loans, and countless other advocacy efforts to help those in need. These are signs of the kingdom.

In other words, we are not results-oriented so much as prophetic-oriented. With our actions we prophesy a bright tomorrow, even while living amidst the chaos of a broken today.

The plague of AD 250 powerfully illustrates this idea. A deadly pandemic had broken out across the Roman Empire infecting thousands, perhaps even millions. Thousands died daily, afflicted with diarrhea, vomiting, burning eyes, loss of limbs, loss of hearing, and loss of sight.[5] Pontius, a deacon in the congregation at Carthage, noted how the city was littered with "no longer bodies, but the carcasses of many."[6] The stench of death must have been unbearable as the plague ravaged house after house. Dionysius, the pastor of the congregation at Alexandria, relates the following description:

> They pushed away those with the first signs of the disease and fled from their dearest. They even threw them half dead into the roads and treated unburied corpses like refuse in hopes of avoiding the plague of death, which, for all their efforts, was difficult to escape.[7]

But even as fear and panic shot through the hearts of the people, the Christians, in contrast, responded differently. Rather than abandoning their loved ones, they bravely cared for their own, making sure the sick had the necessary provisions and sanitation to get better. In the ancient world, nursing someone who is sick from a communicable disease was extremely risky. Dionysius goes on to tell us how severe it was:

> They would also take up the bodies of the saints, close their eyes, shut their mouths, and carry them on their shoulders. They would embrace them, wash and dress them in burial clothes, and soon receive the same services themselves.[8]

Undaunted by death, without putting their own well-being first, Christ-followers reached out to the dying pagans around them, as well. And Christian leaders urged their flocks to extend this love to even their enemies.

---

5. Cyprian, *Mort.* 14.

6. Pontius, *Vit. Cyp.* 9 (p. 270).

7. Eusebius, *Hist. eccl.* 7.22.7 (pp. 240–41).

8. Eusebius, *Hist. eccl.* 7.22.9, 7 (p. 240).

> Then afterwards he [Cyprian] subjoined, that there was noth-
> ing wonderful in our cherishing our own people only with the
> needed attentions of love, but that he might become perfect who
> would do something more than the publican or the heathen,
> who, overcoming evil with good, and practicing a clemency
> which was like the divine clemency, loved even his enemies,
> who would pray for the salvation of those that persecute him, as
> the Lord admonishes and exhorts.[9]

At great personal risk, our Christian brothers and sisters reached out to the infected pagans and nursed them back to health or, failing that, they provided care in the last moments along with an honorable burial. Although believers died in great numbers, their fellow brothers and sisters regarded them fortunate to have given their lives on behalf of others. They were even considered martyrs! Now, some may criticize such self-sacrificial love, practiced in such a risky and costly way, for its lack of effectiveness in ending the plague—or for how it endangered the Christian community. As it turned out, however, this pestilence coincided with one of the greatest periods of growth for third-century Christianity. After their families abandoned them, how eager would the sick have been to hear the gospel when Christians scooped them off the streets and nursed them back to health? Of course, converting the pagans wasn't the primary motivation, but nonetheless, it happened.

In addition to caring for people, the kingdom likewise predisposes us to care for our world. After all, if the Earth is our permanent home, it only makes sense to steward it well. Now, to be clear, the biblical view does not elevate nature over humanity, but it does teach that we humans are God's agents appointed to manage creation. God has given us dominion "over the fish of the sea and over the birds of the heavens and over the livestock and over all the earth and over every creeping thing that creeps on the earth" (Gen 1:26). According to our original mandate, we are to govern and care for creation.

How should we manage this world? I suggest that we ask the question, "How will Christ run things in the kingdom?" as a starting point.

Now, if we believe Jesus is coming back in our lifetimes to whisk us off to heaven then we are not going to give a thought to creation care.[10] However, if we believe this is God's good world that he put us in charge of, both

---

9. Pontius, *Vit. Cyp.* 9 (p. 270).

10. For a popular expression of this sentiment, see the song "I'll Fly Away" by Albert E. Brumley.

now and in the age to come, then we will likely steward our little corners of it in a more responsible and more godly manner.

One last example of how an accurate understanding of the kingdom affects us today relates to tribalism—an all too prevalent feature of our polarized society. Greg Lukianoff and Jonathan Haidt describe how this mindset works in their *Coddling of the American Mind:*

> When the "tribe switch" is activated, we bind ourselves more tightly to the group, we embrace and defend the group's moral matrix, and we stop thinking for ourselves. . . . In tribal mode, we seem to go blind to arguments and information that challenge our team's narrative. . . . Any kind of intergroup conflict (real or perceived) immediately turns tribalism up, making people highly attentive to signs that reveal which team another person is on. Traitors are punished, and fraternizing with the enemy is, too. . . . What happens when you train students to see others—and themselves—as members of distinct groups defined by race, gender, and other socially significant factors, and you tell them that those groups are eternally engaged in a zero-sum conflict over status and resources?[11]

Lukianoff and Haidt focus on college campuses, but this phenomenon has permeated vast swaths of Western society today. In contrast, the biblical vision of the kingdom militates against hyperpolarization based on traditional identity markers. For example, the last book of the Bible portrays an age of peace, wholeness, and diversity, when Christ makes people "from every tribe and language and people and nation, . . . a kingdom and priests to our God, and they shall reign on the earth" (Rev 5:9–10). In Christ, old boundaries dissolve as God invites disparate groups in to become his children. Thus, a kingdom-focused Christianity welcomes people across tribal, linguistic, ethnic, and national boundaries.

From the divisive councils of the fourth and fifth centuries, to the crusades and inquisitions, to African chattel slavery in America, to the xenophobia of the war on terror, to the extreme polarization between Democrats and Republicans today, we have repeatedly failed to embody kingdom unity among ourselves, much less the watching world. I can't help but wonder how church history would be different if we had not lost the kingdom message so long ago.

Furthermore, the kingdom hope can help us in relating to those outside of Christianity. Rather than looking at Muslims, Hindus, or atheists as enemies to fight, we can see them as potential members of God's kingdom

---

11. Lukianoff and Haidt, *American Mind,* 58–59.

family. After all, God wants male and female, black and white, rich and poor, Western and Eastern, city and country, Republican and Democrat, gay and straight, atheist and agnostic people to be with him forever. Simply put, God does not want that "any should perish, but that all should reach repentance" (2 Pet 3:9).

Unlike so many other social adhesives, kingdom Christianity has the glue necessary to bind together diverse people around a common identity, without requiring them to abandon their unique cultures and mindsets. One can be a same-sex-attracted Christian, a Chinese Christian, a lumberjack Christian, or an ex-convict Christian so long as one puts allegiance to Christ the king above his or her own desires. As Jesus comes to reign over every aspect of life, old identities and boundary markers become relativized in light of the new reality. This makes possible new partnerships, relationships, and cooperation across old barriers.

The kingdom age is when diversity and unity will finally reach a harmonious balance—where individuality and commonality will lay down their weapons and recognize the value each has to offer.

To summarize, believing in the kingdom clarifies and motivates our response to the hope of Christ's return. It helps us understand Jesus's identity, message, and ministry—not to mention his present and future roles. The kingdom is the critical target toward which all biblical theology points. It is the climax of the meta-narrative, the dénouement of the great drama of human history. It not only motivates human flourishing, but it also inspires prophetic and meaningful lifestyles that embody the future in the present. It calibrates our moral compasses so we can figure out what's right and wrong in our own lives. It produces in its citizens a sense of ownership of our world, resulting in creation care since Earth is our lasting home, rather than a temporary way station. Lastly, it has the prosocial power to either demolish or relativize identities that enable tribalism and divisiveness. In short, the kingdom changes everything!

But we lose out on all of these benefits the moment we allow "heaven-at-death" to eclipse the Bible's grand vision of the kingdom. The time is ripe for a paradigm shift on this important subject. We know that God's plan is to spread this gospel over the whole world as a testimony to all nations before the end comes. Many of us have seen this truth and allowed it, like a mustard seed, to grow within our own hearts and take over. But how many of us have stopped short of telling our friends, coworkers, pastors, or family members? We nod our heads and mouth the words when the heaven lyrics blare out during worship on Sundays, rather than having that hard conversation with the music team. We smile and nod at funerals, when Mrs. Smith is put in heaven and only her "mortal coil" remains behind for us to bury.

We sit passively while the preacher blithely equates the "kingdom of heaven" with "heaven" and makes up all kinds of fancies about what heaven is supposed to be like. We look on the bright side when we see countless tracts printed that tell people half the gospel and then promise them a cartoonish fate fit for children's stories. Should we remain silent?

Isaac Asimov, the prolific science fiction author, serves as a premium example of what happens when we remain silent. He masterfully expresses how flaccid the traditional heaven gospel sounds to many.

> Imagination has never managed to build up a serviceable Heaven. . . . The Islamic Heaven has its *houris*, ever available and ever virginal, so that it becomes an eternal sex house. The Norse Heaven has its heroes feasting at Valhalla and fighting each other between feasts, so that it becomes an eternal restaurant and battlefield. And our own Heaven is usually pictured as a place where everyone has wings and plunks a harp in order to sing unending hymns of praise to God.
>
> What human being with a modicum of intelligence could stand any of such Heavens, or the others that people have invented, for very long? Where is there a Heaven with an opportunity for reading, for writing, for exploring, for interesting conversation, for scientific investigation? I never heard of one.
>
> If you read John Milton's *Paradise Lost*, you will find that his Heaven is described as an eternal sing-along of praise to God. It is no wonder that one-third of the angels rebelled. When they were cast down in Hell they *then* engaged in intellectual exercises (read the poem if you don't believe me) and I believe that, Hell or not, they were better off. When I read it, I sympathized strongly with Milton's Satan and considered him the hero of the epic, whether Milton intended that or not.
>
> . . . There is nothing frightening about an eternal dreamless sleep. Surely it is better than eternal torment in Hell or eternal boredom in Heaven.[12]

Asimov wants to read, write, explore, have interesting conversations, and perform scientific investigations. He thinks the traditional myths about the afterlife are too one-dimensional—reducing eternity to sex, warfare, eating, or singing. He's right. Before long, any of these "heavens" would become tedious. Asimov wants variety, where he can go on expeditions, produce creative works, and engage with others who have different perspectives.

In short, Asimov, the atheist, wants the kingdom of God.

---

12. Asimov, *I. Asimov*, 108.

When he looked within his own heart at his deepest longings, what did he find? He discovered the very future our creator intends to bring about on Earth. The tragedy is that no one ever told him about the Bible's core message. Having written more than five hundred books and tens of thousands of letters, Asimov died in 1992, an atheist without hope.

What if someone had directed this brilliant man to Isaiah or Daniel? What if he had seen the grand visions of Amos or Micah? Would that have made a difference? Would the biblical hope have wooed him, or would he have remained resolute in his atheism?

Of course, questions like these are impossible to answer now, but how many Asimovs are out there today? These are intelligent people who are looking for something real to sink their teeth into; people who will not find satisfaction in tales of disembodied bliss.

How can we sit comfortably, marveling at the priceless pearl and say nothing to the others who have inherited costume jewelry from their pastors, Sunday school teachers, and TV preachers? Can we buy the field and take possession of the treasure but close our mouths to our fellow sisters and brothers while they search field after field with their broken metal detectors?

Even worse, most are not even aware that they are supposed to be seeking kingdom pearls and treasures. Instead, they stay home and contentedly sing hymns like "This World Is Not My Home," which teaches that heaven is our home.[13] Heaven is *not* our home! We were not born there; we do not live there; we will not move there one day. This world *is* our home even if it remains, to a great degree, enemy-occupied territory. We, like Abraham before us, look for a city whose designer and builder is God (Heb 11:10).

Jesus himself said, "And this gospel of the kingdom will be proclaimed throughout the whole world as a testimony to all nations, and then the end will come" (Matt 24:14). We know that this is his plan and, as such, will happen with or without us. The question is: will I get on board with his plan, or let others do the work?

13. Reeves, "This World Is Not My Home."

Appendix 1

Has the Kingdom Already Come?

Throughout this book, I have laid out a positive case for a well-rounded understanding of God's kingdom, how this precious truth was lost, and how by God's grace we found it again. I realize some may have this or that verse rattling around in the back of their minds. "What about 'absent from the body and present with the Lord,' or 'the kingdom is within you'?" Of course, I cannot in these little appendices answer every objection or anticipate every challenge, but I can at least outline some thoughts on a few of the most misunderstood texts in an effort to relieve the reader of lingering doubts.

THE KINGDOM IS WITHIN YOU (LUKE 17:21)

Sometimes people combat the idea of an external, future kingdom by quoting Jesus's statement "the kingdom of God is within you." I typically only hear this phrase from those who prefer older translations, like the King James Version or the New King James Version. In virtually all modern translations, the words are either "in the midst of you" or "among you," but not a single one of them says "within you." Here is the text from the English Standard Version:

> Being asked by the Pharisees when the kingdom of God would come, he answered them, "The kingdom of God is not coming in ways that can be observed, nor will they say, 'Look, here it is!' or 'There!' for behold, the kingdom of God is in the midst of you." (Luke 17:20–21)

Now, the words "in the midst" are from the Greek word ἐντὸς *(entos)*, which can certainly mean "within." However, as Albert Nolan points out, "In the present context to translate it 'within' would mean that in answer to the Pharisees' question about when the kingdom of God would come (17:20) Jesus told them that the kingdom of God was within *them!*"[1]

Needless to say, this translation would contradict so much of what Jesus says about the Pharisees elsewhere. Jesus is either telling the Pharisees that one day they will wake up to discover the kingdom has suddenly arrived in their midst or that Jesus himself *is* the kingdom. In other words, Jesus, as the Messiah, is the chief ambassador, who represents the kingdom wherever he goes. Thus, seeing Jesus in action is seeing the kingdom.

THIS GENERATION WILL NOT PASS AWAY (MATT 24:34)

In his Olivet Discourse, Jesus spoke about stars falling from heaven and the appearing of the sign of the Son of Man. He told his disciples that the angels would come forth with a trumpet call and gather his elect from the four winds. Then he says,

> From the fig tree learn its lesson: as soon as its branch becomes tender and puts out its leaves, you know that summer is near. So also, when you see all these things, you know that he is near, at the very gates. Truly, I say to you, this generation will not pass away until all these things take place. (Matt 24:32–34)

In this section, Jesus says that "this generation" will still be on earth when the events that he's describing occur. What do the words "this generation" mean? How can they help us make sense of this prophecy?

Three options for understanding the phrase "this generation" include (1) the time of his original apostles, in which case "all these things" have already occurred twenty centuries ago; (2) "this generation" refers to this race or kind of people; and (3) "this generation" applies to the future generation living when the abomination of desolation stands in the holy place. Let's work through each of these in turn.

Option one is to understand Jesus's statement as directed to the people standing before him. From a historical perspective, this is easily the most natural way to take the phrase, "this generation." Jesus's disciples had asked about the temple and he told them it would be destroyed. By telling them it would happen within their own generation, Christ prepared them for a

---

1. Nolan, *Jesus before Christianity*, 58–59.

coming cataclysm of events that not only ended thousands of lives, but also the Jewish temple sacrificial system.

Two ways of thinking about this are to see this preterist approach as either (1) that all the events Jesus mentioned found fulfillment, or (2) that some of them happened, while others still await future realization. Many Christians find the full preterist view of the Olivet Discourse troubling because it posits not only that the abomination of desolation and great tribulation occurred long ago, but that the coming of the Son of Man and the gathering together of the elect did, as well. If all these events have already come to pass, then where is the kingdom today?

I have been to Jerusalem and it is not a city ruled by King Jesus. In fact, Christianity is a minority in Israel today, making up only about 2 percent of the population. If the Son of Man has come and the kingdom has been established, what happened?

Sadly, some who have taken this view regard Jesus as a false prophet. Others perceive a break between the destruction of the temple and the coming of the Son of Man. In this view, the events of AD 70 relate to the final events that will occur when Christ comes, but are not the final fulfilment of those events. Darrell Bock explains,

> In Jesus's view, the events of A.D. 70 and the end-time are inseparably linked, so that the fall of Jerusalem guarantees the completion of the other event. . . . [T]he end has begun with events leading to the fall. . . . Jesus is saying that this group of disciples will experience the catastrophe of A.D. 70 within their lifetime, an event that itself pictures the beginning of end-time events. As such, experiencing the fall in A.D. 70 is as good as experiencing the end, because one event pictures, guarantees, and reflects the others.[2]

Thus, in this first perspective, the prophecy of Jesus mirrors the events of the future but is merely a partial fulfillment of what is to come.

The second overall option is to understand Jesus's phrase "this generation" to mean "this type of people." The word γενεά (*genea*) means not only "a generation" but also "a race" or "kind." The standard lexicon for New Testament Greek includes a definition for *genea* as "those exhibiting common characteristics or interests, race, kind."[3] Three subvarieties of this view include defining "this kind" as Jewish people, humanity at large, or rebellious unbelievers. If we take the last possibility, Jesus is saying that this type of unbelieving generation will not pass away until the consummation of the

2. Bock, *Luke*, 1691.

3. Bauer et al., *BDAG*, c.v. "Genea."

kingdom occurs. This reading is rather like Jesus's statement, "The poor you always have with you" (John 12:8). However successful the disciples and their heirs are, the unbelievers "you always have with you" until Christ returns.

Lastly, Jesus could have meant "this generation" to apply not to the generation standing before him, but to the future generation that sees the abomination of desolation set up in the temple. The sense then is that once the great tribulation begins, everything will proceed quickly right up through the coming of the Son of Man and the gathering of the elect—all within one generation.

We may question how Jesus could be talking to a particular generation and say to them "this generation" without referring to them. Once again, Bock is helpful here:

> The main objection to this view is that γενεά [*genea*] usually re-
> fers to the present generation, rather than to a deferred genera-
> tion, a correct point. Nonetheless, in the discourse's prophetic
> context, the remark comes after making comments about the
> nearness of the end to certain signs. As such it is the issue of the
> signs that controls the passage's force, making this view likely.[4]

Just prior to saying "this generation will not pass away until all these things take place," Jesus had remarked about a fig tree. Observant people know that summer is near when they see fig tree branches putting out leaves. So it is with those who see all these things. What things? He had mentioned the abomination of desolation, the great tribulation, and the visible coming of the Son of Man in the clouds. The immediate context, therefore, is not necessarily those standing before him, but the generation that sees all these signs. This third option seems the most convincing to me.

However, I wonder if somehow options one and three could both be right. Could it be that Jesus intentionally spoke in such a way that his words applied to both his immediate audience as well as his ultimate audience way off in the future? Perhaps Jesus grouped the two periods together because of their similarity in content, not their synchronicity in timing. Craig Keener puts it this way:

> Old Testament prophets often grouped events together by their
> topic rather than their chronology, and in this discourse, Jesus
> does the same. He addresses what are grammatically two sepa-
> rate questions: the time of the temple's destruction and the time
> of the end.[5]

---

4. Bock, *Luke*, 1692 (emphasis in original).

5. Keener, *IVP Bible Background Commentary*, 111–12.

We have reports from later historical sources that say the Christians of the first century took Jesus's words to heart. When the Roman army marched on Jerusalem, the Christians escaped rather than fighting. This spared them the staggering horrors of starvation, crucifixion, and death that Josephus describes in gory detail in his *The Jewish War*. Still, the Son of Man has yet to return, so we remain vigilant, watching and waiting for him to come back.

NOT DIE BEFORE SEEING THE SON OF MAN COMING (MATT 16:28)

Just before the transfiguration in Matthew, Mark, and Luke, we find Jesus making a puzzling statement about the timing of the kingdom's arrival. In fact, it sounds like a guarantee that at least some of the disciples would live to see the kingdom consummated.

> Truly, I say to you, there are some standing here who will not taste death until they see the Son of Man coming in his kingdom. (Matt 16:28)

Four interpretive options come to mind: (1) Jesus believed the Son of Man (either himself or someone else) would soon arrive and got it wrong; (2) Jesus predicted the kingdom's imminent arrival and fulfilled it spiritually (perhaps on Pentecost); (3) The kingdom really was going to come within their lifetimes, but got postponed because the leaders of Israel rejected Jesus as Messiah; or (4) Jesus referred to a vision of the kingdom his disciples would soon experience at the mount of transfiguration.

As a Christ-follower, I find position one utterly untenable because it leaves me with Jesus as a false prophet. In light of the rock-solid evidence favoring the historicity of Jesus's resurrection, it is particularly unconvincing. The second position is possible from this text, but it strongly contradicts so much of the tactile language the Scriptures use to speak about the kingdom, not to mention its political dimension. The third option is intriguing since it makes Jesus's prophecy conditional, like Jonah's proclamation of doom to Nineveh, but seems like a stretch in the absence of any explicit texts that mention postponement.

I lean toward the fourth view, that Jesus's transfiguration was a vision of the kingdom. Let's consider what the text says:

> And after six days Jesus took with him Peter and James, and John his brother, and led them up a high mountain by themselves. And he was transfigured before them, and his face shone like the sun, and his clothes became white as light. And behold,

> there appeared to them Moses and Elijah, talking with him. And Peter said to Jesus, "Lord, it is good that we are here. If you wish, I will make three tents here, one for you and one for Moses and one for Elijah." He was still speaking when, behold, a bright cloud overshadowed them, and a voice from the cloud said, "This is my beloved Son, with whom I am well pleased; listen to him." When the disciples heard this, they fell on their faces and were terrified. But Jesus came and touched them, saying, "Rise, and have no fear." And when they lifted up their eyes, they saw no one but Jesus only. And as they were coming down the mountain, Jesus commanded them, "Tell no one the vision, until the Son of Man is raised from the dead." (Matt 17:1–9)

Although some have suggested this incident involved the actual Moses and Elijah, we know from verse 9 that it was, in fact, a "vision," not a historical event. Peter, James, and John saw it, but we should not press it too hard for historical details. They saw the glorified and exalted Jesus with his face shining like the sun and his clothes white as light. (This description aligns quite well with the returning Christ in Rev 19.) They did see Moses and Elijah, but in their future resurrected bodies.

This, then, was a snapshot of the age to come, when Jesus, Moses, Elijah, and all the saints will enjoy conversation and fellowship one with another. The aims of the vision then were twofold: (1) to convince Jesus's inner circle that he truly was the Messiah who will receive glory in the age to come; and (2) to impress upon the disciples that they should listen to what Jesus has to say—trust him. They would soon go through tragedy, as Jesus's enemies seemingly outmaneuvered and then tortured and executed him. Certainly they needed encouragement at this juncture to make it through the dark times ahead.

Later, Peter refers back to the transfiguration:

> For when he received honor and glory from God the Father, and the voice was borne to him by the Majestic Glory, "This is my beloved Son, with whom I am well pleased," we ourselves heard this very voice borne from heaven, for we were with him on the holy mountain. And we have the prophetic word more fully confirmed, to which you will do well to pay attention as to a lamp shining in a dark place, until the day dawns and the morning star rises in your hearts. (2 Pet 1:17–19)

The words "honor and glory" are probably kingdom terminology. For example, in Daniel's vision of the Son of Man, he wrote, "to him was given dominion and glory and a kingdom" (Dan 7:14). What is the Messiah's glory and honor? Is it not to rule and reign over God's kingdom in the age to come? The writing of 2 Peter occurred many years after the transfiguration—still, after such a lengthy period of reflection, the takeaway is clear: the mount of transfiguration authenticated Jesus's identity as God's Son, which, in turn, should make us take the prophetic word seriously. Thus, Jesus's claim that some there would not die before the Son of Man came in glory found its fulfillment when three of the apostles experienced the transfiguration.

Appendix 2

Is the Kingdom in Heaven?

IN ADDITION TO THE three texts mentioned in Appendix 1, Bible readers often misinterpret three Scriptures: Phil 3:20, John 14:2, and John 18:36. As we saw from a myriad of texts in both the Old and New Testaments, the ultimate destination of the righteous is the earth, healed and renewed. However, many Christians, even Bible-believing ones, continue to locate the realm of ultimate redemption off-world in heaven, pointing to these three texts as evidence that the kingdom of heaven is in heaven.

CITIZENS OF HEAVEN (PHIL 3:20)

Heaven is the storehouse. It is where Jesus told his followers to lay up treasures, "where neither moth nor rust destroys and where thieves do not break in and steal" (Matt 6:20). Even so, that doesn't mean we need to relocate to heaven to get our reward. That would be like retiring and moving into the bank! No, we empty out what we've stored up to use it on earth. We store up our good deeds in heaven; then, when Jesus comes, he will reward us appropriately. Nevertheless, some get confused by this text about citizenship:

> But our citizenship is in heaven, and from it we await a Savior,
> the Lord Jesus Christ. (Phil 3:20)

Citizenship was important in the Roman empire, especially in a Roman colony like Philippi. N. T. Wright explains:

> "We are citizens of heaven," Paul declares in verse 20. At once many modern Christians misunderstand what he means. We

naturally suppose he means "and so we're waiting until we can go and live in heaven where we belong." But that's not what he says, and it's certainly not what he means. If someone in Philippi said, "We are citizens of Rome," they certainly wouldn't mean "so we're looking forward to going to live there." Being a colony works the other way round. The last thing the emperors wanted was a whole lot of colonists coming back to Rome. The capital was already overcrowded and underemployed. No: the task of the Roman citizen in a place like Philippi was to bring Roman culture and rule to northern Greece, to expand Roman influence there.[1]

Our citizenship is in heaven presently, reserved with Christ until he comes. In the meantime, we are heaven's ambassadors, commissioned to give the world a foretaste of what is to come. Then, when Christ returns, he will fully enact our role as citizens within his kingdom as he extends God's rule to earth as it is already in heaven.

I GO AND PREPARE A PLACE FOR YOU (JOHN 14:2)

During the upper room discourse in John 14–16, Jesus spoke about going to prepare a place for his disciples. Many have interpreted this to mean that Jesus would go to heaven to prepare living areas for his followers to go to at their death. Here is the text:

> Let not your hearts be troubled. Believe in God; believe also in me. In my Father's house are many rooms. If it were not so, would I have told you that I go to prepare a place for you? And if I go and prepare a place for you, I will come again and will take you to myself, that where I am you may be also. And you know the way to where I am going. (John 14:1–4)

If we assume this text refers to going to heaven, we are left with a couple of questions. Do we believe Jesus is leading the housekeeping staff of his Father's house, preparing rooms for guests? Should we think Jesus returns every time believers die as a personal valet to conduct each soul to their new home? Surely another interpretation can make better sense of these verses in the context of the upper room discourse.

Jesus's focus throughout this section is preparing his disciples for his departure. He knows that he is going to be leaving them soon, and he wants to prepare them for their next phase of life. He is not going to abandon them

1. Wright, *Paul for Everyone*, 126.

as orphans, but via the spirit of truth, or advocate, he will come to them. With this in mind, let's proceed to Thomas's follow up question and Jesus's response:

> Thomas said to him, "Lord, we do not know where you are going. How can we know the way?" Jesus said to him, "I am the way, and the truth, and the life. No one comes to the Father except through me. If you had known me, you would have known my Father also. From now on you do know him and have seen him." (John 14:5–7)

Like many Christians today, Thomas interpreted Jesus's statement about going away and bringing them along literally. He didn't understand where Jesus was going, and he didn't have the directions to get there. But how did Jesus reply? Did he say, "Well, Thomas, I'm talking about the afterlife; when the time comes, I'll guide your disembodied soul on its way"? No: Jesus was not talking literally, and we know that by his response. He said that *he* is the way to the Father. He wasn't talking about physical location, but relationship and spiritual reality. He would leave them soon, but shortly thereafter, he would come again via the Spirit so they would not be without him.

Craig Keener explains,

> The rooms here (lit., "dwelling places") could also allude to rooms in the new temple, where only undefiled ministers would have a place (Ezek 44:9–16; cf. 48:11). Whatever the particular background of the image (perhaps simply an ordinary house), John presumably understands this language figuratively for being in Christ, where God's presence dwells (2:21); the only other place in the New Testament . . . where this term for "dwelling places" or "rooms" occurs is in John 14:23, where it refers to the believer as God's dwelling place.[2]

Jesus is going away to prepare a place for them in his Father's household or presence. Then he will come again via the paraclete (Spirit) to receive them unto himself. The Father and Son will dwell within the disciples. The whole focus is on what will shortly come to pass, not on the afterlife.

MY KINGDOM IS NOT OF THIS WORLD (JOHN 18:36)

When Pilate asked Jesus if he was the king of the Jews, Jesus replied with a disarming, though honest, answer. He said,

2. Keener, *John*, 145–46.

> Jesus answered, "My kingdom is not of this world. If my king-
> dom were of this world, my servants would have been fighting,
> that I might not be delivered over to the Jews. But my kingdom
> is not from the world." (John 18:36)

In the ESV, we find the following three phrases:

1. My kingdom is not *of* this world

2. If my kingdom were *of* this world

3. But my kingdom is not *from* the world

In the first two instances, the word "of" is the Greek preposition *ek*, which may mean "of," but also means "from" or even "out from." Jesus's kingdom is not *from* this world, but it certainly is *for* this world.[3] In fact, this is precisely why Jesus is returning. So many of the messianic prophecies remain unfulfilled. His purpose for coming is to realize his messianic destiny by ruling over our world. His kingdom does not arise as a result of a military coup d'état or a democratic campaign for votes. He is not going to marry into a royal family or convince the United Nations to appoint him chancellor. No: Jesus's kingdom does not originate from our world, but from heaven. God anointed Jesus to be the Messiah and it is the Father's delight to confer upon the Son authority to rule the nations. Thus, this text in no way challenges the future, physical, and political nature of Christ's coming kingdom.

---

3. N. T. Wright said it this way: "'The world,' as we've seen again and again, is in John the source of evil and rebellion against God. Jesus is denying that his kingdom has a this-worldly *origin* or *quality*. He is not denying that it has a this-worldly *destination*. That's why he has come into the world himself (verse 37), and why he has sent, and will send, his followers into the world (17.18; 20.21). His kingdom doesn't come from this world, but it is for this world. That is the crucial distinction." Wright, *John for Everyone: Part 2*, 115.

Appendix 3

Isn't God Going to Destroy the Earth?

In our materialistic age, it's not uncommon for preachers to stress the transience of the material world to combat greed, selfishness, and consumerism. The go-to text for such sermons is 2 Pet 3, where we read about a terrifying and totalizing eschatological fire that will destroy not only earth, but also heaven. Here is the text in question:

> But the day of the Lord will come like a thief, and then the heavens will pass away with a roar, and the heavenly bodies will be burned up and dissolved, and the earth and the works that are done on it will be exposed. Since all these things are thus to be dissolved, what sort of people ought you to be in lives of holiness and godliness, waiting for and hastening the coming of the day of God, because of which the heavens will be set on fire and dissolved, and the heavenly bodies will melt as they burn! But according to his promise we are waiting for new heavens and a new earth in which righteousness dwells. (2 Pet 3:10–13)

This text is problematic in light of the many Scriptures we've seen that say God plans to heal and restore our world. To be sure, most eschatologies place this conflagration at the end of the age, just prior to the eternal state, what is often called the "new heaven and earth." Still, the idea that God will nuke the planet and the stars with an annihilating heat introduces a discontinuity between our present earth and the one to come.

So, when Jesus said, "Blessed are the meek, for they shall inherit the earth," was he referring to some other earth? Is this a new earth, perhaps even in a distant galaxy? Or does he refer to the same planet—but only after it's been charred to a crisp, with all the mountains melted to fill in the valleys and all the seas dried up?

Allow me to present another option.

The prophets regularly portray God's anger as a furious fire that will burn up his adversaries.[1] Sometimes, instead of specifying the wicked as the object of God's burning wrath, the prophet pictures the fire as consuming the entire earth (Deut 32:22; Zeph 1:17–18; 3:8). Although those of us living in a post-nuclear age can imagine the destruction of the entire planet's surface, this is not what the ancients had in mind. We know this because often the judgment texts mention survivors.

Joel's famous proclamation of cosmic cataclysm, when God will "show wonders in the heavens and on earth, blood and fire and columns of smoke" (Joel 2:30), does not indicate the elimination of all humanity. For afterwards Joel says, "the survivors shall be those whom the LORD calls" (Joel 2:32). After Malachi proclaims, "the day is coming, burning like an oven, when all the arrogant and all evildoers will be stubble" (Mal 4:1), he talks of a time of healing when "you shall tread down the wicked, for they will be ashes under the soles of your feet" (Mal 4:2–3). Immediately following Zephaniah's prophecy that "in the fire of my jealousy all the earth shall be consumed" (Zeph 3:8), we read, "For at that time I will change the speech of the peoples to a pure speech" (Zeph 3:9).

Thus, Richard Bauckham explains, "In OT texts the function of this fire is to consume the wicked, not to destroy the world."[2] To read these Scriptures woodenly is to miss the hyperbole and therefore conclude these texts refer to the wholesale destruction of earth rather than judgment limited to the wicked.

Now, the text lurking in the background of Peter's proclamation of pyro-punishment was probably Isa 66. I say this because, in this Old Testament prophecy, we find not only an oracle of judgment by fire, but also the unusual phrase "the new heavens and the new earth." Here's the relevant part of the chapter:

> For behold, the LORD will come in fire,
>   and his chariots like the whirlwind,
> to render his anger in fury,
>   and his rebuke with flames of fire.
> For by fire will the LORD enter into judgment,
>   and by his sword, with all flesh;
>   and those slain by the LORD shall be many.

1. Isa 29:6; 30:27, 30, 33; 66:15–16, 24; Joel 2:30; Nah 1:5–6; Mal 4:1–3.
2. Bauckham, *Jude, 2 Peter*, 300.

Those who sanctify and purify themselves to go into the gardens, following one in the midst, eating pig's flesh and the abomination and mice, shall come to an end together, declares the LORD.

For I know their works and their thoughts, and the time is coming to gather all nations and tongues. And they shall come and shall see my glory, and I will set a sign among them. And from them I will send survivors to the nations, to Tarshish, Pul, and Lud, who draw the bow, to Tubal and Javan, to the coastlands far away, that have not heard my fame or seen my glory. And they shall declare my glory among the nations. And they shall bring all your brothers from all the nations as an offering to the LORD, on horses and in chariots and in litters and on mules and on dromedaries, to my holy mountain Jerusalem, says the LORD, just as the Israelites bring their grain offering in a clean vessel to the house of the LORD. And some of them also I will take for priests and for Levites, says the LORD.

> For as the new heavens and the new earth
>> that I make
> shall remain before me, says the Lord,
>> so shall your offspring and your name remain.
> From new moon to new moon,
>> and from Sabbath to Sabbath,
> all flesh shall come to worship before me,
> declares the Lord.

And they shall go out and look on the dead bodies of the men who have rebelled against me. For their worm shall not die, their fire shall not be quenched, and they shall be an abhorrence to all flesh. (Isa 66:15–24)

Isaiah portrays God's judgment as coming in fire upon all flesh. In the text, however, he says the LORD will slay many (not all). The targets of God's wrath are those who violate his commandments—not all of humanity, much less the destruction of planet Earth. The mention of sending survivors to spread God's fame to those who have not heard of him clearly confirms that God's fire did not result in extinction. Finally, in verse 22, we get the language of new heavens and earth; but this can't be a new planet, since God's people will "look on the dead bodies of the men who have rebelled" (v. 24).

The only other place in the Hebrew Bible that mentions "new heavens and a new earth" is Isa 65:17. Here it is clear that it refers not to destroying the old and starting over from scratch but recreating out of what remains. God tells his people to "rejoice forever in that which I create; for behold, I create Jerusalem to be a joy, and her people to be a gladness" (Isa 65:18). The United Bible Societies commentary states, "The purpose of this recreative work is to introduce a new age, the future God wants for his chosen people."[3] Once again, the point is not demolition of our planet, but the transformation of it. "This hyperbolic statement," notes the NET, "likens the coming transformation of Jerusalem to a new creation of the cosmos."[4] God's portrayal of his renovation of the earth as making a whole new world is hyperbole, and missing this fact results in an eschatology that more resembles science fiction than biblical truth.

Before returning to 2 Pet 3, let's read the words of Jesus himself, who spoke frequently about the coming judgment. In his parable of the tares and the wheat, he gives the following interpretation:

> Just as the weeds are gathered and burned with fire, so will it be at the end of the age. The Son of Man will send his angels, and they will gather out of his kingdom all causes of sin and all law-breakers, and throw them into the fiery furnace. In that place there will be weeping and gnashing of teeth. Then the righteous will shine like the sun in the kingdom of their Father. He who has ears, let him hear. (Matt 13:40–43)

Jesus mentions judgment by fire but makes it clear that this is targeted on the wicked. In fact, the whole point of judgment is to bring about a new age in which righteousness dwells. No longer hampered by persistent darkness all around them, the righteous will shine like the sun in the kingdom of their Father.

In sum, we have strong biblical precedent to interpret judgment-by-fire language—even when it includes statements that explicitly state the earth will be consumed—as referring solely to the fate of the majority of the wicked, not the extinction of humanity nor the demolition of our entire world.

Once again, here is our text:

> But the day of the Lord will come like a thief, and then the heavens will pass away with a roar, and the heavenly bodies will be burned up and dissolved, and the earth and the works that are done on it will be exposed. Since all these things are thus to be dissolved, what sort of people ought you to be in lives of holiness and godliness, waiting for and hastening the coming of the day of God, because of which the heavens will be set on fire and dissolved, and the heavenly bodies will melt as they burn! But

3. Ogden and Sterk, *Handbook on Isaiah*, para. 1821.

4. Harris, *NET Bible Notes*, para. 51399.

> according to his promise we are waiting for new heavens and a
> new earth in which righteousness dwells. (2 Pet 3:10–13)

Now, some older English versions read differently in verse 10. Instead of saying, "the earth and the works that are done on it will be exposed" as the ESV has it, they read, "the earth and the works that are in it will be burned up" (NKJV). This is not so much a translation issue as a textual problem. In fact, the textual specialists struggled with this decision so much that this verse received one of only four "D" ratings in Bruce Metzger's *Textual Commentary on the Greek New Testament.*

This rating refers to how certain the committee of textual scholars was about which reading is original: "A" meaning the text is certain, "B" that the text is almost certain, "C" that they have difficulty deciding which reading, and "D" that they have extreme difficulty picking one. Thus, we should exercise restraint in building a whole doctrine on this one word.

Nevertheless, as I've already shown, even if the text describes the complete burning up and destruction of heaven and earth, this could just as well be typical prophetic exaggeration, designed to communicate the certainty, thoroughness, or intensity of the coming judgment.

Even if Peter's apocalyptic language is somewhat opaque for modern sensibilities, his point is easy to grasp. He asks the question in light of the coming conflagration, "what sort of people ought you to be in lives of holiness and godliness" (v. 11)? If he has in mind the destruction of all of creation: the stars, the planets, Earth, and everything else, how does that motivate holiness?

Perhaps an analogy will help us think this through. Let's say astronomers detect an asteroid on a collision course with Earth. They predict we have one year to live. How will people respond? Sure, some will "get religion," but others will embrace hedonism, quitting their jobs and acting on their baser impulses, knowing that it's all going to burn anyhow. But what if, instead, the asteroid was smart—able to limit its destruction only to those who act wickedly? To be sure, some would still rebel, either disbelieving the coming judgment or defying it altogether, but most would straighten out their lives. My contention is that the judgment of 2 Pet 3 refers to the latter. It's a specific, targeted judgment, not one that brings indiscriminate, wholesale doom. This aligns nicely with many other Scriptures in the New Testament that speak of God's judgment on the wicked.[5]

Even so, what is God's purpose in bringing about such an irreversible punishment? The apostle Paul explains. He personifies creation itself as groaning, anticipating the redemption of God's people, knowing that when

5. Mark 4:22; Luke 18:17; John 3:21; 1 Cor 3:13; 14:25; Eph 5:13.

this occurs, creation itself "will be set free from its bondage to corruption and obtain the freedom of the glory of the children of God" (Rom 8:21). The final judgment is not about destroying God's good creation but rescuing it from evil.

What's more, the frame of reference Peter uses for thinking about the coming destruction is the past destruction at the time of Noah. Prior to our text, we read,

> For they deliberately overlook this fact, that the heavens existed long ago, and the earth was formed out of water and through water by the word of God, and that by means of these the world that then existed was deluged with water and perished. But by the same word the heavens and earth that now exist are stored up for fire, being kept until the day of judgment and destruction of the ungodly. (2 Pet 3:5–7)

What was destroyed in the flood? Did planet Earth perish? No, it was merely covered by water for a time. Nevertheless, Peter is quite comfortable saying "the world that then existed was deluged with water and perished" (2 Pet 3:6). Furthermore, he does not see the future destruction as targeted at the world, instead he says that the fire is for the "destruction of the ungodly" (2 Pet 3:7).

The problem God used the flood to remedy was wickedness among humanity. Likewise, the aim of the coming judgment is sinful people, and the purpose is ultimate renovation and recreation.

Gene Grene writes about the verses at issue:

> In spite of the destructive forces of the divine judgment (3:7, 10–12), the Christian hope is the renovation of creation and not its annihilation. As the ancient world destroyed by the flood (2:5; 3:6) gave way to the present order, so also the present world will suffer divine judgment (3:7), but in turn God will usher in the new creation.[6]

Richard Bauckham strikes a similar note when he writes,

> The essential element in most Jewish and Christian references to the eschatological conflagration is the destruction of the wicked by the fire of divine judgment; this idea, which differs from the Zoroastrian fire of purification and from the Stoic idea of a natural, deterministic cycle of destruction and renewal, is fundamentally Jewish and biblical. The author of 2 Peter, who is

---

6. Grene, *Jude and 2 Peter*, 334.

really interested in the conflagration as judgment on the wicked, follows this Jewish tradition.[7]

So the judgment is for the wicked, not for our physical planet itself.

Before concluding, we have one more important text to address. In the Bible's last book, we read,

> Then I saw a new heaven and a new earth, for the first heaven and the first earth had passed away, and the sea was no more. And I saw the holy city, new Jerusalem, coming down out of heaven from God, prepared as a bride adorned for her husband. (Rev 21:1–2)

When many of us read "the first heaven and the first earth had passed away," we think destroyed, as if God blew up the planet and made a new one *ex nihilo*. However, Christians have not always looked at it this way. For example, Oecumenius, who lived in the seventh century, said,

> They do not say this as though heaven and earth and sea are destroyed and pass into nonexistence and that other things come into being in their place. Rather, they mean that the present realities have cast off their corruption and become new, putting off their filth as though it were an old and dirty garment. For that is called "new" which is not such as it was formerly but is as it has now become.[8]

Once again, renewal is the idea—not destruction and recreation. Nevertheless, in John's apocalyptic vision of Rev 21, he may very well have *seen* the destruction of the old and the genesis of the new. When reading Revelation and similar prophetic literature, it's important to distinguish between the revelation itself and the reality the vision represents. Previously, John saw death and hades cast into the lake of fire (Rev 20:14). This visual experience represented the second death (see Rev 21:8). Then he saw the passing away of the heaven and earth followed by the new heaven and earth. The fact that the transitional period between the old and the new wasn't part of John's vision does not mean God will one day disintegrate our universe and conjure up a new one in its place.

As for the absence of a sea ("the sea was no more," Rev 21:1), in Jewish apocalyptic literature, the sea generally represents the source of chaos and destruction in the world (see Dan 7:2–3; Rev 13:1). G. K. Beale makes the point that the sea is done away with because "The sea is a part representing

7. Bauckham, *Jude, 2 Peter*, 301.

8. Weinrich, *Ancient Christian Commentary*, 354.

the whole of the cosmos, but not so much in a geographical manner. Rather, the evil nuance of the sea metaphorically represents the entire range of afflictions that formerly threatened God's people in the old world."[9] As such, it wouldn't make sense to have a "sea" in God's new world, although there will probably be plenty of large bodies of water.

In conclusion, the language of 2 Pet 3 and Rev 21 depict a cosmic conflagration in apocalyptic imagery—"a sphere where," to quote Michael Green, "literalism is always dangerous."[10] He goes on to summarize in the following:

> Judgment by fire is one of the great Old Testament pictures of the Day of Yahweh; the same holds good of intertestamental literature and the New Testament. It means purification and the destruction of evil when God comes to judge his world. And so here, while we may not exclude the possibility that Peter is envisaging the fiery destruction of the whole universe (by no means incredible to a generation which lives after Hiroshima), all that he actually says is that the heavens and earth are kept in store for fire in anticipation of the judgment of ungodly men.[11]

Thus, the kingdom hope is unshakable. Even if the final judgment seems like it would annihilate everything in its path, its true aim is the removal of the ungodly to pave way for the fulfillment of all of the kingdom promises God has made throughout the Bible. I can imagine no better text to encapsulate this truth and end on than this one:

> At that time his voice shook the earth, but now he has promised, "Yet once more I will shake not only the earth but also the heavens." This phrase, "Yet once more," indicates the removal of things that are shaken—that is, things that have been made—in order that the things that cannot be shaken may remain. Therefore let us be grateful for receiving a kingdom that cannot be shaken, and thus let us offer to God acceptable worship, with reverence and awe, for our God is a consuming fire. (Heb 12:26–29)

9. Beale, *Book of Revelation*, 1042–43.

10. Green, *2 Peter and Jude*, 144.

11. Green, *2 Peter and Jude*.

Appendix 4

The Intermediate State

Strictly speaking, what happens immediately after death and what happens ultimately are two separate doctrines. It's possible to have faith in a conscious intermediate state and also believe in God's age of restoration when Jesus returns to this earth. However, in my experience, those who believe in heaven-at-death tend not to care very much about the kingdom. This is only natural; what's next is what we typically focus on, rather than what happens after an unknown period of waiting. This is why I decided to intertwine the doctrines of a terrestrial hope and an unconscious intermediate state in the main body of this book.

Nevertheless, I realize that a handful of often misunderstood texts may cause the reader difficulty in accepting the powerful combination of a coming kingdom along with the sleep of the dead. Before looking at the smattering of texts that seem to teach an immediate reward upon death, I'd like to offer a brief look at the common theological options.

When it comes to the intermediate state, Christians have broadly held three major views:

1. Immortal Soul: the body dies but the soul lives on in heaven, hell, purgatory, or a subterranean netherworld.

2. Soul Sleep: at death the soul becomes unconscious, causing the person to be unaware of the passage of time until resurrection.

3. Soul Death: when the body dies, the soul ceases to exist, awaiting recreation at resurrection.

The idea of the immortal soul is also called "natural immortality" since in that view everyone has a soul that cannot die. The question is not *whether* one will live again, but *where* one will go on living. Souls don't die, the logic goes, so they must go somewhere.

This understanding is very common in antiquity, from the Egyptians to the Norse to the Greeks to the Hindus. Although not represented in the Hebrew Bible, the idea of the immortal soul began making inroads into Judaism about a century or two before Christ through contact with Greek culture (Hellenism). Throughout the time of Jesus, until the end of the first century, significant portions of Judaism embraced the immortal soul. Hélène Dallaire explains,

> It was during such turbulent periods that the concept of heaven and hell developed to a high degree of complexity in Jewish literature. . . . The belief that the soul survived death and that the body would one day be resurrected and reunited with the soul became the traditional Jewish view during this period and for many subsequent centuries.[1]

Nevertheless, the NT, though written in Greek, appears to have escaped the Hellenizing corruption that was beginning to pervade Judaism, especially outside of the land of Israel. After Lazarus died, Jesus tells his disciples, "Lazarus has fallen asleep, but I go to awaken him" (John 11:11). He mentions a day when "all who are in the tombs will hear his [Jesus'] voice and come out" (John 5:28–29). Once he even proclaims, "No one has ascended into heaven" (John 3:13). When Stephen died, Luke writes, "he fell asleep" (Acts 7:60). Paul believed that David "fell asleep and was laid with his fathers and saw corruption" (Acts 13:36). Peter confirms this fact when he says, "David did not ascend into the heavens" (Acts 2:34). Throughout his epistles, Paul regularly refers to the deceased as those who have fallen asleep (1 Cor 11:30; 15:6; 1 Thess 5:10). Likewise, Peter perceived even the patriarchs of the past as asleep (2 Pet 3:4).

Still, perhaps no NT text is clearer than Paul's extensive treatment of resurrection in 1 Cor 15. Here is an excerpt:

> And if Christ has not been raised, your faith is futile and you are still in your sins. Then those also who have fallen asleep in Christ have perished. If in Christ we have hope in this life only, we are of all people most to be pitied. But in fact Christ has been raised from the dead, the firstfruits of those who have fallen asleep. For as by a man came death, by a man has come also

---

1. Dallaire, "Judaism and the World," 54–55.

> the resurrection of the dead. For as in Adam all die, so also in
> Christ shall all be made alive. But each in his own order: Christ
> the firstfruits, then at his coming those who belong to Christ. (1
> Cor 15:17–23)

Paul doesn't see a third option where people live on temporarily out of their bodies in another realm, whether celestial or subterranean. The dead, he writes, "have fallen asleep" (18) but not perished—if Christ's resurrection happened. In that case those sleeping in death will "be made alive . . . at his coming" (22–23). This provides a clear anchor for timing; it is at Christ's return that the dead become alive.

Now, this metaphor of saying the dead are asleep can have multiple meanings depending on whether one is a dualist or monist. That said, however, what sleep cannot mean is awake. The dead must be unconscious for the metaphor to work. And it won't do to say, "Yes, the body is asleep, but the soul lives on." Not only is such language entirely missing from the Scriptures, but the many texts that say the dead are asleep refer to the whole person, not just the body. Besides, sleep is a unified experience. It's not as if my body can sleep while I remain awake. Nor can I be asleep while my body is awake.

The last two positions I mentioned above, soul sleep and soul death, fall under the umbrella of conditional immortality (in contrast to natural immortality). Conditional immortality posits that immortality is conditional rather than innate. What is the condition that brings about immortality? Paul explains it nicely, once again, in 1 Cor 15:

> Behold! I tell you a mystery. We shall not all sleep, but we shall
> all be changed, in a moment, in the twinkling of an eye, at the
> last trumpet. For the trumpet will sound, and the dead will be
> raised imperishable, and we shall be changed. For this perish-
> able body must put on the imperishable, and this mortal body
> must put on immortality. (1 Cor 15:51–53)

Immortality depends on resurrection, which occurs not at death but "on the last day" (John 6:39–40, 44, 54). Without resurrection, humans are mortal, perishable, without hope. With resurrection, we have a way out of the greatest problem we face.

Of course, I could go on to build a much more extensive case for conditional immortality, but my interest in this appendix is in dealing with the troubling texts that perennially arise when discussing the afterlife. Those interested in going deeper can avail themselves of the many excellent books[2] and online resources[3] available on conditional immortality.

In what follows I will work through what I consider to be the most significant texts that lead some to doubt conditional immortality.

DEPART AND BE WITH CHRIST (PHIL 1:23)

Paul was facing incredibly difficult circumstances when he wrote his letter to the Philippians. He was in prison, suffering, while other Christians were wreaking havoc on the churches he had planted, attempting to wrest them away from Paul. He was in such distress that he wasn't sure if he should even continue to fight on or just give up and die.

> I am hard pressed between the two. My desire is to depart and
> be with Christ, for that is far better. But to remain in the flesh is
> more necessary on your account. (Phil 1:23–24)

For those who don't believe in an unconscious intermediate state, this text supports the notion that, immediately at death, Paul would be with Christ. Obviously, this reading assumes, Jesus is currently in heaven, therefore Paul would go to heaven at death.

However, this reading ignores the first-person perspective of the deceased. The moment someone dies, he or she enters a dreamless "sleep" that lasts until the resurrection day comes. From the point of view of the dead, no time passes whatever. From Paul's perspective, he would die and then, in his very next moment, he would be with Christ. It would make no difference to him if an hour or two thousand years had passed after he died; his next conscious moment would be the second coming of Christ. Resurrection happens when Jesus comes, not the moment of death, as Paul clearly explains in 1 Cor 15:23.

But what about his statement that dying would be far better than continuing on in life? How is unconsciousness better than living? To answer this, we need to remember Paul's situation: he wrote in prison awaiting trial.

In those days, incarceration was incredibly uncomfortable, especially for older people like Paul. We know he had some kind of "thorn in the flesh" that dogged him throughout his life (2 Cor 12:7). We also know that he was repeatedly beaten during his missionary journeys, likely leaving him

2. See Fudge, *Fire That Consumes*; Prestidge, *Life, Death and Destiny*; Buzzard, *Our Fathers*; Froom, *Conditionalist Faith of Our Fathers*.

3. See https://www.afterlife.co.nz/, https://rethinkinghell.com/, https://conditional-ism.org/, and the debates of Chris Date.

with chronic pain. Add to that the stress and anxiety commensurate with planting churches in the face of relentless opposition both from within and without, and it is easy to see why he would have preferred the sleep of death to fighting another day.

Perhaps Elijah can provide us a good comparison here. He had hidden from Ahab and Jezebel's attempts to seize him for years. Finally, he had a showdown with four hundred prophets of Baal on Mount Carmel. He came away the overwhelming victor, and *still* Jezebel wanted to kill him, now more than ever. He escaped to the wilderness where he summarized his heartbroken state with the words "It is enough; now, O LORD, take away my life, for I am no better than my fathers" (1 Kgs 19:4). Discouraged and ready to quit, Elijah would rather depart from his work and let God find someone else to do what needed to be done. However, God did not let Elijah off the hook; instead, he ministered to him and gave him more work to do. Similarly, Paul did not give up, but kept on fighting to stay alive and complete the work God had given him to do.

ABSENT FROM THE BODY, PRESENT WITH THE LORD (2 COR 5:8)

Christians often employ this text to argue that at death our souls immediately leave our bodies and go home to be with the Lord. It reads as follows:

> So we are always of good courage. We know that while we are at home in the body we are away from the Lord, for we walk by faith, not by sight. Yes, we are of good courage, and we would rather be away from the body and at home with the Lord. (2 Cor 5:6–8)

Before getting to the specifics of this passage, we do well to remember that Paul repeatedly calls death "sleep" (1 Cor 15:6, 18, 20, 51; 1 Thess 4:13, 14, 15; 5:10; Eph 5:14). Now, we recognize that the way the Scriptures use sleep for death must be a metaphor. Even so, whatever actually happens in the intermediate state, we should not, indeed cannot, say that the dead are awake. For if sleep means anything, it cannot refer to the state of being awake. We are left with a puzzle: if Paul believed the dead are asleep rather than awake, what could he have meant in 1 Cor 5:8 when he said, "we would rather be away from the body and at home with the Lord"?

Once again, we must back up to the beginning of the passage and get some context to understand what he is saying. Here are the first five verses:

> For we know that if the tent that is our earthly home is destroyed, we have a building from God, a house not made with hands, eternal in the heavens. For in this tent we groan, longing to put on our heavenly dwelling, if indeed by putting it on we may not be found naked. For while we are still in this tent, we groan, being burdened—not that we would be unclothed, but that we would be further clothed, so that what is mortal may be swallowed up by life. He who has prepared us for this very thing is God, who has given us the Spirit as a guarantee. (2 Cor 5:1–5)

To follow Paul's line of thought here, we have to understand his analogies. He talks about our tent (or earthly home) and contrasts that to a building, or house, "eternal in the heavens." Paul is comparing our current bodies to our resurrection bodies. Those in which we live now are temporary, like a tent, and originate from the earth.[4]

We do not seek to be naked or unclothed, to be a disembodied soul, but rather to be further clothed with our heavenly dwelling. Keeping up with the analogy here, our heavenly dwelling is not the idea of relocating to the heavens to live, but of a heavenly body coming down to swallow up our mortal bodies with eternal life.

We must be careful to remember that Jews often used heaven to refer to God. Our dwelling, or building, is heavenly because it originates from God himself. This is all explained at length in the prequel to the text at hand—in 1 Cor 15—where Paul writes about God's plan to upgrade our physical bodies to be imperishable and immortal.

Now we can return to the verses we started with in order to see what they mean in context. Paul said, "We know that while we are at home in the body we are away from the Lord. . . . And we would rather be away from the body and at home with the Lord." While we remain in our present bodies, we are away from the Lord, who now lives in his resurrected body. We would rather be away from our present corruptible and feeble bodies and be with the Lord (in our new resurrected and immortalized bodies). Paul doesn't have to say all of that, because he just said the whole plan is not to go naked but to become further clothed.

---

4. God made Adam out of the earth, hence the Hebrew word *adamah*, which means soil or ground. To a Jewish or Hebrew thinker, humanity's relationship to the earth is obvious because the first human's name was derived from the word for ground.

SOULS UNDER THE ALTAR (REV 6:9)

By anyone's reckoning, Revelation is a tricky book. It is a collection of apocalyptic visions, like Zechariah and Daniel. As a result, we must be careful not to interpret everything literally, but recognize when something is a vision. I believe such is the case in this text:

> When he opened the fifth seal, I saw under the altar the souls of those who had been slain for the word of God and for the witness they had borne. They cried out with a loud voice, "O Sovereign Lord, holy and true, how long before you will judge and avenge our blood on those who dwell on the earth?" (Rev 6:9–10)

Here, contrary to what we see in the rest of Scripture, the dead are awakened to make a statement. They ask how long God will delay judgement upon those who took their lives. Looking at the next verse helps us to understand why we should take this particular section symbolically.

> Then they were each given a white robe and told to rest a little longer, until the number of their fellow servants and their brothers should be complete, who were to be killed as they themselves had been. (Rev 6:11)

How can a soul wear a white robe? The whole scene is a vision, like a dream that expresses a truth. The martyrs need to be avenged. God plans to bring their persecutors to judgment but not yet. They must continue resting until the full number is complete. Then God will act decisively against the perpetrators.

THE RICH MAN AND LAZARUS (LUKE 16:19–31)

A detailed exegesis of this passage would take too much space here. I have written about it in detail elsewhere.[5] I will just make a few remarks to provide a general framework for understanding this parable (Luke 16:19–31). First, I must establish that it is, in fact, a parable. Some argue that this is not a parable because it starts with the phrase "a certain man." But this assertion is groundless because the parable of the Unjust Steward in Luke 16:1 starts just this way.

A second commonly cited reason not to see this as a parable is that it never calls itself a parable. But eleven out of the twenty-six parables in Luke's

5. For my article on the rich man and Lazarus visit https://restitutio.org/ and see "Articles."

Gospel do not self-identify as parables. A third reason is that Lazarus is named. However, Lazarus means "God has helped," which would certainly be an appropriate fictitious name considering the irony of the story.

Furthermore, the story tangles itself in knots if taken as a literal tour of the afterlife. Repeatedly, the parable mentions body parts, such as eyes, the tip of a finger, and a tongue. Besides, what kind of joy could people have in paradise if they could not only see but converse with their loved ones while they undergo incessant torture? Additionally, Jesus never mentioned heaven or hell or souls. Last of all, how would a drop of water satisfy the thirst of a man burning in agony?

I will have to admit that upon first inspection, instantaneously our minds go to the typical modern picture of someone burning mercilessly in hell while others are up in heaven. But the audience of Jesus had an ancient worldview and would have read this parable differently. In order to bring out what Jesus's hearers would have understood, we need to look at the parallels in their own literature, or we risk mistaking Jesus's meaning.

For example, if I make a reference to Trinity from *The Matrix*, what would come to mind? Probably one would think of an attractive woman who wears black leather clothing and does incredible martial arts. Obviously, no one would think about the Father, the Son, and the Holy Spirit. This is because we share the context of the word "Matrix." We understand that *The Matrix* is a movie. However, if someone a thousand years from now looked back on a conversation between two people about *The Matrix* and Trinity they would be more likely to associate a matrix with a grouping of numbers and the Trinity as the Father, the Son, and the Holy Spirit (three yet one). They could totally miss the point because of their ignorance of our cultural context.

If we are not familiar with the stories of a culture, we can miss a reference to a well-known character or theme and end up taking everything the wrong way.

It just so happens that there was a story going around during the time of Jesus in which fates were reversed after death. Edward Fudge explains,

> The plot of the parable, the reversal of earthly fortunes after death, was familiar in popular Palestinian stories of Jesus's times. Hugo Gressmann cites a Greek parallel from a first-century Egyptian papyrus, and he says there are at least seven versions of the story in Jewish literature. One of the most famous involved a poor student of the Law and a rich publican named Bar Ma'jan. There are differences between these stories and Jesus', of course,

and therein lies the Lord's uniqueness. But the basic plot was well-known folklore.[6]

It was as if the Jews had watched movies in which this idea of two people whose fates were reversed in the afterlife was common. If this story was in fact common in the time of Jesus, then what matters is not so much the idea of fates reversed in the afterlife but what Jesus does with the parable, how he sharpens it up to prick the Pharisees' hearts.

In fact, the whole story is actually about money, not the afterlife. The rich man and Lazarus is sandwiched between two other parables that deal with money, as well. The point, it seems, is not to roll out a topographical survey of the underworld but to convince the wealthy to give generously to the poor.

Sadly, this point is all too often missed completely when we use this story to prove that the dead are conscious and experiencing rewards or suffering. Warren Prestidge summarizes the point nicely:

> No, Jesus is not endorsing the story's paraphernalia. He is using it simply to meet his opponents, the Pharisees, on their own ground: using a story familiar to them, in order to convict them out of their own mouths, as it were, for their indifference to the poor, and perhaps to "sinners" and even Gentiles in general. All that he actually endorses here is "Moses and the prophets" (29). . . . [H]e does not intend here to give a preview of life after death. On this almost all commentators agree.[7]

In conclusion, we should not literalize this parable, but take from it the essential truth Jesus taught about generosity and compassion.

TODAY YOU WILL BE WITH ME IN PARADISE (LUKE 23:43)

While Jesus hung on the cross, one of the criminals next to him mocked him, saying, "Are you not the Messiah? Save yourself and us" (Luke 23:39). The other confronted him, defending Jesus as an innocent. Next, we read,

> And he said, "Jesus, remember me when you come into your kingdom." And he said to him, "Truly, I say to you, today you will be with me in paradise." (Luke 23:42–43)

6. Fudge, *Fire That Consumes*, 203–4.

7. Prestidge, *Life, Death and Destiny*, 39.

Some Christians see Jesus's response as giving his listener a one-way ticket to heaven upon death. They identify paradise as heaven and think Jesus guaranteed this man entry that very day. Others argue that paradise refers to a subterranean waiting room where disembodied souls await resurrection. However, we know for certain that Jesus himself did not go to heaven when he died. For just after he arose from the dead, he told Mary, "Do not cling to me, for I have not yet ascended to the Father" (John 20:17). Rather, he was in "the heart of the earth" until resurrection (Matt 12:40). Why didn't Jesus go to heaven? If this thief went to heaven, then certainly it was open for business, right? What precluded Jesus from enjoying a three-day respite?

Context is the key to understanding the passage. The thief asked Jesus for a simple favor: "Remember me when you come into your kingdom." Jesus had a sign hanging above his head that read, "This is the King of the Jews" (Luke 23:38). The other criminal mocked the sign, while this one put his faith in it. He really thought Jesus was the Messiah, the king of the Jews, and would come into his kingdom some day in the future. Now, considering the criminal was Jewish, it's not hard to imagine where he got the idea of a coming kingdom; prophecies about it are sprinkled throughout the Hebrew Bible. Wouldn't it be strange if Jesus responded, "Today you will enter heaven"? Such a rejoinder would be wholly out of place with the Jewish notions of the messianic age. However, the whole issue dissipates like a mirage in a desert if we move a single comma.

At this point, it's important to remember that the Greek manuscripts we have contain little to no punctuation. Translators add in commas, periods, quotation marks, semicolons, etc. when they believe the text warrants it. These punctuation marks are a matter of opinion, not inspiration.

If a translator believes Jesus gave this man a free pass to heaven, then he or she may (even subconsciously) assume the comma belongs before the word "today."[8] However, if we look at it the other way, Jesus says, "Truly, I say to you today, you will be with me in paradise." I prefer this reading. The man had asked Jesus to remember him when he came into his kingdom—an undisclosed future date. Jesus responded by telling the repentant criminal he didn't have to wait until his kingdom arrived. He was telling him today, right here and now, that he will be with him in his kingdom (or paradise). Jesus gave him a free ticket to his future kingdom that very day. The man subsequently died and waits in his grave for resurrection on the dawn of the age to come.

---

8. At least one important manuscript seems to put punctuation after the word "today": Codex Vaticanus, originating from the fourth century.

Another possibility is to read the text with the comma in its traditional place. In that case, Jesus says, "Today you will be with me in paradise." From the perspective of that man, he would see Jesus in paradise on that very day. After he died on his cross, he would cease to have consciousness. Thousands of years can pass, but without him noticing anything. Then at the return of Christ, he awakes to paradise. From his subjective perspective, everything did happen that same day while from an objective perspective, many days had passed.

ENOCH AND ELIJAH

Enoch and Elijah sometimes come up in discussions about the afterlife. About Enoch, we read two extremely brief details: "Enoch walked with God, and he was not, for God took him" (Gen 5:24). The author of Hebrews picks up on this, elaborating a little. "By faith Enoch was taken up so that he should not see death, and he was not found, because God had taken him" (Heb 11:5).

Likewise, when Elijah's time came to die, horses and chariots of fire appeared, separating Elijah from Elisha. Then, "Elijah went up by a whirlwind into heaven" (2 Kgs 2:11). On the strength of this data, many see these two as both paradigmatic and exceptional. They are paradigmatic because they went up into heaven, setting precedents for all the righteous. They are exceptional in that they never died, transitioning immediately to their reward. Sadly, interpreted in this way, Enoch and Elijah lend credence to a system of belief that undermines the hope of the kingdom, substituting in its place the hope of a celestial home.

Why not look at Enoch and Elijah as exceptional and not paradigmatic? There's nothing in the text that indicates either of them are examples for what will happen to others. It's entirely possible that God chose to do something different with these two than the rest of his people. Even if they currently reside in heaven, that in no way counters the biblical teaching on the intermediate state. After all, on a surface level reading, neither die, so neither can be paradigmatic of the intermediate state. Whether they are living in some other dimension or transported directly into the future kingdom or ended up dying later, their unusual departures in no way dislodge the overwhelming biblical evidence for the sleep of the dead.

THE WITCH OF ENDOR (1 SAM 28)

The incident when Saul asked the witch of Endor to call up Samuel from the dead is full of mystery and, therefore, susceptible to multiple interpretations. Although God repeatedly and emphatically commanded his people not to talk to the dead,[9] and Saul himself had outlawed the necromancers from Israel, still, we find him in the company of such a woman.

Disguised to conceal his identity, he asks the medium to conjure up Samuel from the dead for him. In the text, the witch cries out with a loud voice, apparently seeing Samuel, and suddenly realizes that the inquirer was indeed King Saul. The "spirit Samuel" asks, rather grumpily, "Why have you disturbed me by bringing me up?" (1 Sam 28:15). Then, the two proceed to converse a bit before the medium utters an accurate prediction of defeat at the hands of the Philistines and doom for the royal family, saying "tomorrow you and your sons shall be with me" (1 Sam 28:19).

Going back to at least the time of Origen of Alexandria, Christians have struggled to sort out what actually happened here. Interpreters have several options to choose from:

1. Samuel remained dead, but the medium impersonated him and made up the prediction.

2. Samuel remained dead, but an unclean spirit spoke through the medium, enabling her to accurately impersonate him and predict the future.

3. Samuel remained dead, but God hijacked the operation, providing the medium a vision of Samuel and enabling her to accurately predict the future.

4. Samuel really spoke, because the medium really did have the power to interact with the dead.

5. Samuel really spoke because God enabled the séance to work.

It is beyond our present scope to analyze each of these five options and select one that makes the most sense. My point is simply that this incident is vulnerable to several interpretations and therefore should not undermine the Bible's normative teaching about the intermediate state. Even if, under certain extraordinary circumstances, a necromancer *can* wake the dead for a brief conversation, that does not disprove that the dead are normally in a state of unconsciousness.

---

9. Lev 19:31; 20:6, 27; Deut 18:9–12; Isa 8:19.

THE SPIRIT RETURNS TO GOD WHO GAVE IT (ECCL 12:7)

Advocates of natural immortality point to this text for evidence for a separation of the soul from the body. The verse ends a depressing rumination on aging, where the preacher urges his readers to remember their creator in their youth before all the consequences of aging set in and, at last, they die. He describes this last event with the words, "the dust returns to the earth as it was, and the spirit returns to God who gave it" (Eccl 12:7). I doubt anyone struggles to understand the first clause, but the second one depends greatly on how the reader defines "spirit." Does spirit refer to breath, as it does many times throughout the Bible? Does it refer to the soul as a separable component containing one's essence?

I lean towards the idea that the preacher is explaining death as the reverse of creation. In the beginning God formed the first person from the dust of the ground and breathed into his nostrils the breath of life (Gen 2:7). At death our bodies return to dust and our breath "returns" to God. "This is not an optimistic allusion to some kind of consciousness after death," says Tremper Longman, "but simply a return to a prelife situation."[10]

But even if Eccl 12:7 means that our spirit or soul returns to God, that doesn't require consciousness in the intermediate state. Although he stops short of explicitly saying the soul is unconscious, John Polkinghorne's technology illustration is helpful:

> It would be altogether too crude to say that the soul is the software running on the hardware of the body—for we have good reason to believe that human beings are very much more than "computers made of meat"—but that unsatisfactory image catches a little of what is being proposed. While the soul, understood in this way, has a dynamic and changing character, it is perfectly possible to suppose that, amid its evolving change, each individual soul carries specific elements of its patterning which are the signature of its own abiding and unique personal identity. . . . If these ideas contain some truth, we have to acknowledge that this information-bearing pattern will, in the course of nature, be dissolved by the decay of our bodies after death. There is, therefore, no intrinsic immortality associated with the soul in this way of understanding it. Death is a real end. However, it need not be an ultimate end, for in Christian understanding only God is ultimate. It is a perfectly coherent hope that the pattern that is a human being could be held in the

10. Longman, *Book of Ecclesiastes*, 273.

divine memory after that person's death. Such a disembodied existence, even if located within the divine remembrance, would be less than fully human. It would be more like the Hebrew concept of shades in Sheol, though now a Sheol from which the Lord was not absent but, quite to the contrary, God was sustaining it. It is a further coherent hope, and one for which the resurrection of Jesus Christ provides the foretaste and guarantee, that God in the eschatological future will re-embody this multitude of preserved information-bearing patterns in some new environment of God's choosing.[11]

So whether Eccl 12:7 refers to death in a poetic way or something far deeper, the text does not require the soul's immortality nor offer a significant rebuttal of conditional immortality.

11. Polkinghorne, *God of Hope*, 106–8.

Appendix 5

The Millennium

Throughout this book, I have endeavored to focus primarily on the kingdom in broad terms rather than tangling with various contested theories about the millennium or the rapture, since, to my mind, these are secondary issues. Jesus never said, "this gospel of the rapture must be preached to all nations," nor did he ever mention a period of a thousand years. Sadly, many have gotten the biblical teaching about the kingdom so intertwined with their view of the millennium that they cannot separate the two. However, I'm convinced that whether Christians hold to premillennial, post-millennial, or amillennial positions, they can and should still hold fast to the Bible's doctrine of the kingdom. Even so, I don't want to duck out of addressing the question of the millennium and how it relates to the kingdom age. So, with this brief disclaimer, let's delve into the swirling waters of systematic theology to consider the various millennial positions.

The three classical views are amillennialism, post-millennialism, and pre-millennialism. Although these perspectives are mutually exclusive, each has certain advantages to which we do well to listen. I'll begin with the amillennial position, which, as its name implies, is the idea that there is no literal millennium. Amillennialists point out that the prophets never spoke of a millennium, Jesus never did, nor did Paul, James, Jude, or Peter. We only encounter it in one chapter in one book of the whole Bible: Rev 20. This book is famously enigmatic and, therefore, difficult to interpret. Indeed, Revelation is full of visions and symbolic language, and the twentieth chapter is no exception. But before going any further, we would do well to read the text in its entirety first, so that it is fresh in our minds.

> Then I saw an angel coming down from heaven, holding in his
> hand the key to the bottomless pit and a great chain. And he
> seized the dragon, that ancient serpent, who is the devil and
> Satan, and bound him for a thousand years, and threw him into
> the pit, and shut it and sealed it over him, so that he might not
> deceive the nations any longer, until the thousand years were
> ended. After that he must be released for a little while.
>
> Then I saw thrones, and seated on them were those to whom
> the authority to judge was committed. Also I saw the souls of
> those who had been beheaded for the testimony of Jesus and for
> the word of God, and those who had not worshiped the beast
> or its image and had not received its mark on their foreheads
> or their hands. They came to life and reigned with Christ for a
> thousand years. The rest of the dead did not come to life until the
> thousand years were ended. This is the first resurrection. Blessed
> and holy is the one who shares in the first resurrection! Over
> such the second death has no power, but they will be priests of
> God and of Christ, and they will reign with him for a thousand
> years.
>
> And when the thousand years are ended, Satan will be
> released from his prison and will come out to deceive the na-
> tions that are at the four corners of the earth, Gog and Magog,
> to gather them for battle; their number is like the sand of the
> sea. And they marched up over the broad plain of the earth and
> surrounded the camp of the saints and the beloved city, but fire
> came down from heaven and consumed them, and the devil
> who had deceived them was thrown into the lake of fire and
> sulfur where the beast and the false prophet were, and they will
> be tormented day and night forever and ever. (Rev 20:1–10)

This passage naturally breaks into three roughly equal sections. In the first,
a great angel binds Satan for a thousand years (hence "millennium"). In the
second, God resurrects the martyrs and those who did not receive the mark
of the beast so they can reign with Christ for a thousand years. Putting these
two together, we get the image of a millennium without Satan but with resurrected Christians ruling. Lastly, we learn about a final rebellion whereby
Satan tricks the nations into surrounding the city of the saints. But God
intervenes and burns Satan and his cohorts in fire.

This is the vision, but what is the interpretation? R. C. Sproul helpfully
explains.

> Amillennialists believe that the binding of Satan took place
> during Jesus's earthly ministry; Satan was restrained while the
> gospel was preached to the world, and this restraint continues

today. Insofar as Christ presently rules in the hearts of believers, they have some influence in the culture in which they live, but they will not transform the culture. Toward the end, the growth of evil will accelerate, resulting in the great tribulation and a personal Antichrist. Christ will return to end history, resurrect and judge all men, and establish the eternal order. In eternity, the redeemed may be either in heaven or in a totally renovated earth.[1]

For amillennialists, the millennium symbolizes a long period of time between Jesus's first and second comings. Jesus's ascension is his official coronation to become king of kings and lord of lords. Already we are living in the kingdom age and the church just is the kingdom. Although Christ's reign is invisible, the church's role is, according to John Calvin, to make Christ's reign visible to the world.[2] Also, all the kingdom prophecies of the Hebrew Bible have found and continue to find their fulfillment in the church. Even so, Jesus will come back and consummate the kingdom, renovating our world into a new heavens and earth.

What I appreciate about the amillennial position is how seriously it takes Jesus's ministry and salvific accomplishments, especially with respect to him defeating the devil. The Gospels portray Jesus battling Satan right from his birth, when Herod slaughtered the innocent children in Bethlehem, forcing Joseph and Mary to take refuge in Africa. Then, even before Jesus began his ministry, the Spirit drove him out into the desert to face Satan directly. After overcoming the devil's temptations, he initiated his itinerant preaching and healing ministry. A significant part of Jesus's work was liberating those oppressed by unclean spirits. Then in his death and resurrection, he delivered the final defeating blow to Satan and his minions and "disarmed the rulers and authorities and put them to open shame, by triumphing over them" (Col 2:15). Thus, the world after Christ is different from the way it was before he came. His life and ministry had cosmic consequences that affect all of those who call upon the name of the Lord. Through Christ, God "has delivered us from the domain of darkness and transferred us to the kingdom of his beloved Son" (Col 1:13). Thus, by association, Christ's followers likewise experience victory and authority over malevolent spiritual forces. I can see why amillennialists believe that Christ bound Satan. These are important truths that premillennialists, for example, often do not emphasize, focusing instead on future victory.

1. Sproul, *Everyone's a Theologian*, 313.
2. See Sproul, *What Is Reformed Theology?*, 144.

Even so, the amillennial view strains credulity when we take a moment to consider the last twenty centuries of human history. If Satan is bound, then why has there been so much gratuitous pain and suffering? For example, why did the demonic Nero execute Paul and Peter in the first century? Why didn't Christ protect these apostles from the devil's agent of wickedness? How could he let the Roman government torture and execute thousands of Christians in incredibly gruesome ways during Diocletian's reign in the early fourth century? What about the pagan Vikings and their pillage and slaughter of innocent Christian monks in Ireland in the eighth century? Or what of the unspeakably inhumane torture of the Japanese Christians in the sixteenth and seventeenth centuries?

Over the centuries it does not appear as though Satan was bound with respect to the church. He appears to have been prowling "around like a roaring lion, seeking someone to devour" (1 Pet 5:8). Far from "having authority" or "reigning with Christ," Christians over the centuries have sometimes struggled to even survive (Rev 20:4).

Additionally, this view fails to adequately explain how the martyrs came to life and reigned with Christ (cf. Rev 20:4). By definition, martyrs are those who died for their faith. Do amillennialists believe that God resurrected all the martyrs at some undisclosed time in history? Also, Rev 20 sounds as though this group whom the beast persecuted and murdered were the same ones who reign for a thousand years. If so, where are they?

Lastly, it's hard to identify any who hold an amillennial interpretation of Rev 20 prior to Augustine in the fifth century. Surely, if this view was clear, it would not have taken four hundred years to develop.

In light of these problems, it is no wonder that some amillennialists have adopted a different way of looking at this chapter. B. B. Warfield argued the millennium was a picture of the intermediate state.

> The picture that is brought before us here is, in fine, the picture of the "intermediate state"—of the saints of God gathered in heaven away from the confused noise and garments bathed in blood that characterize the war upon the earth, in order that they may securely await the end. The thousand years, thus, is the whole of this present dispensation, which again is placed before us in its entirety, but looked at now relatively not to what is passing on earth but to what is enjoyed "in Paradise."[3]

Warfield's interpretation solves two of the major problems of the this-worldly amillennial view; Satan really is bound with respect to the saints (in the intermediate state), and the very same martyrs who died at the hands

---

3. Warfield, *Biblical Doctrines*, 649.

of the beast are still reigning. However, this position elicits new problems. Firstly, the chapter begins with an angel binding Satan, not a relocation of people from earth to another realm where Satan cannot touch them. The plain reading leaves us with the impression that Satan is out of the picture *on earth*. Secondly, what does it mean that the devil is released for a little while at the end of the "thousand" years? Does that mean the saints who are enjoying a heavenly existence will once again become subject to Satan's bullying and terror?

Thirdly, Rev 20 describes the coming to life and reigning with Christ as "the first resurrection." We don't have to guess at what resurrection means, because we have Christ as our example. It means an embodied existence— one that uses up the matter of the old body, resulting in a transformed, physical, resurrected body. Can anyone argue that Christian graves contain no bodies? What kind of world would it be if believers' bodies disappeared just as they took their last breath? It won't work to say that the first resurrection of Rev 20 happens at the moment of each believer's death.

Of course, committed amillennialists have responses to the issues I've raised here about these two versions of their belief. Furthermore, there are probably other theories that I haven't encountered yet. I'm not saying that amillennialism is indefensible, nor am I denigrating those godly people who hold this view. However, even if good answers can assuage the issues I just raised, what is not negotiable is belief in God's ultimate kingdom to come. In some strands of amillennialism, the kingdom of God as the hope for our world and the gospel we preach has taken a back seat to a conscious intermediate state or the rather nebulous phrase "new heavens and new earth."

Another problem with amillennialism is its assertion that all the kingdom prophecies are fulfilled in the church. Now it's fitting for the church to enact and embody the kingdom prophecies found in the OT; but whatever we can do, it will always be partial and temporary. Nevertheless, we should not regard the church's role as the final application of the kingdom prophecies. To do so would not only require adopting metaphorical or allegorical interpretation strategies across the board, but it would also tie many of Jesus's sayings in knots. "The kingdom is not the church," writes George Ladd. He continues, "The apostles went about preaching the kingdom of God (Acts 8:12; 19:8; 28:23); it is impossible to substitute 'church' for 'kingdom' in such passages."[4] To be clear, the church contains the citizens of the kingdom, who preach the gospel of the kingdom while looking forward to the coming of the kingdom and doing what we can to embody the kingdom,

---

4.. Ladd, "Kingdom of God," 313.

but strictly speaking, the church is not the kingdom. This is an important distinction amillennialists do well to retain.

Next up is postmillennialism, which, like amillennialism, sees the millennium as a period between the two comings of Christ. However, unlike amillennialists, postmillennialists believe the purpose of the church is to prepare the world for Christ to return. Kenneth Gentry Jr. provides the following description.

> Postmillennialism holds that the Lord Jesus Christ established his kingdom on earth in the first century through his preaching and redemptive work. Since then he has continued to equip his church with the gospel, empower her by his Spirit, and charge her with the Great Commission to disciple all nations. Postmillennialism expects that eventually the vast majority of men living will be saved. Increasing gospel success will gradually produce a time in history prior to Christ's return in which faith, righteousness, peace, and prosperity will prevail in the affairs of men and of nations. After an extensive era of such conditions, the Lord will return visibly, bodily, and gloriously, to end history. Associated with his return will be the general resurrection and the final judgment after which the eternal order follows.[5]

Like amillennialism, postmillennialism does not take the thousand years of Rev 20 literally, rather, it promotes the view that it is a long period of time—perhaps centuries or even millennia. Although amillennialists recognize the church's ability to transform culture, they do not believe Christianity must succeed for Christ to return. In contrast, postmillennialists do not see Jesus's command to make disciples of all nations as a wish but an inevitability. Eventually the gospel will spread to all nations and our world will enjoy a long period of unprecedented peace and righteousness. Thus, postmillennialism is undoubtedly the most optimistic of the three main views of the millennium; both amillennialists and premillennialists believe Jesus must return in order to fix our world, whereas postmillennialists hold that Christ will achieve widescale healing and wholeness through the church prior to his return.

I find postmillennial optimism attractive and its emphasis on our present role in the world refreshing. Sometimes premillennialists embrace historical pessimism—the view that each generation is worse than the one that preceded it. This can lead to throwing up our hands or, even worse, complicit endorsement of an evil government or cultural movement with the understanding that such rampant evil may hasten the end, a tragic

5. Gentry, "Definition," para. 2.

vulnerability of that end-times belief. Furthermore, I appreciate the post-millennial focus on the corporate church, rather than the individual. Western Christianity has sometimes embraced a very private and individualistic mindset that abdicates cultural institutions to the fallen world, but postmillennialists actively seek not only to press forward in the Great Commission generation after generation, but also to get involved in our broken world to bring healing and lasting change.

Even so, we cannot ignore history. We've seen so many problems when Christians have taken over the government, from Constantine to Charlemagne to the Spanish Inquisition to the European wars of religion. Rather than a golden age of wholeness and human flourishing, Christian governments have left oppression and bloodshed in their wake. Furthermore, movements like the radical Christians who took over Münster, forcibly converting the citizens, establishing communism, and mandating polygamy held the same kind of thinking as the postmillennialists. Why did the Münsterites act this way? They believed that if they could get the city population up to 144,000 then Christ would return. I'm not saying postmillennialists endorse polygamy or communism or any of the other weird and ungodly behaviors that occurred at Münster, I'm merely pointing out that they employed the same logic to their situation. Other examples include state churches all across Europe that historically marginalized, persecuted, and even executed Christians in the name of Christ. Interestingly enough, these state-sponsored churches have been declining, not thriving, throughout Europe as people have turned to secularism or free churches.

A second historical issue with postmillennialism is the amount of bloodshed and suffering over the last century. It's easy to see how believers in the nineteenth century could extrapolate out from the Reformation of the sixteenth century to their own day, extoling the many improvements so many people enjoyed, whether governmental, technological, medical, or otherwise. However, the twentieth century showed us how despots could use new forms of transportation, technology, and medical knowledge to kill countless millions of people with planes, machine guns, and biological weapons. Rather than a golden age of unprecedent peace, abundance in food, and economic prosperity, we saw nearly constant war, repeated famines, and total economic collapse in the Great Depression. Twisted leaders like Pol Pot (killed 1.7 million), Adolf Hitler (killed 17 million), Joseph Stalin (killed 20 million), and Mao Zedong (killed 50 million) slaughtered, persecuted, and exploited swaths of the population during the period. Wars raged at the staggering rate of more than two per year, leaving most postmillennialists disillusioned by the dawn of the twenty-first century.

Our own century has witnessed breakthroughs in communication, access to information, and medicine. Nevertheless, we simultaneously find ourselves living in a time of unprecedented political polarization, spiking levels of anxiety, depression, suicide, and increasing amounts of fake news and misinformation on social media—not to mention a pandemic that has claimed the lives of millions. Access to clean drinking water, sanitary waste disposal, and public education remain major problems in much of our world. Murder rates, teen pregnancies, and crime in general are significantly lower (at least in the US) than previous years; and yet so many languish, trying to escape mountains of debt through jobs that do not pay what they used to. From a biblical perspective, many have shifted away from absolute truths and the biblical metanarrative into the individualist fog of post-modernism. Western culture has gone from seeing the Bible's sexual ethics as arcane to outright offensive and even proclaims recipients of sex reassignment surgery as heroes. Where does all this confusing data leave us? It's hard to say. Is our time better or worse than someone living two generations ago? Honestly, I'm not sure how one could even objectively figure that out.

It does not appear that God has bound Satan, eliminating his ability to deceive the nations. Over the last two centuries, the nations, if anything, appear more deceived than ever. Prognosticating about the future is even less certain.

Postmillennialism could still be true—at least the idea that mankind will yet enter a golden age of human flourishing prior to Christ's return—but we have little reason to suspect that we are now in that period. And even if Christianity grew from one-third of the population to two-thirds, that wouldn't necessarily prove postmillennialism right, either.

Another problem with the postmillennial interpretation relates to explaining the particulars of these verses:

> Then I saw thrones, and seated on them were those to whom the authority to judge was committed. Also I saw the souls of those who had been beheaded for the testimony of Jesus and for the word of God, and those who had not worshiped the beast or its image and had not received its mark on their foreheads or their hands. They came to life and reigned with Christ for a thousand years. The rest of the dead did not come to life until the thousand years were ended. This is the first resurrection. (Rev 20:4–5)

This text reads as though resurrected Christians will have continuous authority to rule in the government for the entire millennium. Certainly, postmillennialists aren't expecting martyrs to be resurrected to rule prior to the return of Christ, are they?

Lastly, to my knowledge, we lack any evidence that early Christians held this view. Charles Hodge, himself a postmillennialist, acknowledges this when he says, "In opposition to this view [postmillennialism] the doctrine of a pre-millennial advent of Christ has been extensively held from the days of the Apostles to the present time."[6] This now transitions us to the last of the three main options—premillennialism.

This view more or less takes this whole chapter in Revelation at face value. In it, an angel will actually "bind" Satan, eliminating his influence on our world while the saints reign with Christ for a thousand years—or, at least, a long time. Because in this view Jesus returns prior to the millennium, we call it "premillennialism." In it, the millennium serves as a transitionary time between the world as it currently is and how it will be in the eternal state. Christ returns to show the world what it looks like when God's will is done on earth as it is in heaven.

The prophets seem to be aware of this period when they prophecy about idyllic conditions in a time when death still occurs. Here is one example:

> I will rejoice in Jerusalem
> and be glad in my people;
> no more shall be heard in it the sound of weeping
> and the cry of distress.
> No more shall there be in it
> an infant who lives but a few days,
> or an old man who does not fill out his days,
> for the young man shall die a hundred years old,
> and the sinner a hundred years old shall be accursed.
> They shall build houses and inhabit them;
> they shall plant vineyards and eat their fruit.
> They shall not build and another inhabit;
> they shall not plant and another eat;
> for like the days of a tree shall the days of my people be,
> and my chosen shall long enjoy the work of their hands.
> They shall not labor in vain
> or bear children for calamity,
> for they shall be the offspring of the blessed of the LORD,
> and their descendants with them. (Isa 65:19–23)

Widely recognized to be eschatological, this vision includes stereotypical kingdom-of-God language, when God makes what is wrong with the world

---

6. Hodge, *Systematic Theology*, 861.

right. However, death still occurs, though lifespans are much longer. People who die after celebrating their centennial birthday are still considered young. How can we fit this prophecy in apart from a transitionary period like the millennium? It makes sense that when Christ returns the world will begin getting better year by year rather than all at once. At the same time, this first stage of the kingdom includes not only the resurrected saints, but also many who survive the cataclysmic events prior to the coming of Christ.

Another Scripture that fits quite nicely with the premillennial scheme is Paul's mini-apocalypse:

> For as in Adam all die, so also in Christ shall all be made alive. But each in his own order: Christ the firstfruits, then at his coming those who belong to Christ. Then comes the end, when he delivers the kingdom to God the Father after destroying every rule and every authority and power. For he must reign until he has put all his enemies under his feet. The last enemy to be destroyed is death. For "God has put all things in subjection under his feet." But when it says, "all things are put in subjection," it is plain that he is excepted who put all things in subjection under him. When all things are subjected to him, then the Son himself will also be subjected to him who put all things in subjection under him, that God may be all in all. (1 Cor 15:22–28)

Here we observe a transitionary period between the coming of Christ to resurrect and the time when he hands the kingdom over to God "so that he may be all in all." What occurs in the interim? "For he must reign until he has put all his enemies under his feet" (v. 25). Presumably, this will take some doing. I don't imagine the nations of the world will instantly fall into line the moment Jesus returns. At the conclusion of this interim period, death itself—the last enemy—is destroyed. This nicely dovetails with the final judgment that happens after the millennium in Revelation:

> And the sea gave up the dead who were in it, Death and Hades gave up the dead who were in them, and they were judged, each one of them, according to what they had done. Then Death and Hades were thrown into the lake of fire. This is the second death, the lake of fire. (Rev 20:13–14)

Thus, the millennium is the first phase of the kingdom. It initiates the changes that will eventually result in a new heavens and earth in which righteousness dwells. It's little wonder that after the preparatory work of the messiah, the very next chapter of Revelation contains the following words:

> And I heard a loud voice from the throne saying, "Behold, the
> dwelling place of God is with man. He will dwell with them,
> and they will be his people, and God himself will be with them
> as their God. He will wipe away every tear from their eyes, and
> death shall be no more, neither shall there be mourning, nor cry-
> ing, nor pain anymore, for the former things have passed away."
> (Rev 21:3–4)

The millennium helps us make sense of the sequence of events following the coming of Christ but preceding the eternal state.

Within premillennialism, we can identify two main branches: (1) historic and (2) dispensational. Historic premillennialism tends to define the rapture as the church meeting the Lord in the air to escort him down to earth rather than going to heaven for several years. Dispensationalism, on the other hand, in most of its varieties, envisages the rapture as an event that occurs prior to the coming of Christ. In this view, the consequence of the rapture is that humanity is left to its own devices without the restraining influence of God's children. Then, after the inhabitants of earth have suffered terribly, Christ returns with his saints to establish the kingdom.

A second difference between classic and dispensational premillennialists arises from how each interprets OT prophecies. Dispensationalist's literal approach to kingdom predictions results in affirming that "in the millennium, the Jewish temple will be rebuilt, and the entire sacrificial system reinstituted, according to the prophecies of Ezekiel 40–48."[7] Historic premillennialists, however, interpret these OT prophecies typologically, rejecting any eschatological Torah observance. Of course, there are plenty of other divergences between historic and dispensational premillennialists, and lots of varieties within each camp, so I encourage interested readers to delve into any of the helpful multi-view books in print.[8]

For me, one of the main reasons I find classic premillennialism attractive is that I can find advocates of this position in early church history. Robert Clouse nicely summarizes the history.

> During the first three centuries of the Christian era premillennialism appears to have been the dominant eschatological interpretation. Among its adherents were Papias, Justin Martyr, Tertullian, Hippolytus, Methodius, Commodianus, and Lactantius. During the fourth century when the Christian church was

7. Ladd, "Historic Premillennialism," 26.

8. Hultberg et al., *Three Views on the Rapture*; Blaising et al., *Three Views on the Millennium*; Ladd et al., *Meaning of the Millennium*; Blaising and Bock, *Progressive Dispensationalism*; Gentry and Wellum, *Kingdom through Covenant*.

given a favored status under the emperor Constantine, the amillennial position was accepted. The millennium was reinterpreted to refer to the church, and the thousand-year reign of Christ and his saints was equated with the whole history of the church on earth, thus making for the denial of a future millennium. The famous church father, Augustine, articulated this position, and it became the dominant interpretation in medieval times. His teaching was so fully accepted that at the Council of Ephesus in 431, belief in the millennium was condemned as superstitious.[9]

As a restorationist, I'm interested in the earliest forms of a doctrine or practice. I ask myself, "What did Jesus or the apostles believe about this?" and then work from there. The fact that dispensationalism doesn't appear on the scene until the nineteenth century, among the Plymouth Brethren, was one of the original reasons I abandoned the view.

I would like to conclude with some wise words from the late R. C. Sproul:

> Whichever eschatological view we hold, we must hold it humbly because we do not know the future. We can all look backward, but we do not know God's agenda for what's to come. We must be humble and acknowledge that our eschatological view might not be accurate. At the same time, much of the doctrinal teaching in the New Testament has to do with future things, so how we understand God's promises about the future has a dramatic impact on our personal confidence and involvement in the mission Christ gave the church.[10]

What matters most of all is the kingdom. This doesn't mean millennial positions are irrelevant, but they are not primary. Jesus did not say, "Seek first the millennium," but, "Seek first the kingdom." He did not proclaim from town to town, "Repent, the millennium is at hand," but, "Repent, the kingdom of God is at hand." Furthermore, whatever happens is going to happen regardless of our beliefs. Thankfully, holding the wrong view on this (or other doctrines) won't change what God is going to do.

9. Ladd et al., *Meaning of the Millennium*, 9.

10. Sproul, *Everyone's a Theologian*, 314.

Bibliography

Alcorn, Randy C. *Heaven*. Carol Stream, IL: Tyndale, 2004.

Allison, Dale C. *Jesus of Nazareth: Millenarian Prophet*. Philadelphia: Fortress, 1998.

Asimov, Isaac. *I. Asimov: A Memoir*. New York: Random House, 2009.

Associated Press. "Miami Church Brands Members with '666' Tattoos." *Fox News*, February 24, 2007. https://www.foxnews.com/story/miami-church-brands-members-with-666-tattoos.

Augustine. *City of God; Christian Doctrine*. Edited by Philip Schaff. Translated by Marcus Dods. NPNF¹ 2. Peabody, MA: Hendrickson, 2003.

———. *Sermons on the Liturgical Seasons*. Translated by Mary Sarah Muldowney. Fathers of the Church 38. New York: Fathers of the Church, 1959.

———. *Sermons*. Translated and edited by William A. Jurgens. The Faith of the Early Fathers 3. Collegeville, MN: Liturgical, 1978.

Bauckham, Richard J. *Jude, 2 Peter*. Word Biblical Commentary 50. Grand Rapids, MI: Zondervan, 1983.

Bauer, Walter, et al., eds. *A Greek-English Lexicon of the New Testament and Other Early Christian Literature*. 3rd ed. Chicago: The University of Chicago Press, 2000.

Beale, G. K. *The Book of Revelation: A Commentary on the Greek Text*. New International Greek Testament Commentary. Grand Rapids, MI: Eerdmans, 1999.

Billy Graham Evangelistic Association. "Begin Your Journey to Peace." https://peacewithgod.org.uk/.

Blaising, Craig A., and Darrell L. Bock. *Progressive Dispensationalism*. Grand Rapids, MI: BridgePoint, 2000.

Blaising, Craig A., et al. *Three Views on the Millennium and Beyond*. Grand Rapids, MI: Zondervan, 1999.

Bock, Darrell L. *Luke*. Vol. 2, *9:51—24:53*. Baker Exegetical Commentary on the New Testament 3. Grand Rapids, MI: Baker Academic, 1996.

Bonhoeffer, Dietrich. *The Cost of Discipleship*. New York: Touchstone, 1995.

Brown, Francis, et al., eds. *A Hebrew and English Lexicon of the Old Testament*. 1906. Reprint, Peabody, MA: Hendrickson, 2001.

Bullinger, Henry. "Confessio Helvetica Posterior." Translated by Philip Schaff. In *The Creeds of Christendom*, 3:233–306. 2nd ed. 3 vols. New York: Harper, 1877.

Buzzard, Anthony F. *Our Fathers Who Aren't in Heaven: The Forgotten Christianity of Jesus, the Jew*. 2nd ed. N.p.: Restoration Fellowship, 1999.

Calvin, John. *Commentary on the Acts of the Apostles*. Vol. 1, *1–13*. Translated by Henry King Beveridge and John Owen. North Charleston, SC: Createspace, 2017.

———. *Institutes of the Christian Religion*. Translated by Henry Beveridge. Peabody, MA: Hendrickson, 2008.

———. *Psychopannychia*. Translated by Henry Beveridge. Tracts Relating to the Reformation. Edinburgh: Calvin Translation Society, 1844.

Camp, Lee C. *Mere Discipleship: Radical Christianity in a Rebellious World*. Grand Rapids, MI: Brazos, 2008.

Chrysostom, John. *Discourses against Judaizing Christians*. Translated by Paul W. Harkins. Fathers of the Church 68. Washington, DC: CUA, 1979.

Claiborne, Shane. *The Irresistible Revolution*. Grand Rapids, MI: Zondervan, 2006.

Clement of Alexandria. *Clement of Alexandria: Christ the Educator*. Translated by Simon P. Wood. New York: Fathers of the Church, 1954.

———. "Exhortation to the Heathen." In *Fathers of the Second Century: Hermas, Tatian, Athenagoras, Theophilus, and Clement of Alexandria (Entire)*, edited by Alexander Roberts and James Donaldson, 171–206. ANF 2. Peabody, MA: Hendrickson, 2003.

———. *Stromateis, Books 1–3*. Translated by John Ferguson. Edited by Thomas P. Halton. Fathers of the Church 85. Washington, DC: Catholic University of America Press, 2005.

———. "Stromateis." Translated by W. L. Alexander. In *Fathers of the Second Century: Hermas, Tatian, Athenagoras, Theophilus, and Clement of Alexandria (Entire)*, edited by Alexander Roberts and James Donaldson, 299–587. ANF 2. Peabody, MA: Hendrickson, 2003.

Code of Federal Regulations. "Oath of Allegiance." https://www.ecfr.gov/current/title-8/chapter-I/subchapter-C/part-337/section-337.1.

Commodian. "The Instructions of Commodianus." Translated by Robert Ernest Wallis. In *Fathers of the Third Century: Tertullian Part Fourth; Minucius Felix; Commodian; Origen, Parts First and Second*, edited by Alexander Roberts and James Donaldson, 201–19. ANF 4. Peabody, MA: Hendrickson, 2003.

Community Peacemaker Teams. "About Us." https://cpt.org/about.

Constas, Nicholas. "To Sleep, Perchance to Dream: The Middle State of Souls in Patristic and Byzantine Literature." *Dumbarton Oaks Papers* 55 (2001) 91–124.

Copeland, Larry. "Americans' Commutes Aren't Getting Longer." *USA Today*, March 5, 2013. https://www.usatoday.com/story/news/nation/2013/03/05/americans-commutes-not-getting-longer/1963409/.

Dale, A. W. W. *The Synod of Elvira and Christian Life in the Fourth Century: A Historical Essay*. New York: MacMillan, 1882.

Dallaire, Hélène. "Judaism and the World to Come." In *A Case for Historic Premillennialism: An Alternative to 'Left Behind' Eschatology*, edited by Craig Blomberg and Sung Wook Chung, 54–55. Grand Rapids, MI: Baker Academic, 2009.

Dodd, C. H. *The Gospel in the New Testament*. London: National Sunday School Union, 1926.

———. *The Parables of the Kingdom*. New York: Scribner's, 1961.

Dulaey, Martine. *Victorin De Poetovio. Sur L'apocalypse Et Autres Écrits*. Source Chrétiennes 423. Paris: Les Éditions du Cerf, 1997.

Edgecomb, Kevin P. "Victorinus: In Apocalypsin." *Biblicalia* (blog), n.d. https://web.archive.org/web/20230201181817/http://www.bombaxo.com/victorinus-in-apocalypsin/.

Ehrman, Bart D. *Jesus: Apocalyptic Prophet of the New Millennium*. Oxford: Oxford University Press, 2001.

Elliott, J. K., ed. *The Apocryphal New Testament*. Oxford: Oxford University Press, 2009.

Epiphanius. *The Panarion of St. Epiphanius, Bishop of Salamis: Selected Passages*. Translated by Philip R. Amidon. Oxford: Oxford University Press, 1990.

Eusebius. *The Church History*. Translated by Paul L. Maier. Grand Rapids, MI: Kregel, 2007.

———. *Commentary on Isaiah*. Translated by Jonathan J. Armstrong. Downers Grove, IL: InterVarsity, 2013.

"Fast Facts about Agriculture & Food." https://www.fb.org/newsroom/fast-facts.

Fredriksen, Paula. "Apocalypse and Redemption in Early Christianity. From John of Patmos to Augustine of Hippo." *Vigiliae Christianae* 45 (1991) 151–83.

———. *From Jesus to Christ: The Origins of the New Testament Images of Jesus*. New Haven, CT: Yale University Press, 2000.

———. *Jesus of Nazareth, King of the Jews: A Jewish Life and the Emergence of Christianity*. New York: Knopf, 2012.

Froom, LeRoy Edwin. *The Conditionalist Faith of Our Fathers*. 2 vols. Washington: Review and Herald, 1965.

Fudge, Edward. *The Fire That Consumes: A Biblical and Historical Study of the Doctrine of Final Punishment*. 3rd ed. Eugene, OR: Wipf & Stock, 2011.

Gentry, Kenneth L., Jr. "Definition." *Postmillennial Worldview* (blog), n.d. https://postmillennialworldview.com/postmillennialism-defined/.

Gentry, Peter J., and Stephen J. Wellum. *Kingdom through Covenant: A Biblical-Theological Understanding of the Covenants*. Wheaton, IL: Crossway, 2018.

"Geraldine T. Scharoun." *Albany Times Union*, November 19, 2018. https://www.legacy.com/us/obituaries/timesunion-albany/name/geraldine-scharoun-obituary?id=5033519.

Gluckin, Victor. "The Kingdom Story, Part 5: The People." http://kingdomuprising.com/wp-content/uploads/2015/04/Kingdom-Story-Part-5-Kingdom-People.pdf.

Graham, Billy. *Hope for the Troubled Heart*. New York: Bantam, 1993.

Green, Michael. *2 Peter and Jude*. Tyndale New Testament Commentaries. Rev. ed. Grand Rapids, MI: Eerdmans, 2000.

Grene, Gene L. *Jude and 2 Peter*. Baker Exegetical Commentary on the New Testament. Grand Rapids, MI: Baker Academic, 2008.

Harris, W. Hall, eds. *The NET Bible Notes*. 2nd ed. Nashville: Nelson, 2019.

Henry, Matthew. *Matthew Henry's Concise Commentary*. Grand Rapids, MI: Christian Classics Ethereal Library, 2012.

Hiers, Richard H., Jr. "Pivotal Reactions to the Eschatological Interpretations: Rudolf Bultmann and C. H. Dodd." In *The Kingdom of God in 20th-Century Interpretation*, by Wendall Willis, 15–34. Peabody, MA: Hendrickson, 1987.

Hill, Charles E. "Cerinthus, Gnostic or Chiliast? A New Solution to an Old Problem." *Journal of Early Christian Studies* 8 (2000) 135–72.

Hillar, Marian. "Philo of Alexandria." *Internet Encyclopedia of Philosophy*. https://iep.utm.edu/philo/.

Hippolytus. "Commentary on Genesis." Translated by S. D. F. Salmond. In *Fathers of the Third Century: Hippolytus, Cyprian, Caius, Novatian, Appendix*, edited by Alexander Roberts and James Donaldson, 163–68. ANF 5. Peabody, MA: Hendrickson, 2003.

———. "Jerome's Epistle 36 to Pope Damasus." Translated by S. D. F. Salmond. In *Fathers of the Third Century: Hippolytus, Cyprian, Caius, Novatian, Appendix*, edited by Alexander Roberts and James Donaldson, 47. ANF 5. Peabody, MA: Hendrickson, 2003.

———. "On Daniel." Translated by S. D. F. Salmond. In *Fathers of the Third Century: Hippolytus, Cyprian, Caius, Novatian, Appendix*, edited by Alexander Roberts and James Donaldson, 177–85. ANF 5. Peabody, MA: Hendrickson, 2003.

———. "On Six Days Work (Hexaëmeron)." Translated by S. D. F. Salmond. In *Fathers of the Third Century: Hippolytus, Cyprian, Caius, Novatian, Appendix*, edited by Alexander Roberts and James Donaldson, 163. ANF 5. Peabody, MA: Hendrickson, 2003.

———. "Scholia on Daniel." Translated by S. D. F. Salmond. In *Fathers of the Third Century: Hippolytus, Cyprian, Caius, Novatian, Appendix*, edited by Alexander Roberts and James Donaldson, 185–91. ANF 5. Peabody, MA: Hendrickson, 2003.

Hodge, Charles. *Systematic Theology*. Vol. 3, *Soteriology*. Peabody, MA: Hendrickson, 2001.

Holmes, Michael W., ed. *The Apostolic Fathers: Greek Texts and English Translations*. Peabody, MA: Hendrickson, 2003.

Horsley, Richard A. *Jesus and Empire: The Kingdom of God and the New World Disorder*. Philadelphia: Fortress, 2003.

Hultberg, Alan, et al. *Three Views on the Rapture: Pretribulation, Prewrath, Posttribulation Rapture*. Grand Rapids, MI: Zondervan, 2010.

"Infancy Gospel of James." In *The Complete Gospels*, edited by Robert J. Miller, 361–78. Salem, OR: Polebridge, 2010.

Irenaeus of Lyons. "Against Heresies." In *The Apostolic Fathers with Justin Martyr and Irenaeus*, 315–567. ANF 1. Peabody, MA: Hendrickson, 2003.

———. "Against Heresies." Translated by Michael W. Holmes. In *The Apostolic Fathers: Greek Texts and English Translations*, edited by Michael W. Holmes, 751–53. Peabody, MA: Hendrickson, 2003.

Jerome. *Jerome: Letters and Select Works*. Translated by W. H. Fremantle. Edited by Philip Wace and Henry Schaff. NPNF[2] 6. Peabody, MA: Hendrickson, 2003.

———. "On the Lives of Illustrious Men." Translated by Ernest Cushing Richardson. In *On the Holy Trinity: Doctrinal Treatises; Moral Treatises*, edited by Philip Schaff and Henry Wace, 359–84. NPNF[2] 3. Peabody, MA: Hendrickson, 2003.

Johnson, B. W. *The People's New Testament*. St. Louis, MO: Christian Board of Publications, 1891.

Josephus, Flavius. *The Antiquities of the Jews*. Translated by William Whiston. Nashville: Nelson, 1998.

———. *The Jewish War*. Nashville: Nelson, 1998.

Justin Martyr. *Dialogue with Trypho*. Translated by Thomas B. Falls. Washington, DC: Catholic University of America Press, 2003.

Kautzsch, Emil, ed. *Gesenius' Hebrew Grammar*. Translated by Arther E. Cowley. 2nd ed. Oxford: Clarendon, 1910.

Keener, Craig S. *The IVP Bible Background Commentary: New Testament*. Downers Grove, IL: InterVarsity, 1993.

———. *John*. Zondervan Illustrated Bible Backgrounds Commentary: New Testament 2A. Edited by Clinton E. Arnold. Grand Rapids, MI: Zondervan, 2019.

Knight, George R. *A Brief History of Seventh-Day Adventists*. 2nd ed. Hagerstown, MD: Review and Herald, 2004.

Kolenkow, Anitra Bingham. "Chaeremon the Stoic on Egyptian Temple Askesis (From Porphyry, On Abstinence 4:6–8." Translated by Vincent L. Wimbush. In *Ascetic*

Behavior in Greco-Roman Antiquity: A Sourcebook, edited by Vincent L. Wimbush, 387–92. Studies in Antiquity and Christianity. Minneapolis, MN: Fortress, 1990.

Lactantius. "Divine Institutes." Translated by William Fletcher. In *Fathers of the Third and Fourth Centuries: Lactantius, Venantius, Asterius, Victorinus, Dionysius, Apostolic Teaching and Constitutions, Homily, and Liturgies*, edited by Philip Schaff and Henry Wace, 9–258. ANF 7. Peabody, MA: Hendrickson, 2003.

Ladd, George Eldon. *The Gospel of the Kingdom: Scriptural Studies in the Kingdom of God*. 1959. Reprint, Grand Rapids, MI: Eerdmans, 1990.

———. "Historic Premillennialism." In *The Meaning of the Millennium: Four Views*, edited by Robert G. Clouse, 17–40. Downers Grove, IL: InterVarsity, 1977.

———. "Kingdom of God." In *Wycliffe Dictionary of Theology*, edited by Everett F. Harrison, 309–14. Peabody, MA: Hendrickson, 1960.

———. *The Presence of the Future: The Eschatology of Biblical Realism*. Grand Rapids, MI: Eerdmans, 1974.

Ladd, George Eldon, et al. *The Meaning of the Millennium: Four Views*. Edited by Robert G. Clouse. Downers Grove, IL: InterVarsity, 1977.

Landes, Richard. "Lest the Millennium Be Fulfilled: Apocalyptic Expectations and the Pattern of Western Chronography 100–800 CE." In *The Use and Abuse of Eschatology in the Middle Ages*, edited by Werner Verbeke et al., 137–211. Mediaevalia Louvaniensia. Leuven, Belg.: Leuven University Press, 1988.

Layton, Bentley. *The Gnostic Scriptures: A New Translation with Annotations and Introductions*. New York: Doubleday, 1995.

Longman, Tremper, III. *The Book of Ecclesiastes*. New International Commentary on the Old Testament. Grand Rapids, MI: Eerdmans, 1998.

Lukianoff, Greg, and Jonathan Haidt. *The Coddling of the American Mind: How Good Intentions and Bad Ideas Are Setting Up a Generation for Failure*. Harmondsworth, UK: Penguin, 2018.

Luther, Martin. *Luther's Works*. Vol. 32, *Career of the Reformer II*. Translated by George W. Forell. Edited by Helmut Lehman. Philadelphia: Muhlenberg, 1958.

———. *Luther's Works*. Vol. 15, *Notes on Ecclesiastes, Lectures on the Song of Solomon, Treatise on the Last Words of David*. Translated by Jaroslav Pelikan. St. Louis: Concordia, 1972. Kindle ed.

"The Martyrdom of Polycarp." Translated by Michael William Holmes. In *The Apostolic Fathers: Greek Texts and English Translations*, edited by Michael W. Holmes, 306–33. Peabody, MA: Hendrickson, 2003.

Melancthon, Philip. *The Unaltered Augsburg Confession*. Translated by Glen L. Thompson. Milwaukee, WI: Northwestern, 2005.

Miller, William. "Mr. Miller's Apology and Defence." *The Advent Herald*, August 13, 1845.

The Net Bible Notes. 2nd ed. Edited by W. Hall Harris. Nashville: Nelson, 2019.

Neusner, Jacob, and William Scott Green, eds. *Dictionary of Judaism in the Biblical Period: 450 B.C.E. to 600 C.E.* Peabody, MA: Hendrickson, 1999.

Newman, Hillel I. "Jerome's Judaizers." *Journal of Early Christian Studies* 9 (2001) 421–52.

Nolan, Albert. *Jesus before Christianity*. Maryknoll, NY: Orbis, 1992.

Noll, Mark A. *Between Faith and Criticism: Evangelicals, Scholarship, and the Bible in America*. Vancouver, BC: Regent College, 1991.

———. *A History of Christianity in the United States and Canada*. Grand Rapids, MI: Eerdmans, 2003.

Ogden, Graham S., and Jan Sterk. *A Handbook on Isaiah*. UBS Translator's Handbooks. New York: United Bible Societies, 2011.

Origen. "Against Celsus." Translated by Frederick Crombie. In *Fathers of the Third Century: Tertullian Part Fourth; Minucius Felix; Commodian; Origen, Parts First and Second*, edited by Alexander Roberts and James Donaldson, 395–670. ANF 4. Peabody, MA: Hendrickson, 2003.

———. *Commentary on the Song of Songs*. Translated by Rowan A. Greer. The Classics of Western Spirituality. Edited by Kevin A. Lynch. Mahwah, NJ: Paulist, 1979.

———. "A Letter from Origen to Africanus." Translated by Frederick Crombie. In *Fathers of the Third Century: Tertullian Part Fourth; Minucius Felix; Commodian; Origen, Parts First and Second*, edited by Alexander Roberts and James Donaldson, 386–92. ANF 4. Peabody, MA: Hendrickson, 2003.

———. *On First Principles*. Translated by George W. Butterworth. Notre Dame, IN: Ave Maria, 2013.

———. *The Song of Songs Commentary and Homilies*. Translated by R. P. Lawson. Mahwah, NJ: Paulist, 1957.

Osborn, Eric Francis. *Clement of Alexandria*. Cambridge: Cambridge University Press, 2008.

Papias. "Fragments of Papias." In *The Apostolic Fathers: Greek Texts and English Translations*, edited by Michael William Holmes, 732–67. 3rd ed. Grand Rapids, MI: Baker Academic, 2007.

Parmenides. *Fragments of Parmenides*. Translated by John Burnet. In *Early Greek Philosophy*, edited by Paul A. Böer Sr., locs. 5971–6711. 1920. Reprint, N.p.: Veritatis Splendor, 2014. Kindle ed.

Pearcey, Nancy. *Total Truth*. Wheaton, IL: Crossway, 2008.

Philo. "On the Contemplative Life." In *The Work of Philo: Complete and Unabridged, New Updated Edition*, translated by Charles Duke Yonge, 698–706. Peabody, MA: Hendrickson, 1997.

———. "On the Creation of the World." In *The Works of Philo Judaeus: The Contemporary of Josephus*, translated by Charles Duke Yonge, 3–24. London: Bell, 1800.

———. "On the Unchangeableness of God." In *The Works of Philo Judaeus: The Contemporary of Josephus*, translated by Charles Duke Yonge, 158–73. London: Bell, 1800.

———. "The Special Laws." In *The Works of Philo Judaeus: The Contemporary of Josephus*, translated by Charles Duke Yonge, 534–639. London: Bell, 1800.

Plato. "Cratylus." In *Plato in Twelve Volumes*, translated by Harold North Fowler, 1–192. Cambridge: Harvard University Press, 1971.

———. *The Dialogues of Plato*. Vol. 3, *Gorgias; Philebus; Parmenides; Theaetetus; Sophist; Statesman*. Translated by Benjamin Jowett. Oxford: Oxford University Press, 1892.

———. "Phaedo." In *The Last Days of Socrates*, translated by Hugh Tredennick and Harold Tarrant, 93–185. Penguin Classics. Harmondsworth; London: Penguin, 1993.

———. *The Republic of Plato*. Translated by Desmond Lee. Harmondsworth, UK: Penguin, 1987.

———. *Timaeus and Critias*. Translated by Benjamin Jowett. Scotts Valley, CA: Information Age, 2009.

———. *Timaeus; Critias; Cleitophon; Menexenus; Epistles*. Translated by R. G. Bury. Cambridge: Harvard University Press, 2005.

Plotinus. *Enneads*. Translated by Stephen MacKenna. Burdette, NY: Paul Brunton Philosophic Foundation, 1992.

Polkinghorne, J. C. *The God of Hope and the End of the World*. New Haven, CT: Yale University Press, 2002.

Pontius. "The Life and Passion of Cyprian." Translated by Robert Ernest Wallis. In *Fathers of the Third Century: Hippolytus, Cyprian, Caius, Novatian, Appendix*, edited by Alexander Roberts and James Donaldson, 267–74. ANF 5. Peabody, MA: Hendrickson, 2003.

———. *On Abstinence from Animal Food*. Translated by Thomas Taylor. Wiltshire, UK: Prometheus Trust, 1994.

Prestidge, Warren. *Life, Death and Destiny*. Auckland, NZ: Resurrection, 1998.

Priestley, Joseph. *The Corruptions of Christianity*. London: The British and Foreign Unitarian Association, 1871.

Pseudo-Barnabas. *Epistle of Barnabas*. Translated by Michael William Holmes. Grand Rapids, MI: Baker Academic, 2008.

Pseudo-Thomas. *Gospel of Thomas*. Translated by Bentley Layton. New York: Doubleday, 1987.

Sanders, E. P. *Jesus and Judaism*. Philadelphia: Fortress, 1985.

Schweitzer, Albert Montgomery W. *The Quest of the Historical Jesus*. Translated by W. Montgomery. Mineola, NY: Dover, 2005.

Silver, A. H. *A History of Messianic Speculation in Israel: From the First through the Seventeenth Centuries*. Boston: Beacon, 1959.

Sproul, R. C. *Everyone's a Theologian: An Introduction to Systematic Theology*. Sanford, IL: Reformation Trust, 2014.

———. *What Is Reformed Theology?* Grand Rapids, MI: Baker, 1997.

Stone, Barton W., and John Rogers. *The Biography of Eld. Barton Warren Stone*. Cincinnati, OH: James, 1847.

Tertullian. "The Prescription against Heretics." Translated by Peter Holmes. In *Latin Christianity: Its Founder, Tertullian*, edited by Alexander Roberts and James Donaldson, 243–67. ANF 3. Peabody, MA: Hendrickson, 2003.

Trigg, Joseph Wilson. *Origen: The Bible and Philosophy in the Third-Century Church*. Atlanta; Richmond, VA: John Knox, 1983.

Tyndale, William. *An Answer to Sir Thomas More's Dialogue*. Edited by Henry Walter. Cambridge, UK: Cambridge, 1850.

Vaage, Leif E. "Cynic Epistles (Selections)." In *Ascetic Behavior in Greco-Roman Antiquity: A Sourcebook*, edited by Vincent L. Wimbush, 117–28. Studies in Antiquity and Christianity. Minneapolis, MN: Fortress, 1990.

———. "Musonius Rufus. *On Training* (Discourse VI)." In *Ascetic Behavior in Greco-Roman Antiquity: A Sourcebook*, edited by Vincent L. Wimbush, 129–33. Studies in Antiquity and Christianity. Minneapolis, MN: Fortress, 1990.

Victorinus. "Commentary on Revelation." Translated by Robert Ernest Wallis. In *Fathers of the Third and Fourth Centuries: Lactantius, Venantius, Asterius, Victorinus, Dionysius, Apostolic Teaching and Constitutions, Homily, and Liturgies*, edited by Philip Schaff and Henry Wace, 344–60. ANF 7. Peabody, MA: Hendrickson, 2003.

———. "On the Creation of the World." Translated by Frederick Crombie. In *Fathers of the Third and Fourth Centuries: Lactantius, Venantius, Asterius, Victorinus, Dionysius, Apostolic Teaching and Constitutions, Homily, and Liturgies*, edited by Philip Schaff and Henry Wace, 341–43. ANF 7. Peabody, MA: Hendrickson, 2003.

Warfield, B. B. *The Works of Benjamin B. Warfield.* Vol. 2, *Biblical Doctrines.* 1932. Reprint, Grand Rapids, MI: Baker, 2003.

Weinrich, William C., ed. *Ancient Christian Commentary on Scripture.* Vol. 12, *Revelation.* Downers Grove, IL: InterVarsity, 2005.

Weiss, Johannes. *Jesus' Proclamation of the Kingdom of God* [Die Predigt Jesu vom Reiche Gottes]. Translated by Richard Hiers and David Holland. Philadelphia: Fortress, 1971.

Wesley, John. *Notes on the New Testament.* Edited by Nigel Dinneen. Nicholasville, KY: Schmul, 2015.

Wilde, Oscar. *Salome: A Tragedy in One Act.* Boston: Branden, 1996.

Wilken, Robert L. "Early Christian Chiliasm, Jewish Messianism, and the Idea of the Holy Land." *The Harvard Theological Review* 79 (1986) 298–307.

———. *John Chrysostom and the Jews: Rhetoric and Reality in the Late 4th Century.* Eugene, OR: Wipf & Stock, 2004.

———. "In Novissimis Diebus: Biblical Promises, Jewish Hopes and Early Christian Exegesis." *Journal of Early Christian Studies* 1 (1993) 1–19.

———. *The Land Called Holy: Palestine in Christian History and Thought.* New Haven, CT: Yale University Press, 1992.

Williams, George Huntston. *The Radical Reformation.* 3rd ed. Kirksville, MO: Truman State University Press, 2000.

Willis, Wendall, ed. *The Kingdom of God in 20th-Century Interpretation.* Peabody, MA: Hendrickson, 1987.

Wright, N. T. *For All the Saints?* Harrisburg, PA: Morehouse, 2003.

———. "God's Future in Person." http://ntwrightpage.com/2016/03/30/gods-future-in-person/.

———. *Jesus and the Victory of God.* Philadelphia: Fortress, 1996.

———. *John for Everyone: Part 2.* Louisville, KY: Westminster John Knox, 2004.

———. "On Earth as in Heaven." https://ntwrightpage.com/2016/03/30/on-earth-as-in-heaven/.

———. *Paul for Everyone: The Prison Letters.* Lousiville, KY: Westminster John Knox, 2004.

Zarrella, John, and Patrick Oppmann. "Pastor with 666 Tattoo Claims to Be Divine." *CNN,* February 19, 2007. http://www.cnn.com/2007/US/02/16/miami.preacher/index.html.

Zeller, Eduard. *Outlines of the History of Greek Philosophy.* New York: Meridian, 1957.

Subject Index

Scripture and Ancient Sources Index